Restructuring the global automobile industry

The motor industry has undergone a period of rapid and extensive change. The restructuring of the world economy and technological change have led to new patterns of automobile production, distribution and consumption.

This book examines the spatial implications of these changes at world, national and local levels. The motor industry has often been representative of wider patterns of industrial change – hence the widespread adoption of the term 'Fordism'. This is borne out by recent trends. Japanese firms have become major players and this has been reflected in their level of foreign direct investment. But 'Japanization' has also had an impact on companies of European or North American origin, and the adoption of flexible working practices and 'just-in-time' techniques have become commonplace.

Restructuring the Global Automobile Industry brings together the work of North American, European and Japanese geographers, economists and sociologists, and includes perspectives from the components industry, the shop floor experience and local economic policy making.

Christopher M. Law is a reader in geography at the University of Salford. He is the author of *British Regional Policy Since World War I* and *The Uncertain Future of the Urban Core*, and numerous articles in economic and social geography.

Restructuring the global automobile industry
National and regional impacts

Edited by

Christopher M. Law

ROUTLEDGE

London and New York

First published 1991
by Routledge
11 New Fetter Lane, London EC4P 4EE

Simultaneously published in the USA and Canada
by Routledge
a division of Routledge, Chapman and Hall, Inc.
29 West 35th Street, New York, NY 10001

Typeset in English Times
by Pat and Anne Murphy, Highcliffe-on-Sea, Dorset
Printed in Great Britain by
Mackays of Chatham PLC, Chatham, Kent

British Library Cataloguing in Publication Data
Restructuring the global automobile industry: national and
regional impacts
 1. Motor vehicle industries
 I. Law, Christopher M. (Christopher Michael), 1938–
 33.8476292
 ISBN 0–415–04712–9

Library of Congress Cataloging in Publication Data
Restructuring the global automobile industry: national and
regional impacts / edited by Christopher M. Law.
  p. cm.
  "The origin of this book lies in a session of the Institute
of British Geographers' Industrial Activity and Area
Development Study Group held at the annual conference in
January 1989" – T.p. verso.
  Includes bibliographical references and index.
  ISBN 0–415–04712–9
  1. Automobile industry and trade – Congresses. I. Law,
Christopher M.   II. Institute of British Geographers.
Study Group on Industrial Activity and Area
Development.   III. Institute of British Geographers.
Conference (1989: Coventry Polytechnic)
HD9710.A2R46 1991   90-46628
338.4'76292–dc20   CIP

Contents

Figures

Tables

Contributors

Ash Amin is a lecturer at the Centre for Urban and Regional Development Studies, University of Newcastle upon Tyne, UK.

Gerald T. Bloomfield is Professor of Geography at the University of Guelph, Canada. He is the author of *The World Automotive Industry* (1978) and many other works.

David Elliott was Principal Economist for the West Midlands Enterprise Board, Birmingham, UK, and is now a Senior Consultant with KPMG Peat Marwick McLintock.

David Froggatt has lectured in Industrial Economics at the Department of Management Studies, University of Salford, UK. He is now Planning Manager at T & N plc, a leading British-based multinational producer of automotive components.

Philip Garrahan is Senior Lecturer in Politics at Sunderland Polytechnic, UK. He is currently researching industrial change and the local economy.

Patrick Gray has worked at the West Midlands Enterprise Board, Birmingham, UK. He is now a Consultant with Oxford Research 2000.

Robert Gwynne is a lecturer in Geography at the University of Birmingham, UK. He is the author of *Industrialisation and Urbanisation in Latin America* (1985) and numerous articles on the economic geography of the Third World.

Christopher M. Law is Reader in Geography at the University of Salford, UK. He is the author of *British Regional Policy since World War I* (1980) and *The Uncertain Future of the Urban Core* (1988), as well as numerous articles on economic and social geography.

Anders Malmberg is Research Associate at the Department of Social and Economic Geography, University of Uppsala, Sweden. He is currently researching the regional impacts of the growing internationalization of the Swedish economy.

Yasuo Miyakawa is Professor and Head of Geography at Aichi Kyoiku University, Japan. He is the author of *The Systematic Location Theory of Manufacturing Industry* (1977), *The Mutation of Japan's Industry in the World* (1988) and numerous articles on industrial systems and regional planning.

Mike Rawlinson is Research Fellow at the Motor Industry Research Unit, Cardiff Business School, University of Wales College of Cardiff, UK.

James M. Rubenstein is Professor of Geography at Miami University, Ohio, USA, and is the author of several articles on the motor industry in the USA.

Dennis Smith is Senior Lecturer in Sociology at the University of Aston, UK.

Ian Smith is Research Associate at the Centre for Urban and Regional Development Studies, University of Newcastle upon Tyne, UK.

Paul Stewart is Senior Lecturer in Industrial Sociology, Sunderland Polytechnic, UK. He is currently researching industrial change and the labour process.

Preface

The origin of this book lies in a session of the Institute of British Geographers' Industrial Activity and Area Development Study Group held at the annual conference in January 1989. The location of the conference in Coventry suggested that the group take a theme appropriate to the setting, and the obvious one was the motor vehicle industry. The city of Coventry illustrates the predicament of the British motor vehicle industry. At the end of the last century Coventry was one of the principal centres for the newly developing cycle, motorcycle and vehicle industry. It is an admirable example of the idea of the transference of skills whereby a town or city can evolve new industries. In the case of Coventry the textile industry gave birth to textile engineering, which provided skills for the cycle and vehicle industries and thence the aircraft industry. During the twentieth century Coventry grew on the basis of an expanding vehicle industry including the firms of Humber, Hillman, Morris, Rover, Alvis, Standard Triumph and Jaguar, the latter a migrant to the town. However, when the industry collapsed in the 1970s the city experienced high unemployment and the need to attract new activities.

I am grateful, as convener of the session, to all those who offered papers, and for the participants who made the day-long session a success. The papers and discussion during the day emphasized the growing importance and role of Japanese companies in the industry. In compiling the papers of the conference for publication I therefore thought it appropriate to add a paper from a Japanese industrial geographer and was pleased when Professor Y. Miyakawa was able to offer one. I am also grateful to Mrs Moira Armitt, Miss Natalie Cheney, Mrs Marie Partington and Mrs Christine Warr for secretarial and cartographic assistance.

1 Motor vehicle manufacturing: the representative industry

Christopher M. Law

The motor vehicle industry never ceases to attract attention and fascination. There are perhaps many reasons for this. It makes products which are familiar to most people, which are increasingly becoming essential for many, facilitating the mobility which they desire, and around which there is often a certain amount of glamour. Even in its manufacturing processes, principally the assembly line, the public find interest, using it as an example of how industry works. The fact that the industry has spawned some larger-than-life figures, from Henry Ford to Lee Iacocca may also have helped. But above all the industry attracts attention because of its size, it is either the largest or one of the largest industries in the world, depending, of course, on how an industry is defined. By 1979, before the second oil price rise, over 30 million cars were produced each year and it was reckoned that there were 5–6 million jobs dependent on the industry in the major producing nations (Altshuler *et al.* 1984). Beyond this the industry is of interest because of the consequences of the explosion of motor car ownership in terms of increased mobility, congestion on the roads and environmental concerns.

As a result of this prominence, the industry is often called upon to be the representative of modern industry, to supposedly typify the characteristics and trends of contemporary life. Numerous studies are therefore undertaken on the industry concerning production systems, the sociology of work, industrial relations (Willman and Winch 1985) and the reasons why the industries of a particular country are either successful or unsuccessful (Williams *et al.* 1987). Consequently, there is an enormous literature on the industry. Quite obviously, given the diversity of manufacturing, it would be unrealistic to expect any one to be entirely representative. Each industry has its own distinctive characteristics of inputs, outputs, technology and labour systems so that it is impossible to identify a typical one. And yet, because it is so difficult to undertake a complete survey of manufacturing, because it is easier to pick on one industry as an exemplar, commentators will continue to return to the motor industry to discern contemporary trends in modern economic life. In this respect the editors and contributors of this book find themselves in a large company of fellow researchers.

Given the wide range of studies on the industry, it is important to identify the particular viewpoint of this book. This may simply be stated as the spatial implications for society of the contemporary motor industry. For many years geographers have been concerned with the spatial patterns and impacts of the industry at the world, national and local levels. In recent years many sociologists and political scientists have also become interested in the impact of economic restructuring at the local level through the so-called 'locality' studies (Cooke 1989). Physical and economic planners have also been concerned about local and regional economic change and how to secure the future of the areas for which they had responsibility. In this opening chapter we shall review the main themes discussed by these commentators as well as introducing the reader to later chapters.

Geographers have long realized that it is impossible to understand the spatial patterns of industry without placing them in the context of the processes of economic development and organizational change. One currently fashionable view of industrial growth is that it occurs in waves of development at periodic intervals, the so-called long-wave theory of Kondratieff. In Western Europe and North America there have been at least four waves since the Industrial Revolution of the late eighteenth century at approximately fifty-year intervals, and it is possible that we are now at the beginning of a fifth one. Each wave of growth is dominated by a group of industries, new types of production that will propel the economy forwards. Amongst the new industries of the third wave which began in the 1890s was automobile manufacturing. Like the propulsive industries of Perroux's growth pole theory, it grew rapidly, became large in scale and was linked with many other sectors of the economy, thus being very influential in causing economic growth. The dominant industries of one Kondratieff wave do not necessarily stop growing in the next wave, and this has certainly been true of motor vehicles, but their influence on the character of new growth will be less.

Industrial organization is also evolving. By organization we mean the size of firms, their relationships to each other, the way in which labour and technology is used and the relationship of industry to the socio-political systems. For at least the first hundred years following the Industrial Revolution, firms were mainly small or medium-sized, there were strong links between them without dependent relationships developing, labour skills and crafts were important and the use of technology was limited. According to Piore and Sabel (1984), a new form of organization began to emerge at the beginning of the century involving mass production and consumption. They described this as the first industrial divide and the new system has been called 'Fordism' by Aglietta (1979) and others, a term which clearly reflects the influential role of motor vehicles in creating the new system. Because of the importance of this topic we shall deal with it in more detail later in this chapter. Many commentators suggest that a new dominant form of industrial organization is now evolving, a second industrial divide, the key characteristic of which is flexibility. For some this is post-Fordism whilst for others it is neo-Fordism. Linking these ideas with the earlier discussion on growth, it can be suggested that during the third and fourth Kondratieff waves Fordism was the predominant mode of industrial organization whilst for the fifth wave the key feature is likely to be flexibility.

So far new industries have emerged in the countries of Western Europe and North America. Often they have started in several locations but frequently they have quickly become concentrated in a limited number of places where industrial complexes have evolved. These areas have either previously had limited industrial development or experienced industrial decline (Storper and Walker 1989). This is largely true of the motor vehicle industry where, after the early phase, clusters developed in the Detroit area, the British West Midlands, in and around Turin, and in the Middle Rhine area of Germany. Later, industries tended to become more dispersed, partly through a process of decentralization and partly through inward migration of plants from other countries. These patterns evolved under Fordism and may need to be modified in a post- or neo-Fordist period (see below). From the major advanced countries industries spread to other regions in the world, beginning with those where either there is rapid growth (incomes and infrastructure developments) and/or there are sizeable markets. This changing pattern of world industry is an important theme in industrial geography (Dicken 1986) and will be discussed in more detail below. Of tremendous importance has been the rise of Japan as a major industrial power. Significantly motor vehicle manufacturing has contributed in an important way to its growth. The spread of industry to Third World countries is regarded as an important goal by most world authorities, but so far it has been very uneven, and this is certainly true for motor vehicles.

For many people the importance of the motor vehicle industry is because it provides jobs in their town or region. Changes in the scale, structure and organization of production may have considerable effects for them with respect to the economic health of the community. Because of this, local authorities take a keen interest in the industry and as part of economic development policies seek to have an influence. These topics will be discussed in more detail later in the chapter.

FORDISM AND POST- OR NEO-FORDISM

The underlying theme behind these terms is that at any one time there has been a dominant mode of organization within the capitalist system and that from the mid-1970s this mode has been changing. For most of the twentieth century the predominant characteristic of the system was the tendency towards mass production or Fordism. It is argued that since the early 1970s there have been pressures for change, resulting in a new type of organization variously described as flexible specialization (Piore and Sabel 1984), flexible integration (Cooke 1988), flexible accumulation (Harvey 1988), or as post- or neo-Fordism. These ideas have been espoused by commentators from various shades of political opinion. However, political economists would stress that changes in the organization of production should be linked to changes in the socio-political system, and describe Fordism and post-Fordism as regimes of capitalist accumulation. In particular they point to the shift from Keynesian—welfare statism to a resurgence of neo-conservative ideologies. Whilst these ideas appear as non-spatial, the following discussion will indicate how each model has given rise to distinctive geographical patterns.

The key feature of Fordism is that it is based on mass production and consumption. Low costs per unit are achieved through the concentration of production on a limited number of products, through standardization, and high volumes. The latter allows dedicated machinery to be used, which is justified because of the large outputs, and when allied with flow (assembly) line techniques produces economies of scale. Using Taylor's scientific principles of management there is a fragmentation of tasks so that each one requires little skill. There is also a rigid demarcation of tasks with each worker confined to his own particular one. Both these processes result in a de-skilling of the labour force. As large firms evolved they were able to gain organizational economies of scale involving the ability to purchase materials and distribute products more cheaply, and also undertake research and development, both for products and manufacturing processes.

In many of the new industries there were initially a large number of entrants but these were quickly whittled down as a few successful firms gained economies of scale. Competition between firms was intense but, because of the limited possibilities of the machinery, came to be based more on price than on quality and design. Having established itself in the market place, the new large firm continued to grow in various ways, partly through extending its markets geographically across the world, and partly through a process of vertical integration. By purchasing suppliers large firms gained more control over more processes, and sometimes these acquisitions enabled the parent to cut transport and other transaction costs. Unlike earlier periods there appeared to be economies of scope (Scott 1988b). In this way more of the economies of scale for the whole manufacturing process came to be internalized within the firm. Companies became large, as did their factories. The sheer size of plants encouraged strong unionization and collective bargaining. Those suppliers that remained independent, frequently firms using batch productive methods, came to occupy a very dependent position in relation to the large firm. There was intense competition to supply the large firm, and to maintain this, as well as safeguard supplies, there was often dual sourcing. Suppliers were chosen on the basis of price rather than quality. Through the acquisition of other firms, large industrial corporations came to broaden their product base and specialist knowledge and skills.

Whilst the Fordist model of industrial organization exerted tremendous influence through the twentieth century, its methods could not be adopted completely or even partially by all sections of production. It was clearly more suitable for industries like automobiles, consumer electrical goods and mass-produced machinery, than for industries using only a few inputs, such as those processing raw material, and those with a relatively simple product, as well as those where there was only a small demand.

The Fordist system of organization survived for a long time because it was successful. As prices fell, so more people could afford to purchase the product. With high volumes there were further economies of scale and more price cuts. Profits were high and companies could afford union requests for higher wages, which in turn created increased demand, resulting in a virtuous economic circle. Although there were cyclical factors in economic growth, these could be handled through Keynesian macroeconomic policies and welfare state policies.

Initially, as we have seen, new industries appear at several locations, but quickly become clustered. Within these territorial industrial complexes the large firm plays a key role. It functions efficiently when there is clear role specialization within the firm. After a time it becomes possible to relocate particular functions to sites where costs are less. Thus from a position of concentration large corporations have decentralized their activities. Initially, branch plants were close by, then in more distant regions, and perhaps finally in other countries. This filtering-down process approximates to the product life-cycle model. In particular the large corporation was able to benefit from lower labour costs, government subsidies and growing markets in distant areas. In a similar way, as transport improved, some suppliers were able to relocate to gain lower costs. All this was possible because the main assemblers had large warehouses. Sayer (1986) has described this as a 'just-in-case' system. Overall, Schoenberger (1987) has described these processes as a 'spatial de-linking of skills and functions within the large mass production based corporation, and the differential location of various segments of production and other activities of the firm in accordance with geographical variations in factor supply conditions'.

The fact that this type of industrial system was termed 'Fordism' suggests that it draws a great deal of its inspiration from the motor vehicle industry where we should expect to find most of the features present. Economies of scale are very important within the industry (Maxcy 1981; Rhys 1972). For some components such as engines, these continue up to the level of 1 million units a year. However, for the assembly track, economies of scale are limited to about 200,000 units a year. A car producer may, therefore, have one large engine plant supplying several assembly plants which may be in more than one country. Once the industry had become global it was possible to conceive of the world car.

Within the major countries of the US, France, Germany and the UK, there were a large number of entrants to the industry at the beginning of the century, but within 30–40 years their number had been reduced to about half-a-dozen mass producers plus a few catering for the prestige luxury market. At this stage the industries of these countries were protected by tariffs. With the removal of these tariffs there is now competition between the major companies, with the smaller and less competitive ones being eliminated. The industry also illustrates the process of vertical integration as described above, although the extent of integration has varied between firms and countries. Henry Ford's River Rouge plant in Detroit illustrates the greatest degree of vertical integration, with iron ore entering at one end and cars emerging at the other. At the other extreme, Japanese companies still buy-in a high proportion of the cost of a car, although some of their suppliers are partly owned by them.

The motor vehicle industry, as we saw earlier, quickly became clustered in a few localities such as Detroit and the British West Midlands. Subsequently, however, there was a considerable dispersal of the industry. In Western Europe this was encouraged through regional policy which provided grants and loans in assisted areas where there was high unemployment and also in some cases, as in Britain, prohibited unlimited developments in traditional core areas of the industry. Component makers were also encouraged to move to the assisted areas, but with limited success. The major motor companies established foreign plants to serve these markets mainly because of tariffs. As such they tended to be screwdriver plants relying on imported kits with only a small local content. The problems of establishing motor vehicle industries in Third World countries is discussed by Robert Gwynne in Chapter 3.

The proponents of the post- or neo-Fordist hypothesis base their case on the way the industrial system has been changing since the mid-1970s. Outward symptoms of change have been the large loss of manufacturing jobs in Western Europe and North America, the closure of many plants, mergers, acquisitions and sell-offs, the increased role of small firms, burgeoning foreign investment and a wider variety of work practices, including temporary and part-time labour.

The pressure for change has come from several directions and various commentators give different emphasis to each of the factors. Of greatest importance has been the fierce competition in the world economic system with firms fighting to survive, to reverse falling profits and to raise productivity levels (Cooke 1988). This increased competition has arisen from several sources. From the late 1960s tariffs began to fall as a result of General Agreement on Tariffs and Trade (GATT) agreements, whilst common markets such as the European Community (EC) have eliminated many trade barriers altogether within certain regions. The recessions brought on by the oil price rises of late 1973 and 1979 have produced stagnating markets, overcapacity in the productive system and the need to rationalize in many industries and firms. The rise of Japanese companies in world markets has shocked the complacency of many North American and West European giants. Competition is now also beginning to emerge from Third World countries such as Taiwan, South Korea and Hong Kong. At the same time interest rates have risen in many countries, bringing to bear another pressure on company profits. Concurrently there has been an overall increase in affluence in many countries accompanied by widening social polarization which has caused a break-up of the mass markets as richer consumers become more discriminating in their purchases. So firms have had to learn to respond to different markets and fluctuating demands. Many would also argue that because of rigidities, the Fordist system has reached its limits (Sayer 1986). These rigidities include high inventory costs, difficulties in quality control, dedicated machinery, over-rigid task demarcations and the alienation of workers which Taylorism brings. It was thus becoming more diffi-cult within traditional Fordism to maintain productivity improve-ments (Schoenberger 1988). Moreover, the failure of the system impacted on itself as when workers who could not be given higher wages went on strike. To avoid a crisis, significant changes in the system were needed. Fortunately at this time technological advances were creating new possibilities, but it was clear that changes in organ-ization were also needed. The key word of the new system is flexi-bility, but it has many dimensions not all of which may be found in the same plant or firm at the same time (Schoenberger 1989).

These features include the following.

Flexible machines

Under Fordism, machines were dedicated to particular tasks, which could only be changed at considerable cost in terms of lost production owing to long set-up times. Computer-controlled machines can have their programmes changed quickly so that one machine can be used for several tasks and can be changed quickly to respond to changes in demand. It has been argued that these flexible machines reduce econo-mies of scale and enable small firms to compete with large ones. These machines will also be available to design intensive craft industries, in clothing, furniture, etc., and according to Scott (1988b) there has been a revival of these activities both in large cities and in regions such as Emilia-Bologna (Third Italy).

Flexible firms

Increased competition has forced large corporations to examine every activity and adopt a pragmatic approach to its future and mode of operation.

This has involved:

1 Firm restructuring. Many corporations had diversified well beyond their core business. On examination they found that many of their activities were not strong enough to compete in world markets without further investment. Consequently the 1980s has witnessed a massive restructuring of firms with many subsidiaries which had no long-term viability being sold, so that resources could be ploughed back into those activities which were seen as the core business of the future. Some businesses were sold to managers (sometimes later to be sold again) and others to major corporations which were looking to strengthen their own core business.

2 Alliances. Under Fordism many corporations sought complete independence. With increased competition this position is less tenable. Firms have been more willing to collaborate with other companies, to form alliances and partnerships (Cooke 1988). Usually these are based on complementary strengths in technology, production, products and market access. These may operate either world wide or on a limited geographical basis. They may involve existing units or lead to the creation of new units. Each alliance will probably involve a unique set of contributions from the partners.

3 Vertical disintegration. Under Fordism there was a tendency towards integration, whereas under Post-Fordism there is a tendency towards vertical disintegration. The activities of a firm are divided into profit centres, so that to a certain extent each one is like an independent firm. They must also compete with outside firms for the work of other subsidiaries. This is intended to make each section more efficient. Those profit centres which cannot compete maybe sold off, i.e. externalized. In recent years a whole range of activities have been externalized in this way, from the manufacture of components, specialized processing to service activities such as canteens, cleaning, haulage and computer facilities.

4 Networks. In the Fordist system there was a close relationship between companies belonging to the same parent but a more distant one with independent contractors. Now that affiliates have been put at arms length and some sold off, a new relationship is developing between firms which is more of a partnership. Regular suppliers, whether owned by the same parent or not, are likely to be involved much more in the design stage, working together to produce components of the right quality and price. Overall there may be more subcontractors than previously but since these have been structured into a hierarchy each firm will deal with a smaller number.

Just-in-time systems (JIT)

A further change in the relationship between firms is seen in the JIT or kanban system, pioneered by the Japanese. Traditionally as described above, there was a just-in-case system in which materials and components were stored in warehouses so that in the event of a breakdown production could continue. However, this resulted in huge inventory costs as well as capital for warehouses (Estall 1985). In the JIT system goods are supplied just as they are needed, thus saving these costs. Originally the kanban was a simple tag system through which new supplies could be ordered, but today JIT systems involve sophisticated communication systems between assemblers and suppliers, enabling rapid changes in products and quantities. However, proponents of the JIT system maintain that it is more than inventory control (Turnbull 1988). It is also a system of quality control, since suppliers must guarantee 100 per cent reliability and pay heavily for any failures which would cost more in a JIT system than a traditional one. The result is a higher-quality final product with lower failure rates. The introduction of JIT systems has forced firms and workers to think carefully about every stage of manufacture, and as a consequence of this learning experience many other productivity gains have also been made (Sayer 1986).

Flexible labour

There are several aspects of this:

1 Task flexibility. In the Fordist system breakdowns often took much time to repair because of the demarcation of tasks. This weakness and others can be overcome by training workers in several tasks and giving them more responsibilities. Quality circles can be used to help improve productivity. These changes have reversed the deskilling process and created greater functional flexibility.
2 Flexible work practices. Under Fordism, with strong unions, certain work practices developed. Most workers were employed full-time, working within, at maximum, a two-shift-per-day pattern. Under the Post-Fordism system employers seek a greater variety of work practices so that there is greater numerical flexibility. This may involve three-shift working, more part-time workers, the use of temporary staff and even home working. In so far as these work practices are widespread it is likely to exacerbate the dual labour syndrome in which one section of the population has secure, well-paid, full-time jobs, and the other has poorly paid, insecure work.

3 Union power reduced. It has only been possible to introduce these changes as the role of unions has been downgraded. In this, firms have been assisted by rising unemployment and anti-union government stances, as typified by Reagan and Thatcher. When union recognition cannot be avoided, there are single-union deals, if possible involving no-strike agreements. The latter is extremely important where JIT systems are employed. Elsewhere central bargaining has been abolished.

There has been a considerable debate as to whether a new industrial system, based on flexibility, is emerging (Gertler 1988; Pollert 1988a). Some commentators doubt if it is ever possible to suggest that there is a dominant or pervasive system of industrial organization, whether it be Fordist or post-Fordist. Gertler (1988) argues that too much weight has been given to the experience of a few industries, such as automobiles. He finds no evidence for the introduction of flexible systems, and thinks that the use of the term is ironical, given the possibilities of breakdown, the stronger links between firms, and the greater potential power of labour.

It certainly appears doubtful whether flexible manufacturing systems will reduce the importance of large manufacturing systems and introduce a new era for the importance of small and medium-sized companies. Even if production economies are reduced, the large corporations will still benefit from organizational economies of scale. Further, flexible machines will enable the large firm to manufacture a more diversified product range, hitting small firms which had previously found a niche. Flexible machines will be available to all firms, but their cost may put them beyond the reach of many small companies. Since the dominance of large firms is unlikely to be eroded, some commentators prefer the term neo-Fordism to describe what they see as modifications to the system (Sayer 1989).

In so far as the production system is changing or has changed, it has implications for the geography of industry. Under Fordism manufacturing was dispersing, but under flexible regimes there is the possibility of spatial reconcentration. The main reason for this is that in a system of increased vertical disintegration, transactional costs will require plants to be close to each other. These linkage costs involve several components from the traditional physical flows of inputs and outputs, the need to vary flows according to demand, and now the requirement for discussion between firms over both design and production matters. In particular, the JIT/kanban system in which the assemblers hold no buffer stocks and suppliers must provide components just in time, as required, will bring firms closer together

(Estall 1985). There is thus the possibility of new or revived territorial industrial complexes (Schoenberger 1987). This factor will affect several types of production; old Fordist type industries, new industries such as electronics, and the revived design-intensive craft industries (Scott 1988b). Given easier communications today, with a good network of expressways, these industrial complexes may cover a large area, unlike the clusters of the late nineteenth century, which occupied zones within large cities. Even when these complexes are related to restructured Fordist industries it is likely that there will be some shift in location.

How far does the motor vehicle industry show the trends towards flexibility? Certainly the industry has experienced all the pressures for change mentioned earlier. It has been forced to rethink its entire philosophy, from new products, new processes, to new markets. There appears to be a bigger variety of cars in smaller volumes. R. Levy, Chairman of Renault, has said that 'new models are being launched at closer intervals and customer's tastes are diversifying' (*The Economist*, 23 September, 1989). If ever automobile manufacturing was considered a mature industry it has now been rejuvenated or dematured.

Using the features listed above we can discuss how the industry has changed in recent years.

Flexible machines

There have been widespread attempts to introduce flexible manufacturing systems into the industry, although not always with the success that was anticipated (Williams *et al.* 1987). As elsewhere, motor vehicle manufacturing is still on a learning curve. All new plants, such as General Motors' Saturn facility in Tennessee, will be planned from the start to fully involve flexible specialization (Meyer 1984). Production economies of scale have been reduced and this has held out the possibility of smaller companies being able to compete with larger ones (Altshuler *et al.* 1984). However, there is no evidence that this is the case. The financial difficulties of Saab and Jaguar in late 1989, which were resolved by associations with General Motors and Ford respectively, suggest that there is no secure future for the small firm. There is no evidence that Britain's Rover company has found long-term viability on its own, rather its only way forward is through collaboration with Honda. In all these cases it is the high cost of R&D both for products and processes, which puts the small car firm at a disadvantage. On the other hand, new technologies give the large company extra advantages in that its plants can now be used to produce several models instead of one or two. Thus, Volkswagen's Emden plant in northern Germany can easily switch from one model to another (*The Economist*, 23 September 1989, p. 104).

Flexible firms

The major motor vehicle and component firms provide much evidence of restructuring. General Motors has been prepared to give up the unprofitable manufacture of Bedford trucks in Britain, whilst component makers like Lucas have sold off businesses, such as the manufacture of headlights, to former rivals in order to concentrate on what they consider as their core business, braking and engine systems. Some vehicle component makers such as Smiths Industries have virtually left the industry altogether to concentrate on the more profitable area of aerospace parts.

There are also many examples of alliances. Ford (Europe) and Fiat have merged their truck activities in Europe. Volvo and Renault have entered into a partnership. Rover has formed an alliance with Honda; Renault, Peugeot and Volvo have a jointly owned engine plant in northern France. Rover and DAF have combined their truck business, General Motors and Toyota have a joint assembly plant in California. Volkswagen and Toyota jointly assemble light vans in Hanover. These are but a few of the examples of alliances which could be multiplied if more countries around the world were considered.

The relationship of vehicle assemblers and suppliers has been changing in recent years. Formerly the assemblers put out orders to component makers either having undertaken the design and development work themselves, or relying on the knowledge and skills of the suppliers. For each model there could be up to 2,000 suppliers who varied considerably in size. There was much competition between these suppliers for the orders of the car firms, and this was mainly based on price. Today the situation is different. Increasingly the major car firms are looking for large component manufacturers who have specialist knowledge, specialist process equipment, who can undertake R&D, and who can be relied upon to produce quality goods. Increasingly these major suppliers produce component systems and have many contractors working for them who in turn may have contractors working for them, so producing a series of layers (R.C. Hill 1989). The result is a large reduction in the number of direct component suppliers but those that remain have a closer relationship with the car firms, although still remaining in competition with other component firms. Where the major car manufacturers had acquired component manufacturers, as was the case in the United States, these have had their relationship put at arms length and been made to compete with independent firms. In some cases component makers have been sold off, as was the case with British Leyland (Rover). These contractual relationships are discussed by Mike Rawlinson in Chapter 10, whilst David Froggatt and Ash Amin and Ian Smith discuss the components industry in Chapters 7 and 8.

Just-in-time systems

The JIT system was, of course, pioneered in the motor vehicle industry by Toyota in Japan, and so it is not surprising that its diffusion should most clearly be seen in other firms in the industry. After Toyota, it was adopted by other Japanese car makers and it appears that as new assembly plants are built by the Japanese in North America and Japan, the system is incorporated. However, it has been more difficult to change traditional purchasing systems in existing plant, although the severity of competition has forced suppliers to accept the new contracts. Estall (1985) reports that by the early 1980s the major American car firms such as General Motors and Chrysler were attempting to introduce the system. In Europe the change to JIT would appear to have come later. By the late 1980s Ford were reported to be introducing the JIT system to their continental plants whilst Peugeot were enlarging their Sochaux plant with the intention of converting to the system.

Flexible labour

Once again the ideas of task flexibility and group working pioneered by the Japanese are being widely innovated in the North American and West European industry. However, given the strength of unions and the long tradition of Fordist methods this has not been easy and is being introduced on a step-by-step approach. In 1989 General Motors–Vauxhall used the possibility of a new engine plant at Ellesmere Port to force the workers to agree to the introduction of more flexible work practices.

Most car workers continue to work full-time and there is not the part-time or temporary work practices seen in other industries. However, car assemblers are attempting to introduce three-shift working and possibly Saturday working to increase productivity.

Flexible labour practices are seen most clearly in the changing role of unions. From a strong position in North America and Western Europe they are increasingly being marginalized. In countries like Britain where there were many unions at each plant there has been an attempt to introduce single-union deals. In other areas there has been an attempt to have non-unionized plants or only unions which accept no-strike deals. These issues are discussed by Philip Garrahan and Paul Stewart in Chapter 6.

What are the spatial implications for the industry of these organizational changes? The introduction of JIT systems would suggest some reconcentration of the industry with industrial complexes, albeit on a larger geographical scale than occurred in the first half of the century. There is some evidence that new complexes are emerging around the Japanese transplants as the chapters by Rubenstein, and Garrahan and Stewart suggest. With respect to older industries, new patterns are as yet difficult to discern, partly because the changes are only just occurring, but there is clearly a topic for research here.

WORLD SPATIAL PATTERNS

The geographical pattern of world industrial production has been changing rapidly during the past thirty years (Dicken 1986). Modern manufacturing has spread to many more countries, including those of the Third World. The importance of North America and Western Europe has been reduced, and the hegemony of the United States has come to an end. In particular, Japan has emerged as a leading industrial power. Some commentators have postulated a new international division of labour with Third World countries specializing in labour-intensive manufacturing and often including old industries which have filtered down. How far does the motor industry mirror these trends? Is it representative of changing spatial patterns in the world (Table 1.1)?

The rise of Japan as an industrial power has taken the world by storm. Viewed from the aftermath of the Second World War this was completely unexpected. The Japanese have become successful in a wide range of modern industries from consumer electrical products and cameras to shipbuilding and motor vehicles. Much of what is often described as post-Fordism is, in fact, the transfer of best Japanese work practices, and so is sometimes referred to as Japanization. The Japanese began by employing Western technology and management practices, but have frequently gone on to pioneer new systems. Their success is the result of a combination of factors; the

Table 1.1 World car production and changes in GDP

	Output (000s)		Change (%)	GDP (1970–85)[a] Change (%)
	1970	1988		
Japan	3,179	8,198	+ 157.9	+ 550.1
USA	6,550	7,111	+ 8.6	+ 300.2
West Germany	3,528	4,346	+ 23.2	+ 238.7
France	2,458	3,224	+ 31.2	+ 262.2
Italy	1,720	1,884	+ 9.5	+ 256.5
Spain	450	1,498	+ 232.9	+ 346.3
USSR	344	1,319	+ 283.4	—
UK	1,641	1,227	− 25.2	+ 269.5
Canada	940	1,025	+ 9.0	+ 320.6
South Korea	—	872	—	+ 884.4
Brazil	343	782	+ 128.0	+ 420.0
Other major producers	1,483	2,384		
Total	22,636	33,870	+ 50.3	

[a]*Source*: United Nations Statistical Yearbook

thorough use of ideas familiar in the West, their commitment to long-term growth and success, low credit rates and an emphasis on training.

The growth of the Japanese motor industry is described by Yasuo Miyakawa in Chapter 4. Starting from a low base in the 1950s they have become the world's major producer of cars, and the growth of Japanese companies shows no sign of slackening. Initially emphasizing cost-reducing manufacturing processes, such as the JIT system, they are now moving their products up-market into areas previously secure from Japanese competition. Again, for many years Japanese companies preferred to export their products, perhaps fearing that their production methods could not be transferred. However, from the late 1970s this attitude began to change, a consequence of the rise of the value of the yen, the fear of tariffs being raised against them and a perception that sales would rise if there was a local manufacturing base. The 1980s witnessed an explosion of Japanese transplants, including those of the components industry. The main assemblers began to establish manufacturing bases in North America in the early 1980s, and by 1991 there will be 12 assembly plants and 250 automobile component suppliers (Mair *et al.* 1989). In the late 1980s they began to enter Western Europe, where there has been competition to attract transplants. These Japanese factories have attracted enormous attention and questions have been asked such as: are they merely screwdriver (assembly plants); are they buying components from local firms; are they causing an invasion of Japanese component suppliers; what kind of places do they choose; are they causing a new clustering of the industry; how do their work practices compare with indigenous firms; and how do they deal with unions? These questions are dealt with in Chapters 5 and 6.

The impact of the Japanese advance has been felt by the main North American and West European firms. For decades United States' firms dominated the industry and the rise of the Japanese has been a rude shock to them. They have lost sales in their home market and now see Japanese firms constructing factories in North America, such that by the early 1990s they will have 25 per cent of the capacity. They have had to close plants, rethink strategies and even enter partnerships with Japanese firms.

The early post-War period from 1945 to the mid-1970s witnessed rapid economic growth in Western Europe. Many large firms emerged from within their own countries and the prospect of European integration suggested that through mergers, even larger firms could evolve, secure from a large market base, which could help establish Europe as a power to rival the United States. Sceptics suggested that nationalism was so strong that it would prevent cross-national mergers, and that the only beneficiaries would be non-European firms such as those from the United States, who would be able to exploit the common market using the strength of their home bases.

The experience of the European motor vehicle industry gives some credence to the views of the sceptics. In 1967 Ford integrated its European operations to take full advantage of the EC and was later followed by General Motors. Initial European mergers were intra-national rather than cross-national, as with Peugeot and Citroën in France and Fiat, Lancia and Alfa Romeo in Italy. The only significant cross-national links have been between Volkswagen and SEAT (in Spain) and in early 1990 between Renault and Volvo. In 1988 the six largest firms had 75 per cent of the market, but none of them had more than 15 per cent. In that year Japanese firms had 11 per cent of the market, but this is forecast to rise to 20 per cent by 1995, partly based on increased manufacturing capacity. With greater competition in the home market, as well as abroad, European motor vehicles could find it difficult to establish a major world presence, unless they are saved by the opening up of East European markets.

Britain's overall relative decline is again mirrored in its motor vehicle industry. Once the forces of competition were unleashed in the early 1970s, through lower tariffs and integration with Europe, the industry began to decline, output falling by half between 1972 and 1982 (Law 1985). Many features of the industry were blamed for this failure, from poor management and poor products to poor labour relations. The components industry was also badly affected by the decline of vehicle output and this weakened its international role, as described in the Chapters 7 and 8. By 1989 the UK motor industry had a record trade deficit of £6.5 billion, accounting for more than a quarter of the UK's overall deficit. If there is any hope for the industry in Britain it lies in the fact that Nissan, Honda and Toyota have all chosen it for their European manufacturing bases. By the mid-1990s the loss of output in the 1970s could be recovered through the production of Japanese firms.

The shift of modern industries to Third World countries is not fully replicated by the motor vehicle industry. Whilst significant industries have been established in Mexico, Brazil, Argentina, India, Malaysia and South Korea, in most countries of this type the industry is merely represented by screwdriver assembly plants. There are many difficulties in establishing motor vehicle manufacturing in these countries, which are discussed in Chapter 3.

THE LOCAL SCENE

Given the large relative size of many motor vehicle plants it is not surprising they often have a significant local impact which can be examined in various ways. The establishment of a new plant is bound to affect the local labour market, with many workers transferring from existing plants in search of higher incomes and more secure employment (Salt 1967). There is also the potential of local linkages, encouraging the expectation of further employment growth, although in practice this has not been very important. A large community of car workers may have a significant influence on the local culture and politics, a topic discussed by Dennis Smith in Chapter 11. Work practices and union procedures learned in the factory may influence behaviour in neighbouring plants, both in a positive and negative way.

However, the dependence of communities on the motor vehicle industry may be problematical when there is decline and extensive rationalization. Responsible local authorities will naturally be concerned for the state of the industry, seeking to influence trends in a manner which will have a positive effect on their areas. However, their scope for intervention is limited as described by David Elliott and Patrick Gray in Chapter 12.

2 The world automotive industry in transition

Gerald T. Bloomfield

The period since 1973 has been one of substantial, if not turbulent, change in the automotive industry. All firms in this industry now operate in a more competitive environment as the pressures from the Japanese corporations have continued to grow. Few sectors of motor vehicle production and distribution are sheltered from the effects of new production methods, new vehicle designs and technology, and more sophisticated consumer demand. In the face of such powerful movements few places are now protected from external influences.

In the century since Daimler and Benz filed their first patents, the automobile industry has been a major force in technological, economic and social change. Many of the industry's lasting characteristics were established in the 1920s when the Ford–Sloan model of production and marketing became the normal practice in the United States (Kuhn 1986). This model was adopted and adapted by other national motor industries. By the early 1970s the industry was clearly part of a world-system with its production and marketing branches reaching out far beyond its roots in previously autonomous national areas. More recently new forces have begun to undermine the traditional structure of the automobile industry. Among the many forces of change are shifts in the world economy, the redefining of technology and markets, and consequent alterations in the structure of firms and the patterns of location.

The continued internationalization of manufacturing is at the core of many macroeconomic changes. A strong sense of the global forces at work has been conveyed by Dicken (1986) and Ballance (1987). The changing responses of the auto industry have been examined in several studies (Bloomfield 1978, 1981; Bhaskar 1980; Maxcy 1981; Sinclair 1983; Altshuler *et al.* 1984; Foreman-Peck 1986). Few major markets are not influenced or controlled by the multinational motor corporations.

Technological change has not only affected the design and performance of vehicles but has also had profound effects on the production process. Programmable automation and more flexible forms of work organization have begun to transform the traditional elements of mass production which characterized the industry since the Ford Motor Company's innovations of the 1910s. Ford or Fordist methods are now tending to give way to a range of alternatives often pioneered outside the United States (Sabel 1982; Friedman 1983; Ettlie 1988; Gertler 1988). Flexible forms of manufacturing, it is argued, may create new locational patterns involving spatial reintegration (Schoenberger 1987). Such changes would be a reversal of the current moves towards more decentralization.

If Ford's initial world success was founded on the mass production of huge volumes of a standardized car for mass markets (the Model T), General Motors under Alfred P. Sloan in the 1920s developed a different strategy. All income levels were to be served by a broad range of models which would be modified by annual changes incorporating some gradual engineering improvements and regular style changes. The Ford–Sloan model of the industry has now begun to lose its dominance as consumer power has grown. Consumer attention to variety, fashion and quality has placed a new emphasis on product differentiation which is now more possible at reasonable price levels with flexible manufacturing (Sabel 1982; Cohen and Zysman 1987). The traditional oligopolies which have dominated national markets are now being diminished by greater competition from imports (Adams and Brock 1986). Such changes in the market-place are a very significant element in the world shifts taking place in the auto industry.

The rapid convergence of many features of change in the 1970s created the conditions for industrial restructuring, which as Hamilton (1984) has outlined, involves active corporate and government strategies. In this process, old patterns are re-aligned or even destroyed and new patterns are formed and reshaped. The fast pace of change and the complex of elements included in restructuring are well expressed in a growing literature on this field (Massey 1984; Bradbury 1985; Amin and Goddard 1986; Scott and Storper 1986; Henderson and Castells 1987; Peet 1987; Beauregard 1989).

Competitive pressures, global recession and rapid technological change have profoundly affected the motor industry throughout the 1980s. Particular studies of the features of restructuring include Hunker (1983), Cole and Yakushiji (1984), Tolliday and Zeitlin (1986), Hill (1987) and Holmes (1987a). The economic significance of the industry and the sense of crisis in the late 1970s were reflected in the formation of specialized units for the multidisciplinary study of the motor industry. The publications of the Massachusetts Institute of Technology's International Automobile Program (Altshuler *et al.* 1984) and the Science Policy Research Unit at the University of Sussex (Jones 1981, 1988) have developed new insights into this complex world industry.

Change and transition are integral themes in this general overview of world patterns since 1973. In the second part the nature of changing markets, increased competition and the effects on corporate performance are explored in some detail. The problems arising from the coincidence of several forces of change in the late 1970s are examined in the third section where macro features of restructuring are illustrated with reference to General Motors, Volkswagen and Toyota. Finally, some of the spatial effects of structural change are outlined in relation to the re-organization of General Motors operations in Europe.

GENERAL WORLD TRENDS SINCE 1973

The oil crisis which began to affect the world economy in late 1973 acted as a substantial brake on the continued growth of the automotive industry. From 1960 to 1973 world motor vehicle output expanded rapidly from 16.4 million to 39.2 million units. Since 1973 the industry has grown more slowly, reaching 45.6 million units in 1987. In place of the regular annual expansion of the 1960s, the industry has become more cyclical. As illustrated by Fig. 2.1 and Table 2.1 there have been major peaks and troughs in the volume of vehicle production. These cycles reflect macroeconomic forces in oil supply and price and in market demand for cars and commercial vehicles.

Three production regions dominate the industry. Each region has been changing in relative significance since 1973. North America (United States/Canada) has experienced the most violent fluctuations in production. Since this region has the most mature market in terms of market saturation and the oldest production infrastructure, the effects of fluctuating demand have been most substantial. North America's share of world output has continued to decline as new competitors have arisen and as motorization has diffused more widely. In 1977 North America accounted for 35.2 per cent of world vehicle output, a decade later, its proportion had fallen to 27.1 per cent.

Table 2.1 Fluctuations in world motor vehicle output (million units)

	Total world		US/Canada		Western Europe		Japan		Other[a]	
	(million units)	Index	(million units)	Index	(million units)	Index	(million units)	Index	(million units)	Index
1973 (Peak)	39.2	100.0	14.2	100.0	13.3	100.0	7.1	100.0	4.6	100.0
1975 (Trough)	33.3	84.9	10.4	73.2	10.6	79.7	6.9	97.2	5.4	117.3
1978 (Peak)[b]	42.6	108.6	14.7	103.5	12.7	95.5	9.3	131.0	5.9	128.3
1982 (Trough)	36.8	93.8	8.3	58.4	11.6	87.2	10.7	150.7	6.2	134.8
1987 (Peak?)	46.4	118.4	12.5	88.0	14.1	106.0	12.2	171.8	7.5	163.0

Source: MVMA and SMMT data; estimates

[a] Includes Eastern Europe/USSR, Latin America, South Africa/Australia and other Asian producers. See Table 2.2

[b] The peaks and troughs of US/Canada and Western Europe differ slightly after 1978. The post-recession peak in US/Canada was reached in 1985 with an output of 13.6 million (index 95.8)

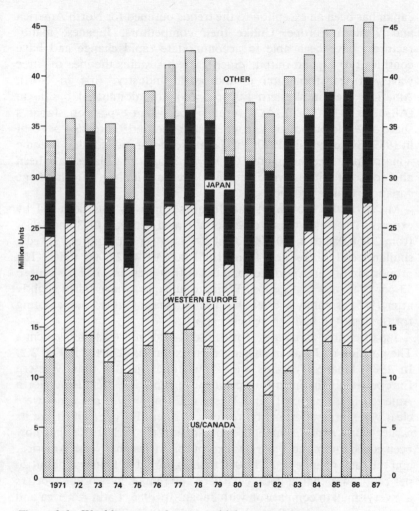

Figure 2.1 World output of motor vehicles, 1971–87
Source: MVMA data

Western Europe's motor vehicle industry has experienced fluctuations in output but not on the same scale as North America. Within the region there have been some locational shifts as the British industry has declined and that of Spain has expanded. Over the period 1977–87 there has been little change in the relative world position of the motor vehicle industry in Western Europe.

Japan in the world automotive industry

Japan has been an exception to the trends outlined for North America and Western Europe. Unlike their competitors, Japanese manufacturers have been able to accommodate rapid change and have continued to expand output. Such growth sustains the idea of three waves of transformation in the world industry, first in North America, then in Western Europe, and now dominated by Japan (Altshuler *et al.* 1984). As a result of persistent expansion, Japan's share of world output grew from 20.7 per cent in 1977 to 26.4 per cent in 1987. Since the mid-1970s the Japanese motor industry has become a major influence throughout the world, so that few places have been able to isolate themselves from the direct and indirect effects of the Japanese vehicle producers.

Much of the growth of the Japanese industry has been led by exports. The total volume of exports tripled between 1973 and 1985, from 2,068,000 to 6,730,000 vehicles. Passenger car exports showed a similar trend, increasing from 1,451,000 to 4,427,000 units. The proportion of car exports to total car output grew from 32 per cent to 53 per cent over that period. While total exports have fallen slightly after 1985, assembly overseas has been increasing, thus compensating for the losses in built-up vehicle exports.

Japan clearly dominates world intercontinental trade movements. The position of Japan in passenger car exports is depicted in Fig. 2.2. In 1986 Japanese exports were four times greater than Western Europe (if all the intra-European movements are excluded). North America (56.4 per cent) and Western Europe (29.0 per cent) were clearly the largest destination regions. Western Europe, which lost its earlier world export dominance to Japan in the early 1970s, has now been edged out of most markets except for Africa and North America, and the total volume of 1,113,000 units exported in 1986 was about 20 per cent lower than a decade earlier. The remaining world exporters are very small in comparison with Japan. In 1986, Latin America and Eastern Europe/USSR each exported about 200,000 units and Canada/US exported only 38,000 cars. South Korea, which increased its car exports from 16,000 in 1983 to 299,000 in 1986, is still a small competitor in world markets.

The continued rise of Japanese car exports can also be expressed in market penetration illustrated in Fig. 2.3. Japanese cars (and often, more importantly, light trucks) dominate much of the world periphery. In the island territories of the Pacific and the Caribbean, for example, Japanese market penetration is virtually 100 per cent. While some

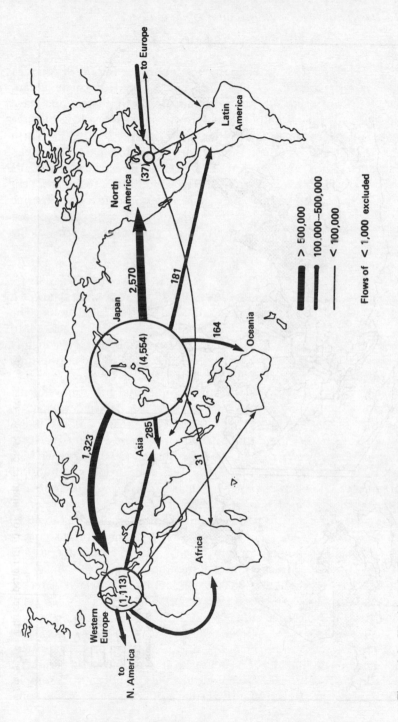

to Europe

Latin
America

North
America

(37)

Japan

(4,554)

2,570

181

164

Oceania

1,323

Asia   285

31

Western
Europe

(1,113)

Africa

to
N. America

> 500,000

100,000—500,000

< 100,000

Flows of < 1,000 excluded

Figure 2.2 World trade flows: passenger cars, 1986

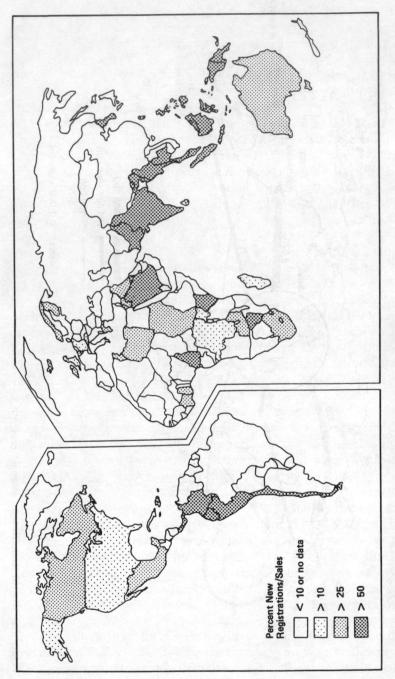

Figure 2.3 Market penetration of Japanese passenger cars, 1986

**Percent New
Registrations/Sales**

< 10 or no data

> 10

> 25

> 50

major market areas such as Argentina and Brazil remain closed to imports, a few, formerly closed markets, have been opened up. In India the joint venture between Maruti and Suzuki, signed in 1982, has begun to transform the national industry. Output of Maruti cars has increased from 175 in 1983 to 94,000 in 1987.

In North America Japanese market penetration reached 26 per cent in Canada and 21 per cent in the United States during 1986. The situation in Western Europe is very variable. Small peripheral markets such as Iceland (69 per cent), Ireland (43 per cent), Finland (40 per cent), Denmark and Norway (35 per cent) had the highest levels of penetration. Intermediate markets such as Belgium, the Netherlands, Sweden and Switzerland averaged between 20 and 25 per cent penetration levels in 1986. In the largest markets with major national motor industries the levels were very variable. West Germany (15 per cent) and the United Kingdom (11 per cent) were fairly open; France (3 per cent), Italy (0.5 per cent) and Spain (0.6 per cent) were clearly very restrictive in their policies towards car imports from Japan.

Why have the Japanese manufacturers been so successful in world trade? The new production management principles, evolved over several decades (Cusumano 1985; Friedman 1988), have been able to deliver lower-cost products of higher quality. In addition, the Japanese methods have been more flexible in adjusting to market changes. It is now clear that Japanese best practice is now replacing many features of the Ford–Sloan model which dominated the industry from the 1920s (Jones 1988: 20–6). The effects of the new principles became clear in the early 1980s when the cost differentials of Japanese and American sub-compact cars were analyzed (Harbour and Associates 1982). Figure 2.4 shows the significance of the management systems and techniques, notably quality control, just-in-time supply lines and other features which raised productivity. Wage rates only accounted for 25 per cent of the cost differential, while the management systems and techniques contributed 63 per cent of the total. Although the differential may have been reduced since 1985 by the appreciation of the yen, Japanese manufacturers still enjoy lower costs.

Until the late 1970s, Japanese manufacturers had only limited overseas investments, which were generally limited to a partial financial interest in ckd ('completely knocked down' kits) assembly or the full ownership of a distributing company (Rae 1982). Since 1980, Japanese firms have not only taken over full control (as in Australia and New Zealand) but have begun large-scale investments in North America and now in Western Europe. Import restrictions, currency fluctuations and the greater self-confidence of Japanese vehicle

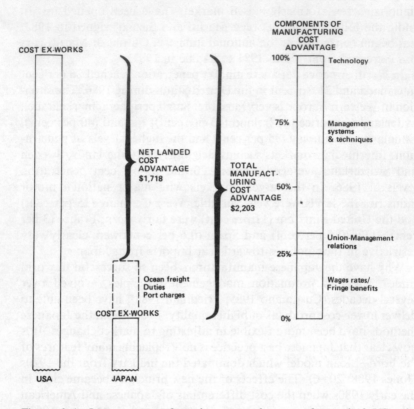

Figure 2.4 Japanese manufacturing cost advantage for typical US sub-compact car, early 1980s
Source: After Harbour and Associates

manufacturers were among the many factors behind the decisions to establish major production bases overseas (Egerton and Thomas 1983). By 1986 Japanese companies had announced plans for ten new plants in North America with a total capacity of 2,120,000 cars, of which 330,000 were to be in Canada (CSCA 1987, p. 9). Results from the earliest wave of development in the United States are now becoming visible. Honda, which began assembly in 1982, is now a major producer and even exports some cars to Japan. The total volume of Japanese assembly in the US had increased from 1,500 units in 1982 to over 760,000 in 1988 and now accounts for nearly 11 per cent of national output.

Honda and Nissan have been active in Western Europe since the early 1980s and other firms, notably Isuzu and Suzuki, are producing light commercial vehicles in Britain (in association with General Motors) and Spain. Toyota has also begun an investigation of potential sites for a major plant investment. In addition to growth in the big market regions of North America and Western Europe, Japanese firms have been investing in South-East Asia. The search for lower production costs and government inducements for export-led manufacturing have been factors. Indonesia is, for example, becoming a significant producer of engines. This substantial growth of overseas investment will eventually have direct implications for the older plants in Japan (*The Economist*, 24 May 1986, p. 67).

The controlling power of Japanese motor corporations has risen in parallel with the growth of production and exports. In 1977 Japanese firms controlled about 21 per cent of world output. By 1986 the proportion had risen to 29 per cent. Over the same period US corporations' share decreased from 46 per cent to 36 per cent and European corporations remained virtually unchanged at 24 per cent. Other corporate shares of firms in Eastern Europe/USSR and South Korea increased slightly from 8 per cent to 11 per cent (Bloomfield 1981: 364 and MVMA 1988: 16). The rising power of Japanese manufacturers is now a key force in the restructuring of the world industry.

Continued world decentralization?

Over the past decade production trends in the other world regions have been variable (Table 2.2). In the late 1970s it was anticipated that more transfer of production would occur as the multinationals sought lower-cost manufacturing bases in the periphery. Changes in production methods, however, focused most investment in the core regions. Consequently there have been few major investments and productivity appears to have stagnated.

The most dramatic changes have taken place in east and south Asia. South Korea has emerged in the 1980s as a significant world producer. Vehicle output increased almost twelve-fold between 1977 and 1987 from 83,000 units to 980,000 and surpassed Brazil (920,000 units). From very modest beginnings in the early 1970s (Odaka 1983), a combination of active corporate development (especially by Hyundai), some external technical linkages, low wages, protected home market and export promotion helped in the creation of a dynamic new industry. Hyundai is the largest company (output 607,000 vehicles in 1987) and has based its growth strategy on exports to North America, first entering the Canadian market in 1984 and the United States two years later. There are two smaller companies in Korea, Kia (linked with Mazda and hence to Ford) with a 1987 production of 197,000 vehicles and Daewoo (owned 50 per cent by General Motors) with an output of 162,000 vehicles.

Table 2.2 Production trends in other world regions (million units)

	1977	1982	1987
Eastern Europe	1.1	1.1	1.4
USSR	2.1	2.2	2.3
Latin America	1.4	1.5	1.5
East and South Asia	0.4	0.6	1.7
Australia	0.4	0.4	0.3
South Africa	0.3	0.4	0.3
Total	5.7	6.2	7.5

Source: MVMA and Ward's data; estimates

China, India and Taiwan have all shown substantial increases in production over the past decade. The decentralization of manufacturing has been most significant not in vehicle-building but in the production of parts and subassemblies. Mexico has become a major supplier of engines, exporting some 1.25 million in 1986, mostly to the United States and Western Europe (170,000 VW engines). Similar developments elsewhere, although difficult to trace in world trade statistics, may well be the new wave of future decentralization.

MARKETS, COMPETITION AND CORPORATE PERFORMANCE

The emphasis on volume and value of production in most industrial studies tends to diminish the significance of markets as the critical challenge for companies and their products. Markets in the 1970s and 1980s have not only become more volatile but have shown very substantial changes. Such changes have been most visible in the United States, the largest mature and most complex market area. But other market areas have also experienced change from the pressures of competition.

As expressed in Fig. 2.5 the market profile of new passenger car registrations in the United States has shifted dramatically since the mid-1960s. The traditional full-size American car which accounted for 50 per cent of the market in 1966, declined in significance to 19.1 per cent in 1976 and to only 9.8 per cent in 1986. Among the many reasons

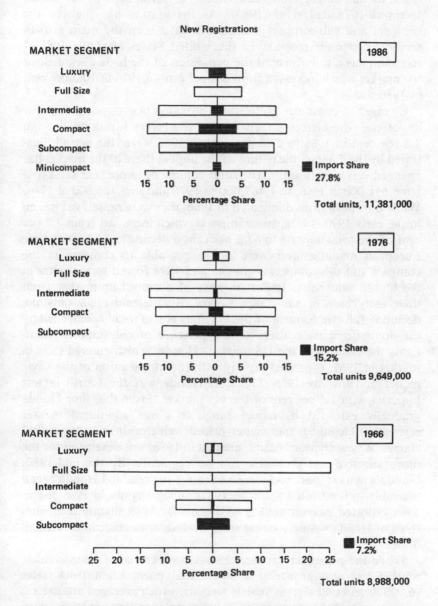

New Registrations

MARKET SEGMENT

1986

Luxury

Full Size

Intermediate

Compact

Subcompact

Minicompact

■ Import Share
27.8%

15 10 5 0 5 10 15
Percentage Share

Total units, 11,381,000

MARKET SEGMENT

1976

Luxury

Full Size

Intermediate

Compact

Subcompact

■ Import Share
15.2%

15 10 5 0 5 10 15
Percentage Share

Total units 9,649,000

MARKET SEGMENT

1966

Luxury

Full Size

Intermediate

Compact

Subcompact

■ Import Share
7.2%

25 20 15 10 5 0 5 10 15 20 25
Percentage Share

Total units 8,988,000

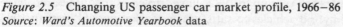

Figure 2.5 Changing US passenger car market profile, 1966–86
Source: *Ward's Automotive Yearbook* data

for this change were the effects of higher fuel prices, general cost inflation in vehicle prices and operating costs, government regulations, as well as deliberate 'downsizing' of car designs by the manufacturers (Crandall *et al.* 1986). As the market has changed the compact and sub-compact size classes have been the main growth sectors. Economic recovery in the United States after the 1981–3 recession has also influenced the expansion of the luxury segment of the market which increased from 5.8 per cent in 1976 to 10.2 per cent in 1986.

Changes in consumer preferences provided new opportunities for importers, who increased their market share very substantially from 7.2 per cent in 1966 to 27.8 per cent in 1986. Over the period illustrated by the diagram the nature of the import share of the market has changed very significantly. The total volume of import car sales rose from 651,000 in 1966, to 1,465,000 in 1976 and to 3,166,000 in 1986. While European firms dominated in 1966, they were rapidly overtaken in the early 1970s by Japanese imports which increased from 7.7 per cent of the total imports to 62.2 per cent a decade later. By this time European manufacturers were no longer able to compete in the compact and sub-compact segments and were forced to specialize in the higher value cars. Importers have also moved up-market from their early base of sub-compact cars. By the mid-1980s only the declining full-size segment of the US market was totally controlled by the domestic manufacturers. The experience of one importer highlights the changes in the US market. Honda, which entered the US market in 1969, expanded rapidly with the introduction of the Civic model in 1974. By 1976 (Fig. 2.6) Honda was the fourth largest importer with 1.5 per cent of the car market. From that time Honda gradually extended its model range to cover additional market segments, including the higher-priced vehicles in the 'specialty' classes. A new division, Acura, created in 1986, was developed for the more selective and profitable market segments. By the mid-1980s Honda's market share had increased to 6.1 per cent and Honda began assembly in the United States in 1982, added engines in 1986 and in 1988 exported Accord models to Japan. By 1986 slightly over one-third of Honda's American car sales were vehicles made in the United States.

While the passenger car market has been changing a new vehicle market has also grown at a substantial pace. Light truck sales (6,000 lb and under gross vehicle weight), which averaged around 1.2 million units each year up to 1982, have tripled as manufacturers have developed hybrid vehicles to satisfy new market possibilities. In 1984

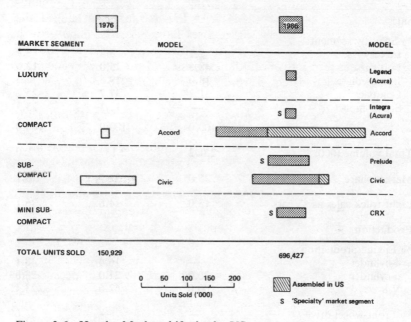

Figure 2.6 Honda: Market shifts in the US
Source: *Ward's Automotive Yearbook data*

light truck sales increased to 2.2 million units and the number rose to 3.4 million in 1987. Sales of the mini passenger van, first introduced by Chrysler in 1983 and designed to fit into the average domestic garage had grown to 550,000 units by 1987. The once clear distinctions between cars and light commercial vehicles are now becoming blurred.

The competitive twists and turns in the market-place have profoundly affected corporations in the world auto industry. Old established domestic manufacturers have seen their basic markets altered and the market share eroded as new entrants have quickly created a niche for their products. Some of the elements of adjustment may be observed in the selected data for the Ford Motor Company (Table 2.3). While the total volume of sales remained fairly stable over the period reviewed, the overall market share declined substantially and the nature of the market was transformed. The break-up of the mass market in the full-size segment has had many implications. There are now many more competitors. In 1966 Volkswagen was the only outsider selling over 50,000 cars in the US; twenty years later there

Table 2.3 Market changes and the Ford Motor Company in the US

	1966	1976	1986
Sales			
% Sales by segment			
Luxury	2.2	5.4	8.7
Full-size	48.6	25.0	12.6
Intermediate	18.0	19.6	30.2
Compact	31.2[a]	37.7	25.2
Sub-compact	—	12.3	23.3
	100.0	100.0	100.0
Total volume (000)	2,042	2,157	2,250
Market share	25.0	22.7	18.1
Light truck sales as % cars	15.02	14.6	36.1
Production			
% Engine production			
4-cylinder	—	16.4	48.1
6-cylinder	20.0[b]	21.0	28.8
V-8	80.0[b]	62.6	23.1
% Front-wheel drive	—	—	55.6
No. of plants			
Car assembly	15	15	8
Light truck assembly	9	8	7
Labour force (000s)	234	220	181

Sources: Annual Reports; *Ward's Automotive Yearbooks*

[a]Includes the very successful 'Mustang' sports model (24.0 per cent of total sales)
[b]Estimates

were 15 foreign companies with annual sales over 50,000 units. Ford has had to reshape its marketing and production strategies to cope with the more competitive environment. Production runs are now smaller as the market has become fragmented. Massive investment has been needed, not only in the design of new lines of cars to cover all market segments but in the production systems to manufacture four-cylinder and V-6 engines in place of the big V-8s of the past. The shift to front-wheel drive meant changes in production methods of transmissions, axles and many other components. All these adjustments had to be made quickly in market conditions which were uncertain and volatile. Similar problems of adjustment to making new types of vehicles had to be faced in other parts of the world where Ford had a major market position.

How well individual corporations have adjusted to the rapid changes in the market has depended on their ability to respond with flexibility and the financial resources which they could command.

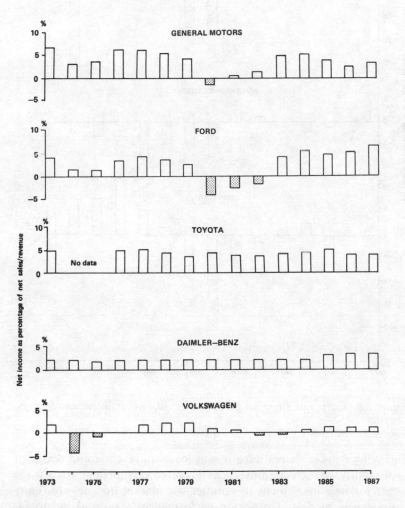

Figure 2.7 Corporate financial performance: GM, Ford, Toyota, Daimler-Benz, VW

Source: Annual reports

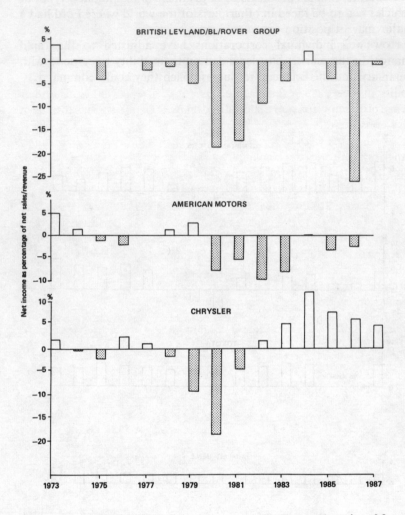

Figure 2.8   Corporate financial performance: BL/Rover, American Motors, Chrysler
Source: Annual reports

Shrinking market shares have meant losses in revenue and declining profitability. In such circumstances it is often very difficult to raise the funds for new investment to counter the market decline with competitive new models. Corporate performance, measured by profitability, has been very variable as companies have struggled to adjust their position (Figs. 2.7 and 2.8).

The large corporations serving all market segments have had the most variable performance. Ford had three years of substantial losses in the early 1980s as it worked to change its models in a period of rapid market decline. Volkswagen experienced losses in the mid-1970s as it had to re-organize after the long dominance of the Beetle car. Toyota is unusual among the mass-market producers in maintaining its profitability in a very consistent fashion over a period of change. Daimler-Benz, producing for more specialized market segments, has also been very consistent.

Not all firms were able to survive the changes. British Leyland and American Motors were financially weak before the rapid market shifts after 1973. Even with infusions of investment capital from the state and from Renault in the case of American Motors the deterioration in financial viability continued. The Chrysler Corporation, which was close to failure in 1979–80, was able to make a remarkable recovery with new management, government loans and a successful new model which was introduced at the critical time (Reich and Donahue 1985).

Some of the broader features of competition and corporate performance are implied in Table 2.4 which shows the ranking of the twenty largest motor corporations in 1977 and 1987. While there has

Table 2.4 Ranking of largest motor corporations by production (000 units)

Rank	1977		1987	
1	GM	9068	GM	7765
2	Ford	6422	Ford	6,051
3	Chrysler	3069	Toyota	4078
4	Toyota	2721	VW	2771
5	Fiat	2282	Nissan	2463
6	Nissan	2278	Chrysler	2008
7	VW	2219	Renault	1965
8	Peugeot	1518	Fiat	1915
9	Renault	1434	Peugeot	1886
10	Mazda	800	Honda	1745
11	Mitsubishi	776	Mitsubishi	1321
12	BL	771	Mazda	1196
13	Lada	725	Suzuki	867
14	Honda	665	Daimler-Benz	832
15	Daimler-Benz	662	Lada	727
16	AMC	382	Hyundai	606
17	SEAT	353	Fuji	605
18	Isuzu	340	Daihatsu	598
19	Moskvitch	320	Isuzu	541
20	Daihatsu	317	Rover Group	508

Source: Bloomfield (1981), MVMA, SMMT and annual reports

been a general increase in size of operations over the period, with twelve corporations producing over one million vehicles in place of nine, there has also been more convergence in size as the dominance of General Motors has been reduced. The major changes in the ranking of the ten largest were those of Chrysler and Honda. Chrysler's lower position reflects the overall down-sizing of the company by the disposal of the earlier loss-making subsidiaries outside North America. Honda, which only began producing cars in 1963, grew very quickly in the period. Three companies, SEAT (to VW in 1987), AMC (to Chrysler in 1987) and Moskvitch disappeared from the list. The newcomers were Suzuki, Hyundai and Fuji (Subaru). British Leyland (BL) declined significantly in rank, reflecting its weak market and financial position. Lada, the largest Soviet car manufacturer, experienced little change in total output over the period.

In the very competitive environment of the world auto industry, the viability of corporations requires a subtle blend of a strong market position and a flexible design production system which can respond to consumer changes. The maintenance of any corporate system depends on profitability which is needed to sustain continuous new investments in R&D, production and marketing operations.

CORPORATE RESPONSES TO THE PRESSURES OF COMPETITION

As outlined in previous sections, all firms in the industry have been subject to more intensified competition in the market as well as from the evolving forms of 'best practice' in manufacturing – largely defined by the Japanese from the mid-1970s (Jones 1988). Rapid changes have influenced corporate financial performance; while the strength or weakness of the corporate financial base and general business confidence have shaped the ability of firms to respond to new competitive pressures. The strategy of most companies in Western Europe and North America has been to attempt to maintain their existing market position. This has meant substantial capital investment and has often been accompanied by some spatial consolidation on core market regions. For Japanese companies, their general strategy of growth has involved an upward move into higher-priced market segments (Fig. 2.6).

The financial costs of responding to change have been enormous. In the US motor vehicle and parts industry, capital investment on new plant and equipment averaged $4.5 billion annually in the 1970s. From 1980 to 1988 the annual average rose to $10.95 billion. Between

1977 and 1988 the US automotive industry spent $120 billion on new equipment and plant (*Automotive News*, 1988: 86). All this investment took place during a period when there was limited overall growth in the volume of production.

Figure 2.9 outlines a series of possible responses by which motor corporations have sought to maintain their competitive position in the world industry. All firms have utilized the basic forms of response, in trimming costs of production and distribution especially by temporary

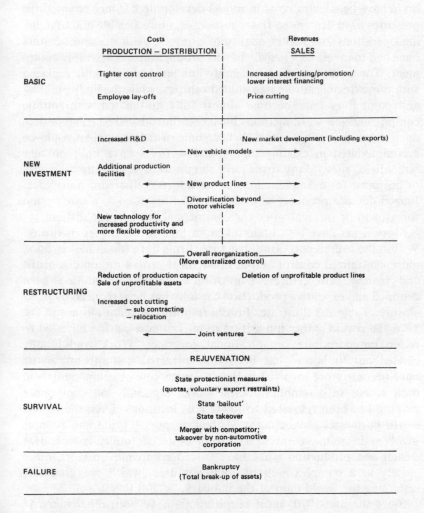

	Costs PRODUCTION – DISTRIBUTION	Revenues SALES
BASIC	Tighter cost control	Increased advertising/promotion/lower interest financing
	Employee lay-offs	Price cutting
NEW INVESTMENT	Increased R&D	New market development (including exports)
	←——— New vehicle models ———→	
	Additional production facilities	
	←——— New product lines ———→	
	←——— Diversification beyond motor vehicles ———→	
	New technology for increased productivity and more flexible operations	
RESTRUCTURING	←——— Overall reorganization ———→ (More centralized control)	
	Reduction of production capacity Sale of unprofitable assets	Deletion of unprofitable product lines
	Increased cost cutting — sub contracting — relocation	
	←——— Joint ventures ———→	
REJUVENATION		
SURVIVAL	State protectionist measures (quotas, voluntary export restraints)	
	State 'bailout'	
	State takeover	
	Merger with competitor; takeover by non-automotive corporation	
FAILURE	Bankruptcy (Total break-up of assets)	

Figure 2.9 Corporate responses to competition in the automotive industry

lay-offs of employees. Attempts to increase market share and sales revenue are regularly pursued through larger advertising and promotion campaigns, lower interest rate financing and even price cutting on model lines reaching the end of their life-cycle.

The more positive and lasting responses require substantial new investment. Market pressures have forced all companies to develop new model lines which incorporate advanced technology. Increased R&D expenditure and the extension of markets by introducing more 'recreation-type' vehicles, and new innovations such as four-wheel drive have been extra costs in model development. Since competitive pressures have demanded faster responses, more flexible manufacturing operations and higher quality of product, vehicle manufacturers have had to invest very heavily in new production and assembly equipment. The traditional final assembly line has been partially replaced with more flexible automated guided vehicles, while the body building and paint lines have become almost fully automated with robotic equipment. New work methods have been introduced to enhance productivity and quality control. While some of the equipment could be accommodated in existing plants, a few firms have built on new 'greenfield' sites. Many firms have sought to diversify into new lines of business; for example, Chrysler has added Gulfstream Aerospace. Indeed defence products have always been regarded as a safe option for growth or survival when the commercial markets are difficult.

Most firms have also undertaken various forms of restructuring. Within the overall corporate structure, firms have sometimes stressed more centralized control and at other times semi-autonomous profit and management centres. Unprofitable product lines have been dropped and expensive production capacity has been reduced by plant closure. Table 2.3 illustrates Ford's response by plant closure in the 1976–86 period. More intensified rounds of cost-cutting have led to rethinking corporate organizational practices. Work traditionally carried out 'in-house' has been subcontracted and subcontractors have become more involved in the design process of components and even whole subassemblies. Some work, especially on component making has been relocated to lower cost locations. Even the largest world businesses have swallowed their corporate pride and become involved in joint ventures. The high costs of totally independent design and production work have forced companies to work more closely in a complex web of joint ventures, which are gradually reshaping the world map of the industry.

Since the mid-1970s most corporations have been rejuvenated in order to retain their competitive position. Such rejuvenation has required many changes in the people and the institutions for whom they work. Leadership for change has become more visible and new figures in the industry have been well publicized, as Michael Edwardes of BL, Lee Iacocca at Chrysler and Roger Smith at General Motors have wrestled with the problems of their respective companies (Edwardes 1983; Iacocca 1984; Nader and Taylor 1986). Competitive responses have, of course, required the active participation of large teams of people throughout the business organizations. New emphases on improved productivity and changes in work practices have led to conflict between managements and workers (Tolliday and Zeitlin 1986).

Not all corporations have managed the transition to a new competitive environment without state support. Indeed, without a degree of state protectionism, many would not have survived without massive reductions in size. Voluntary export restraints were clearly very important for the North American and West European industries in the early 1980s. While a breathing space for new investment and restructuring was allowed, the diminution of some of the Japanese competitive pressure channelled fewer exports into higher and more profitable market segments and into other world markets (OECD 1987). The various forms of survival noted in Figure 2.9 have had to be accepted at one time or another by motor corporations – state bailout (Chrysler), state takeover (British Leyland) and merger with competitor (Citroën with Peugeot, AMC with Chrysler). In the mid-1980s the high cost of state involvement has forced divestment, as exemplified by the sale of Alfa Romeo to Fiat (1986) and the Rover Group to British Aerospace (1988). The links between financial performance (Fig. 2.8) and ultimate corporate survival are obvious.

Total failure, with bankruptcy and break-up of the assets, has been rare. The high economic and political visibility of the large motor companies has compelled some degree of state protection and the implementation of a slower pace of reduction to match the new competitive environment.

Most of the examples of disappearance are in the small firm segment, with such cars as Checker taxis and De Lorean, and in the components manufacturing sector. Restructuring in the tyre industry has led to the disappearance of Dunlop and Firestone, both old firms established in the beginnings of the industry.

The various responses to competitive pressures in the automotive industry have become the basis of new or modified spatial processes which are explored at the world scale through three case studies and in the final section of this chapter.

Three case studies of changing responses

The three corporations selected for further analysis are very different multinational business organizations (Bloomfield 1981). General Motors evolved from a series of mergers beginning in 1908. From the early 1920s the corporation expanded throughout the world in association with semi-autonomous national companies each working within a framework of import substitution. Volkswagen and Toyota are much younger companies and both were created to fulfil distinct national economic objectives while utilizing American production methods. From the late 1950s Volkswagen began to establish production facilities overseas and acquired Auto Union and NSU (reorganized as Audi). Toyota, in contrast to the other two corporations, remains a basically straightforward organization still highly concentrated around the original location in Japan. Variations in corporate complexity are suggested by the data presented in Table 2.5. Rates of change between 1977 and 1987 were very different. Production by GM declined slightly by 3.8 per cent over the period, while VW grew by 25 per cent and Toyota expanded output by 50 per cent. It is clear that General Motors and VW are geographically complex corporations while Toyota is still in the very early stages of decentralized production.

General Motors

As the largest corporation in the automotive industry and the world's largest industrial enterprise, General Motors has had a very difficult task of accommodating to the new competitive environment of the years since 1973. It has been shaken by the massive competition in the North American market which has resulted in declining market share. The 1980 financial results, which showed the first loss since 1921 (Fig. 2.7), also highlighted the need for corporate change. Consequently GM has been involved in virtually every type of corporate response outlined earlier.

The corporation has undertaken several major re-organizations: overseas operations in 1978, the formation of a worldwide truck and bus group in 1981, a new structure for North American passenger car operations in 1984, the formation of the Saturn car division and a new coordinating organization for Western Europe in 1986. With a massive investment programme of over $50 billion between 1977 and 1987, GM has restructured most of its operations in the core areas of North America and Western Europe. New plants have been opened

Table 2.5 World production of three automobile corporations, 1977 and 1987 (000 units)

Production regions	General Motors				VW Group				Toyota			
	1977	%	1987	%	1977	%	1987	%	1977	%	1987	%
US/Canada	6472	80.2	5695	73.3	—		67	2.4	—		44	1.1
Western Europe	1103	13.7	1450	18.7	1626	73.3	2213	79.9	—		—	
Japan	148	1.8	320	4.1	—		8	0.3	2721	100.0	3986	97.7
Other Asia	—		—		1		11	0.4	—		—	
Eastern Europe	—		—		11	0.5	31	1.1	—		—	
Latin America	211	2.6	230	3.0	524	23.6	395	14.3	—		3	0.1
Oceania	116	1.4	70	1.4	57		—		—		45	1.1
Africa	18	0.3	—	0.3	57	2.6	46	1.6	—		—	
World total	8068	100.0	7765	100.0	2219	100.0	2771	100.0	2721	100.0	4078	100.0

Source: Corporation annual reports; MVMA and SMMT data

and redundant ones closed. Various traditional activities have been sold off – Frigidaire appliances in 1979, Terex heavy construction equipment in 1980, heavy trucks to a joint venture with Volvo in 1986. Some diversification has also taken place: GM acquired Electronic Data Systems in 1984 and the Hughes Aircraft Company in the following year. While both acquisitions will remain autonomous they will make contributions to the parent in information technology and electronics.

One of GM's more publicized strategies in the early 1980s was the development of a 'world car'. The J-car (Chevrolet Cavalier in North America, Opel Ascona/Vauxhall Cavalier in Europe and other name-plates) was to be a standardized vehicle produced and sold in all major market areas. Subassemblies, such as engines and transaxles, were to be produced in Australia and Japan and shipped worldwide (Sinclair 1983: 72–4). The plan was flawed from the outset, since the vehicle designed by Opel in Germany was almost totally redesigned in Detroit for the North American market. Thus many benefits of economies of scale were lost (Jones 1988: 33). Inflexibilities in production methods combined with shifts in consumer preferences reduced the possibilities of this concept and limited the overall profitability of the project. The problems of integrating the far-flung activities of GM were among the reasons for later re-organization and the down-sizing of headquarters staff in Detroit.

General Motors has participated in several joint ventures in vehicle building, components and production technology. In 1984 GM joined with Toyota to form New United Motor Manufacturing Inc. (NUMMI) at Fremont, California to build jointly designed vehicles in a Japanese-style work setting. A further major joint venture with Toyota (1989) will transform the Australian subsidiary Holden's. In Canada, the GM/Suzuki joint venture at Ingersoll, Ontario, will add a new line of North American assembled minicars.

Figure 2.10 shows some general world changes of the corporation. Captive imports to North America have increased in the 1980s as GM has continued to battle with the other imports. Mexico has become more closely integrated into North American passenger car operations with some export movements of finished vehicles, engines and small components. The Western European activities have been re-organized with the British operations downgraded to the manufacturing/ assembly activities of cars. Design capabilities were disbanded, engine production ended and heavy commercial vehicle production sold off. New investment in an Austrian engine plant and car assembly in Spain have shifted the centre of gravity southwards (Sinclair and Walker

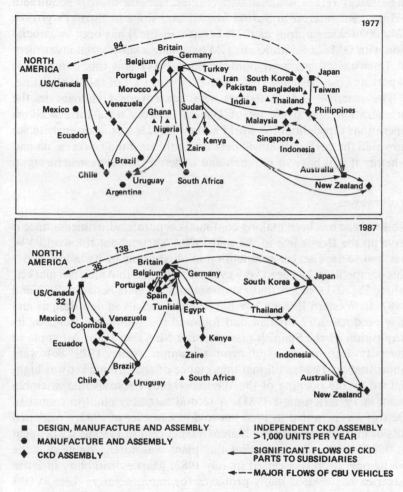

Figure 2.10 World changes in GM, 1977–87

1982). Elsewhere GM operations have been reduced. Argentina was sold off in 1979 and Australia has lost its design capabilities, though a new engine plant ships engines to Europe, South African plants have been sold to local interests. The map has been simplified as GM has retreated in Africa and Asia and supply lines have been truncated. GM's interests in Japan and Korea have been increased as part of a new strategy (Kraar 1984). Isuzu (42.8 per cent holding by GM) has become a major partner in the Asia–Pacific region and elsewhere, as Opel/Isuzu-designed vehicles have a significant role in GM's marketing strategy (e.g. Canada Passport line). General Motors acquired a 5.3 per cent interest in Suzuki in 1981 and some of Suzuki's growth (240,000 vehicle output in 1977; 868,000 in 1987) has been in association with GM. In South Korea GM has made a substantial investment in Daewoo (50 per cent holding since 1981) and this company is exporting Opel-designed vehicles to the US as part of the Pontiac line.

The massive and sometimes very controversial changes in the organization and strategies of General Motors have influenced its operations throughout the world in the 1980s. It is still too early to see how well the corporation will perform in the next major recession and whether it will have to retrench and undergo further restructuring.

Volkswagen

Volkswagen has been making continual corporate adjustments since it gave up the Beetle line in the mid-1970s. Throughout the world VW has had to face severe competition in all sections of its model line – this competition has been very evident in the North American market, where Fig. 2.11 shows that exports shrank by half between 1977 and 1987. In Western Europe VW has invested heavily in new designs and new production equipment and followed the southward trend by its acquisition of the Spanish manufacturer SEAT in 1986. Attempts to diversify into office equipment (Triumph Adler 1979–86) were unprofitable. The traditional importance of the US market was highlighted by the opening of the Westmoreland, Pennsylvania assembly plant in 1978 (Krumme 1981). A second assembly plant in suburban Detroit was acquired in 1980 but sold to Chrysler in 1983. Continued loss of market share from a high of 3.0 per cent in 1980 to 1.9 per cent in 1987, however, meant that this plant was rarely viable and the whole operation was closed in July 1988. Market instability in Latin America has created many problems for manufacturers there. VW's most recent strategy for coping has been the formation of Autolatina (51 per cent VW, 49 per cent Ford) in 1987 to aid restructuring and new investment required in Brazil and Argentina. Exports of the Brazilian-made VW Fox to North America began in 1987. Uncertainties in Nigeria have reduced the operation to a very small size (2,123 vehicles in 1987 with a labour force of 1,300).

Japanese competition forced VW to retreat from South-East Asia. In partial compensation the corporation has established a joint venture in Shanghai (1985) and some production of vehicles in Japan has been undertaken by Nissan since 1984. While Table 2.5 shows that VW extended its worldwide activities between 1977 and 1987, the overall significance of Western Europe has increased. Indeed VW, like other West European firms, has tended to retreat back to its regional roots.

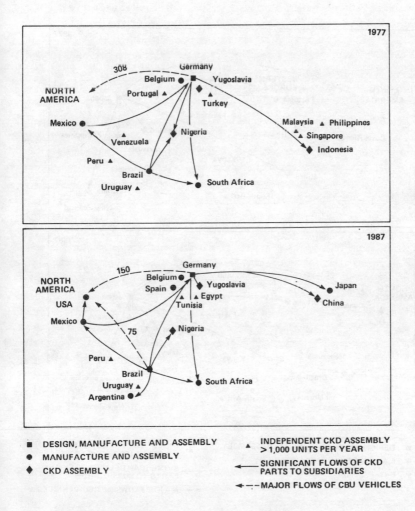

Figure 2.11 World changes in VW group, 1977–87

Toyota

Toyota has been growing substantially in the past decade, a situation different from that of most of its competitors. Exports of vehicles (including ckd) increased from 1,413,000 in 1977 to 2,219,000 in 1986. As the flows to North America and Western Europe shown in Fig. 2.12 testify, Toyota has been able to increase its overall market penetration

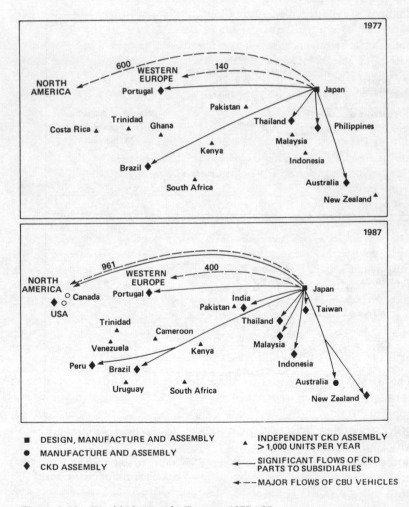

Figure 2.12 World changes in Toyota, 1977−87

despite voluntary export restraint agreements and, since 1985, a rising value of the yen. Toyota is now one of the world's richest companies. But unlike GM and VW which have 75 per cent or more of their sales in the core region, Toyota is more vulnerable to overseas pressures since 43 per cent of its sales are outside Japan.

While the overall geographical pattern has not profoundly changed since 1977, there have been major shifts in strategy. In the past decade Toyota has begun to increase its overseas investment in South-East Asia, Australia and New Zealand as well as on the margins of Latin America. The importance of the North American market and the changes in competition, value of the yen and the earlier established Japanese assembly plants (Honda and Nissan) forced Toyota to consider a stronger base on the continent. The 1984 joint venture with GM (NUMMI) provided an opportunity to learn more about North American production conditions. In 1985 Toyota announced that it was planning to spend at least $1.2 billion on two major assembly plants at Georgetown, Kentucky (200,000 car capacity) and Cambridge, Ontario (50,000 capacity). These plants entered production in 1989 and began the real transformation of Toyota into a full multinational producing corporation. Further investment in engines in North America and South-East Asia will decentralize more activities from Japan.

Toyota used the US joint venture with GM to begin a move to overseas production. A further joint venture with GM in Australia (1989) will restructure Holden's. In West Germany Toyota had a joint venture with VW to assemble Hilux trucks at Hanover in 1989. Western Europe is likely to be the next point of major corporate investment as Toyota attempts to secure its market base. A decision to locate a 200,000-car capacity plant near Derby in the UK was announced in April 1989.

SPATIAL EFFECTS OF STRUCTURAL CHANGE

The structural changes described earlier have had major spatial consequences. Such consequences have been expressed in both the concentration and decentralization of work. This is a continuation of processes which began much earlier at various geographical scales. More integration of production over larger areas, plant rationalization and investment in automation, subcontracting of various jobs previously undertaken in-house have had profound effects, although until more detailed research is undertaken the precise spatial effects are still elusive.

While the final assembly plants are the most visible features of the manufacturing process, changes here have, perhaps, been less profound than in other sectors of the industry. Overcapacity and obsolescence were key factors in Ford's re-adjustment of assembly capacity in the United States (Table 2.3). Ford reduced its car assembly plants from 15 in 1976 to 8 in 1986. Several were closed permanently, others were converted to assembling light trucks. The general trend in the United States has been the closure of plants in the outer regions, notably California, and growth within a somewhat enlarged core region which now includes Kentucky and Tennessee (Rubenstein 1986). Re-adjustment has been most dramatic in Britain where nearly 40 per cent of the car assembly plants were closed between 1978 and 1982 (Law 1985). At least ten commercial vehicle plants have also been closed in the past decade.

The problems of restructuring are not confined to the old core regions of vehicle manufacturing but are to be found throughout the world periphery. Many of the manufacturing/ckd assembly activities developed as part of national import-substitution policies are much less profitable than in the past and in some cases are no longer viable. Some of the smaller operations have been closed and new forms of integration are being organized to maintain viability. Such restructuring has occurred in Australia since the mid-1970s (Rich 1987: 106–16). Many difficulties have arisen in Latin America where markets have not grown as anticipated and export growth has lagged (Kronish and Mericle 1984). The integration of Autolatina (VW and Ford) operations in Argentina and Brazil is indicative of new trends. While political factors have been emphasized, the recent withdrawal of Ford and General Motors from South Africa has a significant economic basis.

Changes in vehicle technology, the search for greater cost savings and improvements in quality have brought new pressures on the component-making sector of the industry. Substantial new investment has been needed in engine and transmission making as well as new items such as fuel injectors and electronic components. Advanced flexible production methods and new forms of inventory control (just-in-time) have also had their effects. The expansion of production facilities in the 1980s has taken place both in traditional manufacturing regions and in new lower cost locations. Engine production, once highly concentrated, has become more decentralized as manufacturers have established plants in Mexico and Spain. Electrical parts have followed a similar pattern.

The components industry is being reshaped by several trends. Auto manufacturers are tending to reduce costs by moving more component work (including R&D) to outside suppliers. Component manufacturers are merging and re-organizing to cope with the new capital demands and to match more Japanese competition as suppliers move in alongside the transplant assembly operations. The spatial effects of these cumulative changes are as yet unclear. It may be that in the future some degree of spatial re-centralization may take place (Glasmeier and McCluskey 1987).

Job loss has been one of the most visible consequences of restructuring as most companies have tended to substitute capital for labour. The Ford Motor Company reduced its world employment by almost one-third between 1978 and 1987, when production declined by only 7 per cent. While the hourly paid workers were most affected, numbers of salaried employees were also reduced substantially. Restructuring of some corporate operations had much more drastic results. In Britain, the integration of Chrysler UK into the Peugeot group from 1978 resulted in total job losses approaching 75 per cent by the mid-1980s.

The employment and economic base of communities and regions has frequently been eroded by restructuring. In Scotland the closure of the Linwood and Bathgate assembly plants and work reduction in the remaining factories reduced employment by 70 per cent between 1978 and 1984. Coventry's auto industry, with the exception of Jaguar, has been devastated by change and overall decline (Thoms and Donnelly 1985). While Detroit has lost jobs in component making and final assembly, the overall significance of this city region has been retained in the proportion of US vehicle production and, of course, in the maintenance of the headquarters of the three large corporations. The social and political costs of decline in Detroit have been very high (Hill 1986).

Cumulative effects of job loss, new productivity levels, the competition from imports and work transfer, show clearly at the national level, especially in Britain and the United States. Trade deficits in motor vehicles and parts have grown very substantially in the 1980s. The US motor trade deficit grew from $10.4 billion in 1980 to $52.7 billion in 1986. Until 1982 Britain had a positive motor trade balance and in 1986 the trade balance in parts and accessories also turned into a deficit. Rapid decline and disintegration of the motor vehicle industry are most evident in Britain, which has experienced all of the traumatic elements of change associated with internationalization of production and the consequences of de-industrialization (Cowling 1986).

While most of the effects of restructuring have generally been negative in most mature production regions, there have been some growth points. Japanese transplant operations and component plants have been developed in new areas and have begun to make a significant economic contribution. As with other sections of the auto industry, competition – in this case between places – has played a significant role in the final decisions about location. Since there has been a strong element of capital support for new developments through regional development grants, there have been 'bidding wars' between nations and regions. The Mazda assembly plant opened in 1987 at Flat Rock, Michigan (metropolitan Detroit) received about $120 million in incentives and subsidies from municipal and state levels of government (R.C. Hill 1989: 98–9).

Since much of the process of restructuring is specific to firms, plants and locations, the following case study examines the effects for one European-wide corporation.

Restructuring GM Europe

Over the past decade the European operations of General Motors have been re-organized to maintain its place among the six large mass-market producers. Changes in the corporate strategy have had significant spatial effects at national, regional and local scales.

General Motors expanded into Europe during the 1920s when ckd assembly plants were opened in London, Copenhagen, Antwerp, Berlin and elsewhere. Deeper roots were established with the acquisition of Vauxhall Motors (1925) and Adam Opel AG (1929). Economic nationalism in the 1930s created new barriers and entrenched a corporate structure which survived for fifty years. The semi-autonomy of the national companies was also reinforced by the divisional structure of the American parent.

Opel and Vauxhall shared in the post-War expansion of the West European motor industry. Both expanded not only in their national markets but also developed a very substantial export trade with North America and other parts of the world. Component making was partly handled by the companies themselves and also by other GM divisions such as AC Delco in Britain. New divisions such as Euclid (renamed Terex in 1968) established plants for making heavy off-highway trucks, first in Scotland and then in Luxembourg in 1971. In the early 1960s Opel and Vauxhall began to decentralize production from their existing congested facilities. In Germany, Opel built a new engine and car assembly complex at Bochum in the Ruhr while Vauxhall developed a similar but smaller plant in Ellesmere Port. The location of each facility was partly shaped by regional development grants. A new plant was opened at Antwerp in 1967 to provide more capacity for North American exports and, more importantly, to cope with the expanding market within the EC.

Several changes in the early 1970s began to undermine the traditional ways in which General Motors had organized its European operations. Export sales began to drop significantly as competition from Japanese manufacturers eroded market potential overseas. Vauxhall's exports of cars, for example, dropped from 66,000 in 1970 to 21,000 in 1975. The overseas exports of Opel cars also fell sharply as the mark appreciated in value. In the United States market, Opel sales (made by Buick dealers) declined from 94,000 units in 1969 to 37,000 in 1975. After this year Buick Opels sold in the US were, in fact, made by Isuzu in Japan.

The overall decline of European export sales increased competition in home markets as manufacturers scrambled to maintain production and increase market shares. In Britain, Vauxhall's market share fell from 13.1 per cent in 1968 to 8.0 per cent in 1974. The fuel crisis of 1973/74 emphasized smaller cars with 1.0-litre capacity engines. General Motors subsidiaries had ignored the so-called mini car segment of the market and were in an increasingly weak position. Ford's introduction of the Fiesta line in 1976 emphasized the need to move into this market segment.

The virtual collapse of Vauxhall in 1975/76 precipitated some changes in strategy. Unlike Ford, which had begun to integrate its European activities in 1967, GM had continued to rely on cooperation between its subsidiaries (Bloomfield 1981: 382–5). But since Opel and Vauxhall had such different roots and were very different in size, cooperation was difficult and GM as a whole tended to be dominated by its American divisions. Over the next decade GM in Europe was restructured in several phases.

During the late 1970s, Opel virtually took over the Vauxhall operations in Britain, transferring most of the car design and engineering activities from Luton to Russelsheim, leaving only a rump of commercial vehicle activities in Britain. General Motors re-organized its Overseas Operations Division in 1978 and concentrated its truck and bus activities in 1982. Major new European investments were announced in 1978 and 1980. In the first decision a new small car (the smallest car ever designed by GM) was designed by Opel to be built in Spain and supplied by a new engine plant in Vienna (Sinclair and Walker 1982). The 1980 announcement was a plan to build five new automotive component plants. Factors involved in the location of all

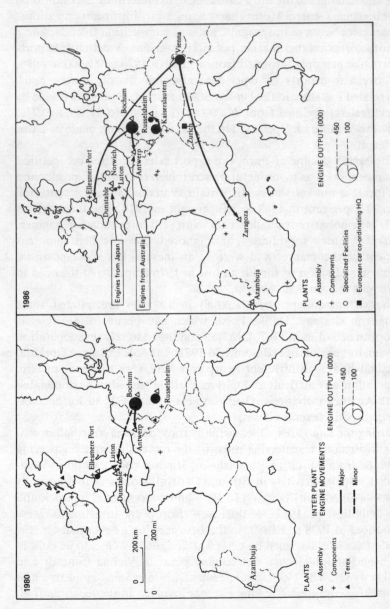

Figure 2.13 GM Europe: spatial organization, 1980 and 1986

the new facilities were lower labour costs and the possibilities of more flexible working practices in the less industrialized areas. Regional development grants also provided incentives to locate in new areas. Other elements of re-organization included the sale of the Terex operations in Scotland and Luxembourg during 1980.

The general situation in 1980 is shown in Fig. 2.13. At this time there were seven assembly plants, including trucks at Dunstable and a small ckd operation at Azambuja, Portugal. There were also ten components plants, mostly controlled by other GM divisions. Vauxhall in Britain was still fairly self-contained, although an increasing proportion of GM's British sales were imported from Germany or Belgium or were Opel designs assembled in Britain. In 1979 only 67 per cent of GM's sales in Britain were assembled by Vauxhall, the others came from Germany and Belgium. At the beginning of the decade 96.7 per cent of sales had been wholly British made. This shift illustrates the major changes which occurred in the 1970s in the internationalization of production. British-assembled vehicles in the UK market fell to a low of 41.6 per cent in 1984 before climbing back to 68 per cent in 1987 after plant restructuring had taken place. In 1980 the British assembly plants were still being supplied by three small-volume engine operations, supplemented by the import of some German-built engines.

During the early 1980s the impact of earlier strategic decisions began to show. The Corsa (Nova in UK) small car appeared in late 1982 from the new Zaragoza plant. At the same time the GM 'world car', the J car (known in Europe as the Cavalier/Ascona) also appeared in the middle-size segment of the market. Given the limitations of GM's European engine manufacturing capacity, the engines were shipped from a new plant in Australia. Further dimensions of restructuring were introduced during 1986. A stronger European car coordinating organization was established in Zurich, replacing the earlier office in London. Lotus, the small sports car firm in Norwich was acquired at this time. Although only a minor producer (704 cars in 1986), Lotus had specialist design facilities of value to GM's worldwide operations. The Bedford heavy truck operations in Dunstable were abandoned in 1986 after several years of declining market share. A decline in the market share of vans in the 1980s forced additional restructuring, first by the assembly of Isuzu and Suzuki vehicles in Luton using mostly imported materials from Japan. In September 1987 a new subsidiary, IBC Vehicles, was formed (60 per cent GM, 40 per cent Isuzu) to produce Japanese-designed vans in the Luton plant.

By 1986 the ways of GM's European activities had changed substantially. The overall pattern was more complex and widespread. Zaragoza had become a major assembly complex with a larger output than the combined British plants. Engine production had virtually ended in Britain and the Russelsheim engine plant had been replaced by an expanded facility at Kaiserslautern. Specialization and greater economies of scale were now possible at Bochum and the new Vienna plant. Component-making plants had been increased to twenty, with significant new growth in Spain, Portugal and Australia. Supply lines had become longer, particularly with engines, not only in Europe but also with the extensions to Australia and Japan.

Restructuring of GM in Europe revitalized the corporate activities in a period of major shifts in the market. Overall market share in cars was maintained (10.8 per cent of new registrations in Europe 1976; 10.9 per cent in 1986) after a sag between 1979 and 1981. The down-market strategy with the Corsa helped to maintain sales against the other big European competitors: VW, Fiat, Ford, Peugeot and Renault. All the changes were expensive and this shows in the profitability of GM's European operations (Fig. 2.14). The corporation had to sustain substantial losses between 1980 and 1986. Indeed over the period 1977–87 there was only a very small positive balance of $26 million. British vehicle operations showed a negative balance on operations throughout the period. Despite the many changes, the total labour force changed little in overall size throughout the period, averaging 122,000 yearly over the period; ranging from a high of 131,000 in 1979 to a low of 113,000 in 1981. In the period of expansion from 1984 GM's earlier investment in more automated equipment did, however, check any growth in the labour force.

The spatial effects of restructuring have been both positive and negative. There have been obvious gains in employment in Spain and Austria and in some peripheral areas where new jobs were created in component plants. New supply linkages and multipliers have been developed in these locations. GM Spain in 1986 was only slightly smaller than the old established SEAT firm and was exporting 70 per cent of its output to markets throughout Europe. Core operations in Germany, Belgium and northern France were maintained and enhanced by new investment.

Negative effects of restructuring were most clearly shown in Britain. The decline of Vauxhall parallels the overall decline of the national industry. For much of the past decade the restructuring of GM's British vehicle subsidiary had all the elements of an emergency as different parts of the manufacturing activities lost their viability.

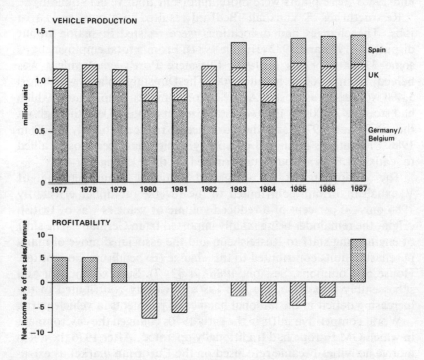

Figure 2.14 GM Europe: production and profitability, 1977–87

Multinational 'sourcing' of vehicles became necessary in the mid-1970s in order to maintain market share and this was achieved in the early 1980s when the share was increased from 8.6 per cent in 1981 to 16.1 per cent in 1984. Export markets, however, almost disappeared in the late 1970s and Bedford's share of the commercial vehicle market declined significantly. Operating costs clearly had to be cut and a viable role for the plants had to be developed. Engine production was phased out after 1980 and effectively ended in 1985. Most design work was transferred from Luton to Germany. By 1984/85 the Ellesmere Port operations were refocused on the making of Astra (Kadette) cars and vans. Re-organizing work at Dunstable and Luton was more difficult. By 1986 the final shape was becoming clearer, as the Dunstable truck plant was to be closed and the Luton complex was to be used for some larger cars and for specialized van production based on Isuzu designs and mechanical components. Throughout the period, the separately organized GM automotive component plants maintained their activities and employment. By the mid-1980s these plants were more important than vehicle-building. Restructuring of Vauxhall—Bedford resulted in a massive loss of jobs. The changes and dislocations were resisted in major labour disputes in 1979 and 1982 (Huckle 1984). From a total employment of some 33,000 workers in 1978, Ellesmere Port's employment was halved, from 9,900 to about 4,700. The Dunstable plant, which had 5,400 workers, was closed. At the Luton complex, employment which had stood at 24,000 in 1959 was stabilized at about 18,000 throughout the 1960s and 1970s and then drastically reduced to only 6,300 in 1986/87. Luton's industrial prosperity, which has been closely allied to Vauxhall, was seriously undermined by these changes.

The disappearance of integrated national manufacturing of Vauxhall in Britain contributed to the reverse multiplier effect. By 1986 only 50 per cent of a reduced volume of vehicles was of British origin, the remainder being mainly imported from Germany. The shift of engineering staff to Russelsheim and the associated move of many purchasing units contributed to this change (Expenditure Committee, House of Commons, Session, 1986—7: 82—7). Such component and subassembly imports in the mid-1980s obviously contributed to the increasing deficit in the national balance of payments in vehicle parts.

World competitive shifts in the early 1970s changed the environment in which GM Europe had traditionally operated. After 1976 the automotive activities became refocused on the European market as extracontinental exports were abandoned. Links to other parts of the world have diminished, except for some component exports and the Opel design work for Isuzu in Japan and Daewoo in Korea. Lotus has also begun specialized consulting work for the Cadillac division. In early 1987 Cadillac introduced the Allante model designed by Pininfarina for the ultra luxury market. Partly erected bodywork is air-freighted to Detroit for final assembly. Sales in the first year amounted to less than 2,000 units.

Drastic corporate restructuring allowed the corporation to maintain its position but at substantial cost. Perhaps if GM had begun to integrate its national activities earlier, some of the changes would have been less traumatic. Competition has, if anything, been intensified since the mid-1980s as the other European firms have been reorganizing. In the 1990s a new wave of competition will emerge with the full operation of the Japanese transplants. More new investment will be needed by GM in order to retain its market share with advanced models and flexible production.

INTO THE 1990s

As the industry enters its second century there is both optimism and pessimism about the future. While the industry is mature, with annual growth rates around 1.8 per cent, there is still growth potential in many developing areas. Since the car is much more than a purely mechanical object for transport it is clear that any epitaphs on its demise are premature. The symbolic value of the car still makes it 'the most psychologically expressive object that has so far been devised' (Marsh and Collett 1986: 26).

Optimism is certainly a quality of most corporations as they expand their production capacity in major market areas. In general, capacity is increasing much faster than demand. The expansion of Japanese transplants in North America is expected to create excess capacity of 5 million units by 1990. In Western Europe the problem of excess capacity may be half that amount, as existing manufacturers lose market share outside Europe and as Japanese transplants expand on a larger scale. Overseas expansion of Japanese firms will lead to a reduction of direct exports, already evident in the export statistics since 1985. Elsewhere in the world there are limited opportunities for protected local industries and for export orientated growth. Hyundai has grown remarkably fast and there may be some opportunities for entry-level cars from new producers such as the Yugo from Yugoslavia and Maruti from India.

The growth of excess capacity will create more competition as manufacturers seek new opportunities or fight to retain market share. More joint ventures to share the high development costs are likely. Middle-sized companies are the most likely casualties, unless they can move to distinct and specialized market niches. There will be a continuation of the process of catching up with Japanese methods so that further restructuring will affect the organization of work, the size of the labour force and the very existence of some plants (Jones 1988: 30).

Most current evidence suggests that the world industry will become even more integrated across national boundaries. Final assembly will tend to become more centred in the large market zones, thus reducing the export flows of built-up vehicles. The manufacture of components and subassemblies (such as engines and transmissions) will continue to become more decentralized as manufacturers extend the production lines into low-cost areas. Such movements will be much less visible than the location of final assembly plants. In this way while the macroscale location pattern may not appear to change very much over the next decade, the microscale patterns will probably exhibit very substantial change. The shift in scale of interest will present many new research challenges in the future.

Most of the varied effects of the world restructuring outlined in this paper will take several years to become clear, just as the globalization process gradually unfolded. As a motor of change, the automotive industry has not yet exhausted its possibilities to surprise and fascinate the observer.

3 New horizons?
The Third World motor vehicle industry in an international framework

Robert Gwynne

The motor car industry has now become a true world industry. From the perspective of newly-industrializing countries and Third World countries attempting to industrialize, the major question is to what extent this global industry can be located in their territories. Can newly-industrializing countries become significant exporters of finished cars, other vehicles (lorries, vans, buses) and components as they have become significant exporters of electronic goods, machine tools, ships, clothing, textiles and footwear?

The global shift of many of these sectors in which Third World production and exports have become significant can be partially explained with reference to the product life-cycle model (Vernon 1979; Gwynne 1990). In this model, Third World countries offer the locational attraction of cheap labour costs for mobile capital and the manufacture of products entering the mature phase of both their product design and process technology. In the context of the product life-cycle model, then, a crucial theoretical question is to what extent the motor vehicle can be seen as a mature product, utilizing standardized technology. In attempting to answer this question, the present chapter will concentrate on the export potentials that Third World countries currently have in terms of the global motor car industry. As a result, this chapter will not focus on those assembly industries that occur in many Third World countries and that are primarily oriented towards their own domestic markets.

It therefore becomes necessary to discuss the motor car industry in an international framework. In the first instance, this will be done by applying the neo-Schumpeterian framework of the early 1980s MIT study on the Future of the Automobile to the potential for growth of the industry in newly-industrializing countries. This analysis will be followed by a brief summary of major locational shifts in global production that have subsequently occurred during the 1980s. Having established an international framework for the evolution of the motor car industry, the potential for an export-oriented industry developing in newly-industrializing countries will then be discussed. In particular, it will be postulated that there seem to be only three strategies that newly-industrializing countries can follow in promoting an export-oriented vehicle industry during the 1990s.

PAST TRANSFORMATIONS IN THE WORLD CAR INDUSTRY

Altshuler *et al.* (1984) argued that the spread of the industry over the world can best be seen in terms of three transformations. Each transformation related to a new innovation in either the product or production process (or both) and, as a result, brought about an increase in domestic demand and exports. Furthermore, each stage became synonymous with a new region of the world becoming predominant in production, and thus in shaping the world car industry.

Stage one was identified as the change from the custom-built car involving short production runs and a great number of manufacturers to a standardized product manufactured on a moving assembly line. This was introduced by Ford in the United States, with the development of the Model T between 1902 and the 1920s, and also involved the division of skills so that jobs became more routinized. These methods were later adopted and developed by General Motors and Chrysler, and resulted in the world car industry becoming dominated by these three companies. In 1923, the American share of world production was 91 per cent, and throughout the 1920s it was generally greater than 90 per cent (Altshuler *et al.* 1984:15).

The second transformation relates to the post-1945 period through to the 1960s, when demand for motor cars had increased and shifted towards a more diversified range of products. European producers had developed separately due to differences in travel patterns, road conditions and consumer tastes. Thus, when the European market opened up, they were able to offer a wide range of models, compared with the standardized American product. Further, they came to pioneer a wide range of new product technologies such as small transverse engines and later front-wheel drive hatchbacks (Jones and Graves 1986). The second stage, then, was characterized by product differentiation and an emphasis on product technology. In the early 1950s, the European producers accounted for only 13.6 per cent of world car production, compared with North America's 85.1 per cent. However, with the removal of tariff walls between the countries of Europe in the 1950s and steady economic growth, producers were able to sell their specialized products in all markets of Europe and produce in quantities which allowed increasing economies of scale to be achieved. By 1970, the West European share of world car production was 46 per cent and the North American share had been reduced to 33 per cent.

Development of the Japanese car industry brought about the third transformation. Altshuler *et al.* (1984) saw this transformation as existing in a well-advanced form by the early 1980s. In the Japanese-inspired transformation, change occurred in labour organization with security of employment and increased worker participation in the form of quality circles. Quality circles assisted in the production process by monitoring the standard of the product at each stage of production. The organization of the manufacturing process was also different, with the use of components direct from the supplier. The arrival of components from the supplier the same day that they would be used by the assembler invalidated the need for large component stocks which had previously been the norm.

This 'just-in-time' system, by reducing inventories, was, however, more vulnerable to error. But it was argued that in this way it was also easier to pinpoint error, particularly in component quality, a feature lacking in previous manufacturing systems based on large stocks. Furthermore, the Japanese manufacturing system provided the framework for continual and multiple improvements to vehicle design, component quality and the production process. This fine tuning of the manufacturing system enabled Japanese producers to combine high-volume output with high quality and the ability to innovate and adapt rapidly. While production in the US and Western Europe stagnated during the 1970s, Japanese production more than doubled. By 1981, the West European share of world car production had fallen to 38 per cent and the North American share to 27 per cent; Japanese world market share was now equivalent to that of the whole of North America.

These three transformations in the world motor car industry have left it dominated by a small number of multinational producers, all with powerful national bases. The home of the first transformation, the United States, still holds the world's two largest producers, General Motors and Ford, as well as Chrysler, now spatially restricting its manufacturing to the North American market (including Mexico). The region of the second transformation, Western Europe, has at least four global corporations that have generally resulted from past mergers and acquisitions (Volkswagen–Audi–SEAT, Renault, Peugeot–Citroën–Talbot, Fiat–Lancia–Alfa Romeo) as well as a variety of more specialized vehicle producers (Rover, Jaguar, Mercedes Benz, BMW, Saab, Volvo).

The strongest and most remarkable corporate growth over the last three decades has, however, been in Japan, where the major industrial groups or 'keiretsu' have invested in motor car manufacturing. 'Keiretsu' are a collection of numerous firms producing a wide range of products and centred around a bank and trading company. Each member company owns a small proportion of the shares of the other companies. 'Keiretsu' have been able to develop motor car firms from scratch partly because of the role of the 'keiretsu' bank providing the necessary funds and partly because of the advantages of mutual ownership and cooperation in providing assistance with technological change and management systems. Nine Japanese car corporations have emerged as a result, although not all are linked to a 'keiretsu' – Toyota, Nissan, Mitsubishi (with 24 per cent Chrysler shareholding), Mazda (25 per cent Ford shareholding), Honda, Isuzu (34 per cent GM shareholding), Suzuki (5 per cent GM shareholding), Daihatsu (important Toyota shareholding) and Subaru (important Nissan shareholding).

THE FOURTH TRANSFORMATION?

The MIT report on the Future of the Automobile predicted that a fourth transformation would affect the industry during the 1980s but thought that the precise nature of the change was a matter of considerable debate. However, as Jones and Womack (1985) pointed out, the nature of the change would have considerable implications for the development of the motor car industry in the Third World. According to one scenario, certain Third World countries would receive major increases in productive capacity; the other scenario gave a different interpretation. The opposing views of the future world car industry can be described as those of the 'world car' and of 'technological divergence'.

The 'world car' concept

Prior to the early 1980s, the prevailing view on the future of the car industry was one in which the 'world car' concept would predominate. The world car has been described as 'a vehicle which shares the same basic design and as many common or interchangeable parts as possible and which will compete successfully in the world's major automotive markets, modified and tuned to their particular requirements' (Gooding 1979).

It was argued that the large automotive multinationals would tend towards increasingly internationalized production networks. Each company would produce a pool of strategic components (engine, gearbox, suspension system) from plants established anywhere in the world, so as to produce parts at the most efficient scale possible. Other components would be bought in from outside suppliers at a low price because of the quantities required.

As a result of the uniform basic design of the 'world car', competition would be based on price, and thus production technology and manufacturing location would be characterized by very large economies of scale at low labour-cost locations. In order to keep costs and prices down, a geographical shift of production from the major markets in developed countries to cheaper labour-cost locations in newly-industrializing countries, such as Brazil and Korea, was envisaged. It was further predicted that by 1990, the international car market would be dominated by a maximum of ten major motor manufacturers, each making a minimum of 2 million vehicles a year.

The model of 'technological divergence'

The rival view of the future, that of 'technological divergence', has been most influentially presented through the four-year, seven-nation study by the Massachusetts Institute of Technology (MIT) on the 'Future of the Automobile' (Altshuler *et al.* 1984). The MIT report argued that the introduction of microprocessor-controlled, flexible production methods, new systems of organization for the production process and the fact that the world's car buyers demand a diverse range of vehicles, would mean the survival of most firms which existed in the early 1980s but with few if any new firms entering the market. The spatial corollary of this argument was that existing automobile corporations in Western Europe, United States and Japan would not only remain intact but would also remain producing principally in their domestic markets or in the markets of other developed countries.

According to Altshuler *et al.* (1984), advances in production technology during the 1980s would enable efficiency to be maintained at lower levels of production. Final assembly plants which formerly needed to produce 240,000 cars a year of one model type on a two-shift work schedule, would be able to spread this volume over a range of models due to increasing use of flexible automation. Further, advances in computer-aided design, engineering and manufacturing would reduce the total number of units a manufacturer has to build in order to recoup development costs and investment in capital equipment. It may be necessary to maintain certain mechanical components, such as engines at a large production level (500,000 units per annum), but increasingly collaborative agreements would be arranged between assemblers, such as between Honda and Rover, or Fiat and Peugeot.

Changes in the organization of the production process were also seen as important by MIT, following along the lines of Japan's 'just-in-time' system. The need for close proximity between component supplier and assembler, required in order to reduce inventories and improve quality control, led MIT to conclude that component production would be likely to become more tightly concentrated at the point of final assembly in the major markets. The type of geographical concentration of component suppliers that occurs around Toyota's four assembly plants in Toyota City (Fig. 3.1) would be the ideal model for other manufacturers to emulate.

Jones and Womack (1985) saw the production of only standardized vehicle systems (lighting, braking, suspension, steering) and minor parts taking place at low labour-cost locations in the future. Furthermore, as vehicle systems incorporate new technology in both product design and productive process, these would be increasingly manufactured near to the supplier's centralized production location. Further benefits would accrue to developed country locations from adopting the more flexible Japanese approach. Closer involvement between workforce and shopfloor management would give the potential for higher quality in production and a source of new ideas for product/component design and the productive process itself. Low inventories would mean less inactive capital, while a more involved, cooperative workforce should indicate less middle management.

Thus, MIT argued that there would be few departures of firms from the industry, because the reduced minimum efficient scale of production would enable the medium-sized and specialist producers to compete with the large multinationals. They may even have a competitive edge in some market niches. At the same time, few if any new manufacturers would emerge due to the very large initial investment required and the great difficulty of car design and manufacture.

The implications for the expansion of export-oriented motor vehicle production in newly-industrializing countries was therefore bleak. Motor vehicle production would continue to be dominated by corporations that had emerged in the geographical areas associated with the first three transformations. Hence, it would be difficult for new corporations to emerge from the newly-industrializing economies.

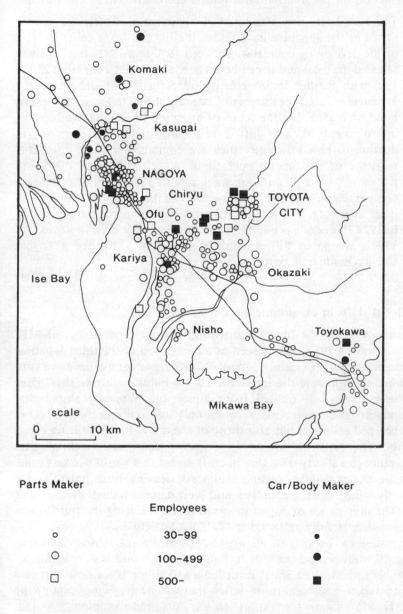

Parts Maker

Car/Body Maker

Employees

○	30–99	●
○	100–499	●
□	500–	■

Figure 3.1 Distribution of motor vehicle plants in Chuk Yo region, 1970

Furthermore, the cost reductions that new technology had brought to the industry meant that low labour-cost locations would offer little attraction for the international vehicle corporations:

> The completely new standards of organizational efficiency established by the Japanese have pulled the rug out from under the feet of the developing countries. Between 1970 and 1981, the Japanese reduced the total number of hours needed to build a car from 250 to 130, with further improvements since then. Not only have the Japanese reduced the number of hours required to assemble a car or build an engine, but the focus of attention in seeking productivity improvements has also shifted from the costs of the factors of production to how efficiently they are combined into an integrated sequence of production operations. As a result, even the South Koreans, with a $1 an hour wage rate in 1980, cannot produce a comparable vehicle for the same costs as the Japanese with a $7 an hour wage rate. The Korean Ministry of Commerce estimated that in 1979 Hyundai's production cost for the Pony built in Korea was $3972, compared with an estimated cost of $2300 for a Toyota Corolla made in Japan.
>
> (Jones and Womack 1985: 400–1)

Global shifts in car production during the 1980s

In many ways, the fourth transformation put forward by the MIT study for the 1980s can be seen as an extension of the third Japanese transformation. Certainly Japan and Japanese companies have continued to dominate the international car industry during the 1980s. The example just quoted from Jones and Womack shows that Japanese production costs were not only undercutting those of other developed countries but also those of the newly-industrializing countries. The Japanese success in orienting continuous technological advance to a steady reduction in costs meant that world markets came to be dominated by Japanese imports, leaving little potential for newly-industrializing countries and their nascent industries.

The dominance of Japan in world markets during the third transformation is fully reflected in Table 3.1. Between 1974 and 1984, Japanese car exports to all world regions, except Africa, increased significantly but particularly to North America and Western Europe. By 1984, the United States recorded a $16 billion trade deficit in cars with Japan, a sectoral trade deficit that was nearly 50 per cent of the total ($35 billion). Car exports to the European Community had an even faster rate of growth.

Table 3.1 Japanese car exports, 1974–84

Importing region	1974	1984	Rate of increase 1974–84
North America	796	1990	2.5
European Community	235	790	3.4
Other Europe	109	240	2.2
Asia	177	450	2.5
Oceania	225	230	1.0
Latin America	84	210	2.5
Africa	101	90	0.9
Total	1700	4000	2.4

The countries of North America and Western Europe responded to such dramatic increases in Japanese car exports with the policy of trade protection. So-called voluntary import agreements were made between Japan and most threatened countries. For example, the United States negotiated a voluntary agreement that Japanese car imports should take no more than 25 per cent of the market; in the United Kingdom, the level was 11 per cent, in France 3 per cent and in Italy imports were simply not permitted. Only West Germany seemed to allow for the relatively free entry of Japanese cars.

The protectionist reaction of the other industrial market economies to Japanese car imports has caused a definite reaction from most Japanese vehicle corporations. The reaction has been very simply one of locating plants within the protected markets. This has been particularly the case in the United States and Canada, and is occurring to a lesser extent within Europe.

The massive plant-building programme of five Japanese manufacturers in North America constitutes the single most important shift in global car production during the 1980s. The use of Japanese process technology and organizational methods has rendered the United States a competitive location for motor car manufacturing in the late 1980s. Production of the first Japanese corporation to locate in the United States, Honda, increased nearly six times between 1983 and 1987 (from 55,337 to 324,064). According to Nissan's head in Mexico, in 1987 production of vehicles in Mexico (with a 1987 wage rate one-tenth of that in the United States) was only 10 per cent cheaper than that in Nissan's Smyrna plant in Tennessee (Johns 1987).

THE THIRD WORLD CAR INDUSTRY: STRATEGIES FOR GROWTH

Therefore, the recent Japanese influence over the evolution of the world motor car industry has meant that costs of production have been declining due to new process technologies and organizational methods. Within this context of declining per unit costs of production, the single factor of low labour costs in less developed countries holds less and less attraction for the location of motor car assembly plants. In contrast to the recent surge of assembly plant construction in the United States, there has been no such comparable growth of motor car assembly plants in the Third World. It appears that the optimistic framework that the 'world car' concept held out for the shift of motor vehicle assembly to Third World countries has been rendered obsolete by the considerable technological and organizational advances that continue to emanate from Japan. What then are the possibilities for Third World countries to establish export-oriented motor car industries?

From an examination of present trends, there seem to be three strategies that Third World countries could follow in terms of export-oriented growth:

1 A technological and financial link between a domestic corporation of a newly-industrializing country and a Japanese multinational.
2 A joint venture between a domestic corporation of a newly-industrializing country and a multinational vehicle corporation whose production strategies are still partially influenced by the concept of the 'world car'.
3 The granting of export incentives by Third World governments to vehicle multinationals already operating in their territories.

Liaisons between domestic corporations and Japanese multinationals

It seems increasingly apparent that Third World car producers cannot just rely on traditional, labour-intensive assembly operations, particularly if they are to be prominent in export markets. According to Jones and Womack (1985: 405), if Third World countries are intent on developing an export-oriented motor vehicle industry, 'the objective should be to maximise the amount of wealth produced per worker using the state-of-the-art social organization and production technology and to create jobs by expanding volume'. If this does not take place, Jones and Womack argue that the Third World country would fall further behind in technological development and have even less chance of ever catching up. The implication of such an analysis must be that Third World motor car producers have to forge stronger links with Japanese vehicle multinationals, particularly in terms of technology transfer and new organizational methods. Because of the numbers of vehicle producers in Japan (nine), it should be possible for either private corporations in or the governments of Third World countries to negotiate such technological and organizational transfers with at least one Japanese multinational.

Third World countries can organize these technological and organizational linkages either through state-controlled corporations or through private conglomerates. The most successful private conglomerate from the Third World to organize and benefit from technological links with a Japanese multinational is undoubtedly Hyundai of Korea. Korea does have the advantage of low labour costs. In 1985, it was reported that 'an average assembly worker in South Korea earns US$2.45 an hour, less than a fifth of a Japanese labourer's cost and a tenth of the cost of a UAW member (in the United States)' (*The Economist*, 2 March 1985). But Hyundai have not just relied on this one international cost advantage and comprehensively invested in new process technology from Japan, mainly provided through Mitsubishi, which owns 15 per cent of the company.

Hyundai is Korea's largest private corporation with a wide variety of activities, ranging from shipbuilding to construction. Its move into motor vehicles can almost be compared with that of the Japanese 'keiretsu'. Because of the small size of the Korean market (mid-1980s sales of 150,000 cars per annum), Hyundai has had to export in order to achieve any reasonable economies of scale. In the early 1980s it was able to export small amounts of cars to such diverse countries as Canada, Chile and the United Kingdom.

Its breakthrough as major exporter, however, came in 1986 when it entered the US market and managed to sell as many as 168,882 cars in its first year. It should be mentioned that such unprecedented first-year car sales were closely linked to US protectionism restricting car shipments from Japan (to 25 per cent of the US market). Following the protective restrictions, the Japanese moved up-market (as US quotas were fixed by reference to number of cars, not value) and thus left a gap for low-priced, small but quality cars. Hyundai supplied its small but well-equipped front-wheel drive Pony Excel and recorded what can only be called dramatic growth in the United States market; sales in the US increased a further 56 per cent in 1987 to reach 263,000 cars. Furthermore, Hyundai has experienced considerable market growth in the Canadian market. As a result of such remarkable export growth, Hyundai's productive capacity has gone up from 150,000 in 1984 to 700,000 in 1988 (Gooding 1987).

However, it should be emphasized that such growth in production and exports has been closely linked to both the advanced product design and process technology that Hyundai has been able to employ and in which Mitsubishi has figured prominently. In particular, Mitsubishi has been of major assistance with the transfer of both engine and transmission technology. Now, in terms of quantities produced, Hyundai is nearly entering the first division of world car producers. One further indication of this has been its decision to build a 100,000-unit assembly plant near Montreal in order to become a true vehicle multinational with a productive base in North America; indeed, production is due to start in January 1989, although only the first stage of the plant has been built, with an annual capacity of 30,000 vehicles.

There are certain similarities between Korea and the newest Far East exporter of motor vehicles, Malaysia. One crucial difference is that whereas Korea's growth in motor vehicle production has been mainly executed through the agency of a large private conglomerate, in Malaysia the government has taken a key role. The Malaysian motor vehicle company, Proton, is 70 per cent owned by the Malaysian government. The remaining 30 per cent contribution comes again from the Japanese multinational, Mitsubishi. Mitsubishi has been very significant in providing the technology, structuring the organization (including quality circles) and designing the production process at Proton's large assembly plant, 8 miles outside Kuala Lumpur. Flexible, automated body welding has been preferred despite the supposed locational advantages of low labour costs. The cars produced are heavily based on Mitsubishi designs (most notably the Colt). The Malaysian Proton has preferential access to the markets of the South-East Asian countries that belong to ASEAN. Furthermore, the company is trying to export to both Western Europe and the United States (entry into the European market is being organized via a British distributor, based in Wythall near Birmingham).

It is too early to judge the success of the Malaysian producer, Proton, in its attempt to enter foreign markets. However, the success of Hyundai in becoming such a major exporter to the North American market in the late 1980s may set the model for any Third World vehicle corporation aiming at international markets. As a result, and linking in with the policy recommendations of the MIT report on 'The Future of the Automobile', it would appear that private and state vehicle corporations from developing countries should attempt to form technological and financial links with Japanese corporations.

Joint ventures between domestic corporations and 'world car' multinationals

Due to the popularity of the 'world car' concept in the late 1970s and early 1980s, there are at least two corporations that have forged technological and financial links with the two major proponents of the 'world car' concept, GM and Ford. They are the Korean conglomerates, Daewoo and Kia respectively. However, it should be stressed that the Korean corporations do have links with Japanese vehicle technology through their partners – GM owns 34 per cent of Isuzu and 5 per cent of Suzuki, and Ford owns 25 per cent of Mazda.

Daewoo's venture into motor vehicle production is perhaps the clearest example of the 'world car' concept boosting car production in Third World countries. Daewoo is in a 50/50 joint venture with General Motors. The joint venture is now selling a cheap Korean-made car in North America as a Pontiac Le Mans. The design is derived from the Opel Kadett produced by GM's German subsidiary with technological improvements provided by GM's Japanese affiliate, Isuzu. This particular case of a European-designed car, incorporating Japanese process technology, being built in a Third World country, primarily aimed at the North American market and all orchestrated by the world's largest vehicle corporation is the best example yet of the optimistic framework provided by the 'world car' concept for increasing vehicle production in Third World countries.

A new car production plant with an annual capacity of 167,000 vehicles is being completed in Korea in order to meet these demands. It will give Daewoo a total annual capacity of approximately 250,000 cars. GM also hopes to use the Daewoo operation to export vehicles throughout East Asia and to produce cheap mechanical parts. A deal was signed with Daewoo to make starter motors and alternators for GM's worldwide operations in 1985 (*The Economist* 1985: 15). However, Daewoo has had considerably less marketing success in the all-important US market than Hyundai during 1988. In the first eight months of 1988, Daewoo's exports to the US were only 46,000 against 255,000 for the same period for Hyundai, despite the fact that the Pontiac Le Mans has been distributed through the extensive GM dealer network; the fact that the Pontiac Le Mans has been priced at a higher level than the Hyundai Excel may be a partial explanation (Ford 1988: 11).

Seeing General Motors expanding rapidly in Korea has brought out a classic example of oligopolistic reaction (Gwynne 1979) from Ford. In 1986, Ford paid US$30 million for a 10 per cent shareholding in Kia 'to show how serious was its intention of drawing that company into its global strategy' and opened a Korean branch office of Ford International Business Development in order to 'develop sources for automotive components in South Korea' (Gooding 1986: 12). With Ford's new capital input and technological assistance from Mazda, Kia has expanded its annual productive capacity to 300,000 units per year. Indeed, during the first eight months of 1988, Kia exported slightly more vehicles (48,000) to the key US market than Daewoo (Ford 1988: 11).

Although Daewoo and Kia have major capital participation from GM and Ford, the importance of the respective links with Isuzu and Mazda has meant that both car assemblers have incorporated Japanese process technology and organizational methods into their operations. Together with Hyundai, they constitute the three major Third World vehicle corporations (with 50 per cent or more local ownership). As a result of the ambitious export-oriented investment plans of these three corporations, by the end of the 1980s, Korea will have the potential capacity to produce 1.2 million vehicles a year.

Furthermore, high local content agreements mean that such growth should be passed on to the diversified components sector. However, here again there is evidence of considerable technological and financial linkages between Korean companies and Japanese components producers. 'In 1982, there were 57 technological cooperations and 17 joint ventures involving major automotive components. These cooperative arrangements had allowed the industry to make the quantum leap from churning out labour intensive replacement parts to complex, state of the art original equipment manufacturing processes' (King 1986: 8).

At present, it could be argued that South Korea and its motor vehicle industry stands as the exception – the only Third World country to genuinely develop a motor vehicle industry geared primarily to export markets. The country has followed a combination of the first two strategies that we noted as open to Third World countries in developing their motor vehicle industries. Other countries, however, have had less control over the development of their motor vehicle industry – and less incorporation of state-of-the-art technology that Jones and Womack saw as so important for the nascent vehicle industries of Third World countries.

Export incentives for car multinationals

The analysis of locational shifts in the world motor car industry during the 1960s and early 1970s tended to be dominated by the increasing significance of economies of scale. During the late 1970s and 1980s, the ability to attain and successfully incorporate state-of-the-art technology has become a much more significant underlying factor. However, in Latin America, the period of expansion in the motor car sector was very much during the 1960s and early 1970s. In that period, Latin America offered the continental perspective of economic growth, expanding markets and considerable capital inflow – three factors that attracted multinational vehicle corporations to invest in large plants in the larger countries and thus benefit from significant economies of scale (Gwynne 1978).

However, the late 1970s and 1980s have, in general, brought a dismal development period to Latin America. Stagnant economies, declining markets and considerable capital outflow mean that the previous favourable trends have been totally reversed. Latin American governments have been faced with the primary need of expanding exports in order to register large trade surpluses that can go some way to paying the huge annual debt repayments that the debt crisis has effectively signified. With declining internal markets for motor cars, governments have turned to the vehicle multinationals to assist in the national need to increase exports by re-orienting their spare capacity to international markets. In order to encourage them, they have been prepared to give considerable export incentives to the multinationals. This is the general background to the third strategy of promoting vehicle exports from Third World countries. However, for most Latin American countries, the vehicle industry was always too high cost for any serious possibility of a re-orientation towards international markets (Gwynne 1978). Such re-orientation has basically been restricted to two countries, Brazil and Mexico, both of which provided contrasting scenarios in the late 1980s.

Recent export trends in Brazil

The Brazilian government had begun to require export commitments from its vehicle multinationals as far back as 1972 with the negotiation of the first of the Special Fiscal Benefits for Exports (BEFIEX) programmes with Ford. One of the major privileges that car multinationals received from the scheme was the reduction in the very high levels of local content that they previously had to comply with – from

99 to 85 per cent. Under BEFIEX vehicle exporters were also eligible for a number of special tax incentives and exemptions from restrictions on imports. Reductions of between 70 and 90 per cent of the Industrial Products Tax on imported equipment and up to 50 per cent of the tax on imported raw materials, components and intermediate products were offered.

> The pressure which forced firms to take up the BEFIEX programme was the control of the Brazilian Council for Industrial Development over the authorization of investment and its ability to offer attractive incentives to the manufacturers. The initial agreement with Ford was signed when the company wished to expand in Brazil through the introduction of the Maverick. In 1973 Volkswagen, worried about the impact of the Maverick on its market share, entered the BEFIEX programme in order to introduce a new model.
>
> (Jenkins 1987: 193)

By 1978 almost all the car multinationals in Brazil had signed BEFIEX agreements. In addition firms were able to benefit from the general fiscal incentives for manufactured exports introduced in the late 1960s and early 1970s. The most important of these were the exemption from the state sales tax in 1967 and the introduction of a tax credit for the industrial products tax in 1969. The total value of incentives received by the industry was 62 per cent of the value of exports in 1971 and 67 per cent in 1975 (Jenkins 1987). Meanwhile, the traditional investment incentives available to the car industry, apart from those related to an export commitment, were all withdrawn in 1974. According to Mericle (1984: 28), 'the message to the automobile producers was clear; any major future expansion was contingent on a commitment to export'.

As a result, Brazil had already begun to record a rapid growth in vehicle exports during the late 1970s and early 1980s. Vehicle exports rose gradually from 13,528 in 1972 to 70,026 in 1977 but then increased rapidly to reach 213,266 in 1981. This 1981 export figure represented 27.3 per cent of all vehicles manufactured in Brazil in that year. The majority of these vehicles were exported to other Third World countries, not only in Latin America but also in Africa and the Middle East; Volkswagen was particularly prominent as an exporter to Third World countries.

However, exports of finished vehicles to other less developed countries proved highly volatile. Whereas 1981 proved a highly successful year with 213,266 vehicles worth US$1227 million being exported, the following year saw increasing problems of debt and recession in the Third World and a concomitant drop in Brazil's vehicle exports to 173,254 vehicles, worth nearly a third less (US$887 million). Nevertheless, the Brazilian government did benefit in the early 1980s from the buoyant exports of Brazil's four vehicle multinationals (Volkswagen, General Motors, Ford, Fiat). In 1981 their exports signified a large trade surplus on the motor industry account of over US$1.5 billion.

During the early 1980s, the Brazilian motor vehicle industry was undoubtedly the largest in the Third World, producing an average of nearly one million vehicles a year. Its large market, that reaches to over one million vehicles a year during times of economic prosperity, has been a major attraction to the automobile multinationals. The only multinational to be allowed in after the 1950s, Fiat, certainly saw it that way. After closing down its plants in Argentina, Chile and Colombia in 1982, a difficult loss-making year for its worldwide operations, Vittorio Ghidela, the head of Fiat's world operations, said: 'The key country in the South American car business will continue to be Brazil and we are determined to stay there, even if the losses continue' (Gwynne 1985).

However, the late 1980s must inevitably have brought second thoughts from the top executives of vehicle multinationals. The problems of Brazil's debt crisis, the mismanagement of the economy and economic stagnation have severely reduced Brazil's internal market for cars – from nearly one million vehicles per annum in the late 1970s to 330,000 in 1987. Almost all these cars are powered by alcohol engines, a technological development that has been rendered idiosyncratic and inappropriate for export by the reduction in the oil price during the 1980s. It seems that Brazil's severe economic problems will continue on until at least the mid-1990s, with the corollary that the domestic vehicle market will remain at only one-third of its former level.

For the multinationals themselves, increasing exports has become a matter of survival for their Brazilian subsidiaries. In April 1987, an agreement was struck between the government and the three Brazilian vehicle subsidiaries (in November 1986, Ford and Volkswagen merged their Brazilian operations to form Autolatina). The vehicle subsidiaries were worried about their increasing losses in Brazil (due to price controls) as well as their increasingly low capacity utilization. Under the deal, the government conceded regular price rises every 30–40 days to combat double-digit monthly inflation. In return, the manufacturers undertook to invest about one billion dollars by the end of 1989 in order to raise export sales to US$7.4 billion and thus leave a US$4.5 billion trade surplus on the motor vehicle account after imports. However, the agreement has subsequently been the focus of much conflict between the multinationals and the government; at the end of 1987, Autolatina took the government to court for breaching the terms of the agreement.

It therefore seems unlikely that the planned one billion dollars of investment will be forthcoming. Such investment is, however, vital both for the multinationals and Brazil. The technological level of the Brazilian motor vehicle industry is rapidly falling behind not only that of the developed world but also that of such East Asian countries as Korea and Malaysia. The year 1987, in fact, was the first year that Korea (790,000) produced more vehicles than Brazil (683,000). The Brazilian industry is increasingly relying on just two locational factors – low labour costs and cheap steel. However, such cost advantages will only have limited applicability in the future unless considerable new investment is made in process technology.

In the meantime, the three vehicle companies have been moderately successful at increasing their vehicle exports. In 1987, an estimated 353,000 vehicles were exported or 51.6 per cent of total production, making 1987 the first year in which production for export was greater than that for internal demand. In contrast to the early 1980s, the majority of these exports now go to the developed world. Fiat uses its Brazilian subsidiary as a supplier of small cars to the European market. Autolatina and GM orient their exports more to the North American market. In particular, the Volkswagen Fox (made in Brazil as the Voyage) has been particularly successful at the low end of the United States market; indeed, the success of the Brazilian-made Fox relative to the US-made Golfs and Jettas in the US market was one reason why Volkswagen closed its Pennsylvania plant at the end of 1988.

However, most Brazilian vehicle exports to developed world markets are now at the lower, cheaper end of the vehicle range. Although this continued to be a market niche for Brazilian exports in the late 1980s, competition from Korea was already making this a highly competitive market segment. In the meantime, the considerable export incentives and subsidies from the Brazilian government combined with the necessity for multinationals to find new markets in the face of a collapsing home market has temporarily made Brazil a major Third World exporter of vehicles. For such a short-term trend to become long-term, however, major new investments are required, particularly in process technology and organizational methods.

Recent export trends in Mexico

The Mexican government has attempted to promote both vehicle and components exports ever since 1969 when an agreement was signed between Mexico's Industrial Ministry and the leading multinationals producing there. Under this agreement, the multinationals would have to steadily increase their vehicle and component exports, with the long-term aim of fully compensating their imports by exports (Bennett and Sharpe 1985: 164). In 1977, this was set for 1982. However, the oil boom of the late 1970s and early 1980s rendered this policy very complicated as the multinationals producing in Mexico found it difficult to even keep up with the rapid increase in internal demand during the period.

The onset of the debt crisis in 1982, the ensuing recession and severe drop in the oil price, has, however, radically changed the feasibility of the policy. After Mexico's vehicle exports (mainly components) climbed slowly between 1972 and 1981 (from US$52.5 million to US$370.3 million), they increased dramatically in absolute terms over the following six years, to over US$2,763.1 million in 1987 (and more equally divided between vehicles and components – see Table 3.2). Incidentally, the trade data do not include the exports from Mexico's border industrialization towns, where numerous components firms, particularly of US origin, have established plants during the 1980s.

Vehicle parts rather than finished vehicles had constituted the majority of exports in Mexico's vehicle sector from the early 1970s (see Table 3.2). Indeed, even by 1985, the export of vehicle parts constituted approximately 90 per cent of the sector's exports. Mexico, therefore, provided a major contrast with Brazil, because the multinationals had primarily used it as a source for parts and components, particularly engines and gearboxes, rather than finished vehicles. One important reason for this was that the three North American companies operating in Mexico (General Motors, Ford and Chrysler) had used their Mexican bases in order to export parts back to Detroit or to other plants in their worldwide operations (as well as to comply with Mexican government regulations). Table 3.3 shows the extent of new investment by the US automobile corporations in Mexico during the 1970s and 1980s. One point to note is that the capacity of engine plants had been much greater than that of assembly plants.

The older assembly plants based either in Mexico City or within a radius of 150 km of the metropolis have been mainly geared to the national market (see Figure 3.2). The small pre-1960s plants within Mexico City have subsequently changed their function to the

Table 3.2　Performance of Mexican vehicle exports, 1972−87

Year	No. of export vehicles	% Share of production	Value (US$ million)			Trade balance (US$ million)
			Vehicles	Parts	Total	
1972	2,212	1.0	5.7	46.8	52.5	− 225.7
1973	20,141	7.0	40.4	80.2	120.6	− 231.3
1974	19,117	5.4	44.7	104.2	148.9	− 356.1
1975	2,938	0.9	8.7	113.3	122.0	− 628.3
1976	4,172	1.3	18.4	173.9	192.3	− 526.4
1977	11,743	4.2	30.0	223.5	253.5	− 385.4
1978	25,828	6.7	67.9	266.0	333.9	− 559.1
1979	24,756	5.5	116.8	260.0	376.8	− 1049.5
1980	18,245	3.7	128.6	275.8	404.4	− 1498.8
1981	14,428	2.4	107.3	263.0	370.3	− 2148.3
1982	15,819	3.4	81.2	449.8	531.0	− 816.5
1983	22,456	7.9	113.3	551.1	664.4	+ 314.4
1984	33,635	9.5	180.8	733.0	913.8	+ 280.3
1985	58,423	12.9	115.3	1013.9	1129.2	+ 421.7
1986	72,429	21.4	314.0	806.8	1120.8	+ 782.5
1987	163,073	41.4	1127.6	1635.5	2763.1	+ 2290.1
1988	173,147	33.9				
1989[a]	137,469	34.5				

Sources: Asociación Mexicana de la Industria Automotriz (1988) La Industria Automotriz de Mexico en Cifras; Jenkins (1987)

[a] January−July

Table 3.3　Investments of US car corporations in Mexico, 1970−86

Corporation	Location	Product	Capacity	Investment (US$ million)
Ford	Chihuahua	Engine	500,000	445
Ford	Hermosillo	Assembly	130,000	500
Ford	Saltillo	Aluminium cylinder heads	860,000	n.d.
GM	Ramos Arizpe	Engine	400,000	300
GM	Ramos Arizpe	Assembly	100,000	
Chrysler	Ramos Arizpe	Engine	400,000	125

Source: Jenkins (1987: 219)

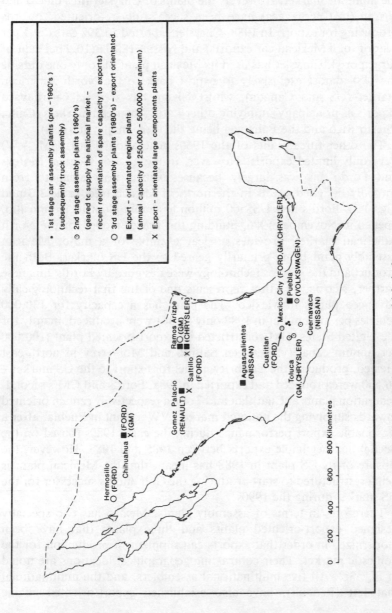

Figure 3.2 Spatial evolution of the Mexican motor vehicle industry

Legend:

- 1st stage car assembly plants (pre-1960's) (subsequently truck assembly)

○ 2nd stage assembly plants (1960's) (geared to supply the national market – recent reorientation of spare capacity to exports)

○ 3rd stage assembly plants (1980's) – export orientated.

■ Export – orientated engine plants (annual capacity of 250,000 – 500,000 per annum)

× Export – orientated large components plants

Plant locations shown on map:

Hermosillo (FORD)
Chihuahua ■ (FORD)
Gomez Palacio ■ (RENAULT)
Ramos Arizpe ○ (GM) × (CHRYSLER)
Saltillo ■ (CHRYSLER)
Saltillo × (FORD)
Aguascalientes ■ (NISSAN)
Cuatitlan (FORD)
Toluca (GM,CHRYSLER)
Mexico City (FORD,GM,CHRYSLER)
Puebla ○ (VOLKSWAGEN)
Cuernavaca (NISSAN)

0 200 400 600 800 Kilometres

production of either commercial vehicles or components. The second-stage plants of the 1960s (with vehicles now having to incorporate a significant amount of locally produced components) were spatially more decentralized but still mainly geared towards producing cars for the domestic market. However, the plants of Chrysler (in Toluca) and Nissan (in Cuernavaca) have been successfully re-oriented towards producing for export. In 1988, Chrysler exported 50,392 cars (29.1 per cent of total Mexican car exports) and Nissan 18,871 (10.9 per cent of car exports). Chrysler has used its Mexican plant (its only one outside the US) almost exclusively to export back to the North American market (US and Canada), whilst Nissan has seen its Cuernavaca exports as principally supplying other Latin American markets (Chile, Puerto Rico and the Bahamas being the three major markets).

The other three plants of the 1960s generation (Ford, GM, VW) have only limited exports. However, in the case of General Motors and Ford, this was largely because exports now emanate from specially designed plants in the north of Mexico (see Table 3.3 and Fig. 3.2). Ford's new US$500 million assembly plant in Hermosillo, opened in November 1986, building the Tracer model for the North American market, provides a clear example of a major Mexican assembly plant being primarily geared to the US market. Both the product and the process technology were designed by Ford's Japanese partner, Mazda, and thus represents one of the first technologically advanced plants in Mexico. The plant has a capacity for 130,000 vehicles per annum but in 1988 only 66,361 were produced, mainly for the United States. GM constructed its export-oriented plant (100,000 per annum capacity) between Saltillo and Monterrey in north-east Mexico, producing the Celebrity model for export to the US market – 36,500 were produced and exported in 1988. Ford's and GM's second-generation plants at Cuatitlán and Toluca respectively remain oriented towards supplying the national market. VW's plant in Puebla, after a reasonable export performance during the early 1980s (based on the Beetle) had negligible exports between 1985 and 1988. However, the closure of its US plant in 1988 has meant that the Mexican plant is being restructured to start producing the Golf and its successor for the US market during the 1990s.

Therefore, in terms of assembly plants, Mexico has two specially designed export-oriented plants and three plants that have been modernized in order that exports can supplement production for the domestic market. Their contrasting geographical locations are noted in Fig. 3.2. All five multinational assemblers, and the multinational that left (Renault), have also established export-oriented engine plants, partly as a response to government legislation and partly due to considerations of labour costs. As a result, the engine plants were constructed with a view to producing for the world supply system of the various multinationals.

It was possible to take advantage of economies of scale and construct plants with capacities around the minimum efficient scale. The capacity of Ford's engine plant at Chihuahua and the engine plants of General Motors and Chrysler at Ramos Arizpe, near Monterrey, 'compare favourably with most estimates of the scale of plant necessary to take advantage of scale economies' (Jenkins 1987: 218). Furthermore, these plants are equipped with modern technology and new machinery. 'The General Motors engine plant in Ramos Arizpe uses automatic transfer machines and is comparable in terms of its technological level to equivalent plants in the United States. Labour productivity is three times as high as the average productivity in previously existing engine plants in Mexico' (Jenkins 1987: 218).

Meanwhile, the US producers in Mexico have benefited during the late 1980s from labour rates nearly one-tenth the US level – in approximate terms, a labour rate of $1 per hour in Mexico as opposed to $10 per hour in the US (Gardner 1987); traditional differences in dollar wages between US and Mexican workers were accentuated due to the Mexican devaluations of the 1980s. High labour productivity levels (due to new machinery), low labour costs and low transport costs to the US market are thus making a Mexican location attractive to the US producers. The fact that fiscal incentives have been used by the Mexican government to persuade the multinationals to come and that these incentives can be worth 'almost half the value of exports' (Jenkins 1987: 216) means that the Mexican location has also become a highly profitable one.

The potential advantages of Mexican proximity to the United States for components and engine production had also been recognized by the non-US firms operating in Mexico. In the last decade Volkswagen has built a large four-cylinder engine plant (400,000 per annum capacity) near its Puebla base, Nissan has completed an engine and stampings plant in Aguascalientes with an annual capacity of 350,000 engines and Renault has built sizeable engine (250,000 per annum capacity) and suspensions (300,000 per annum capacity) plants in the northern location of Gomez Palacio, near Torreón. These plants used to be closely linked to production in the US – indeed, in 1987, Nissan exported 70,000 engines from its plant at Aguascalientes to the Nissan assembly plant in Smyrna, Tennessee (1987 production of 117,334). However, since the closure of the Volkswagen and Renault car plants in the US, engine production at Puebla and Gomez Palacio is now principally geared to European and world supply systems. As with plants of the US corporations, these plants enjoy maximum benefits from economies of scale and employ the latest technology in order to achieve high labour productivity.

However, Mexico's future as an exporter of vehicles may be constrained due to the lack of new technology in the assembly sector (apart from Ford's Hermosillo plant and GM's plant in Ramos Arizpe). As with Brazil, the multinationals set up plants in Mexico principally for access to the internal market. During the years of the oil boom, production of finished vehicles for the internal market increased rapidly, reaching 581,000 in 1981. By 1986, however, production for the internal market had declined to 258,000. In that year, one of the six multinationals producing in Mexico, Renault, closed down its assembly plant at Hidalgo. In 1988, the Mexican domestic vehicle market was divided up between Nissan (24.7 per cent), Chrysler (23.4 per cent), Ford (18.1 per cent), Volkswagen (17.8 per cent) and GM (13.9 per cent).

The second generation of Mexican assembly plants (those designed for supplying the internal market) have not been extensively modernized, particularly those of Ford and GM. Technology still tends to be labour-intensive but the low wage rates of Mexico are often not sufficient compensation in terms of international competition. The most modernized of the second-generation plants is Nissan's plant at Cuernavaca. However, according to the head of Nissan's Mexican operations in 1987, Mr Shoichi Amemiya, 'the costs of producing a Nissan vehicle in Mexico, in spite of lower labour costs, is only 10 per cent less than in the US and slightly more expensive than in Japan' (Johns 1987). In Nissan's case, such relatively high costs of production occur despite low wage rates, the incorporation of quality circles and the employment of 700 Japanese staff in Nissan Mexicana.

The Mexican motor vehicle industry thus makes an interesting contrast to both Brazil and Korea. It has traditionally been a major exporter of components rather than the finished vehicle itself. However, in the late 1980s, it is gradually turning into a significant exporter of finished vehicles as well. Compared to Brazil, there has been considerably more investment during the 1980s, investment furthermore in technologically advanced plant. However, investment in advanced technology at 'greenfield' locations has been limited to engine plants and only two assembly plants, although Nissan has plans to establish a new 'greenfield' site at Aguascalientes during the 1990s.

Unlike South Korea, and despite many historical efforts to promote a 'national' vehicle firm, the Mexican motor vehicle industry relies on foreign corporations, and particularly those from the United States. During the 1980s, the supply of the North American market from a nearby low-cost location became a dominant theme of new investments by the US multinationals in Mexico – first in engines and then in finished vehicles. In 1988, 99.8 per cent of the 153,259 vehicle exports of the three US assembly firms were destined for the United States. However, non-US multinationals have not yet linked their Mexican assembly operations that closely with the US market. Nissan still sees its Mexican plant as a Latin American supply point, Renault has left, and VW substantially reduced its export programme during the 1980s. Although Nissan's Mexican engine plant is closely tied in with Nissan's assembly plant in the US, both VW and Renault have to link their plants in with their worldwide supply networks. However, the 1990s should see some reversal of these trends, particularly with the likely arrival of Toyota as a manufacturer with an export programme directed towards the US market and strong US/Mexican linkages in components.

TECHNOLOGICAL DIVERGENCE: THIRD WORLD AS MARGINAL PRODUCER

At the beginning of this chapter, the spatial development of the motor car industry in the Third World was placed within the context of its technological future, and, in particular, two views of this future. One view of the future saw motor car production being geared to achieving maximum economies of scale and reducing costs; low labour cost locations in the Third World seemed theoretically attractive to multinational producers within this perspective. A rival view of the future saw changing production processes and work practices, combined with increasing use of computer-aided manufacturing as keeping most car manufacturing in the developed countries.

Our survey of recent corporate development has demonstrated that the latter view seems to have been the more correct forecast for the 1980s. The analysis of the Third World motor car industry demonstrated that only three less developed countries have managed to develop car industries with a strong export performance. However, the reasons behind the export success of these countries are different.

The explanation for the original growth of the car industry in Brazil lies in that country's large market and the interest of US and European multinationals in producing for that market. The recent export growth in the car sector is closely linked to subsequent attempts by government to make the multinationals export. However, future growth of the Brazilian industry would now seem difficult if the explanation of Volkswagen's worldwide sales director, Werner Schmidt, behind the decision to merge Volkswagen and Ford in Brazil and Argentina into one company, Autolatina, is taken seriously: 'We think it will take so long for the Brazilian economy to recover, it is best not to wait another 20 years before taking some action' (Gooding 1986). With the Brazilian market likely to be declining for the next decade, the future growth of Brazil's car sector now relies squarely on exports. However, to achieve sustained export growth into the 1990s, considerable investment in new process technology will be required.

Massive investment in motor vehicle plant has only been taking place in the other two countries, Mexico and Korea, during the late 1980s. In Korea, it seems that strategies of linkage with Japanese multinationals have been particularly significant, as in the case of Hyundai. The other two vehicle corporations of Korea, Daewoo and Kia, have registered links with Japanese technology via their North American partners, GM and Ford respectively. Furthermore, they have benefited from direct access to the US market through the distribution networks of GM and Ford. If the successful linking with both Japanese technology and 'world car' corporations of the United States can explain Korean success, Mexican success is inevitably linked to its spatial proximity to the US market. Three US, two European and one Japanese corporation have heavily invested in export-oriented plant in Mexico as a result – mainly in component production but recently in vehicle assembly as well. Again links with Japanese multinationals seem to be increasing through the US multinationals – with Mazda via Ford, Isuzu via GM and Mitsubishi via Chrysler.

The motor vehicle industry remains strongly market-oriented. The most dramatic locational shift in the industry, that of Japanese productive growth, has been caused by technological advances in product design and production process rather than any consideration of labour costs. As a result, the product life-cycle would appear to have little relevance for the industry and its locational future. The motor vehicle is not a standardized product with a standardized technology. Rather, it is an industry continually open to change in product design, process technology and organizational methods, and most particularly in the 1980s. According to the MIT report, only the location of standardized parts such as starters, lighting and suspensions would shift to Third World countries in the future due to the attraction of lower labour costs.

The motor vehicle industry may grow in large markets (such as

Brazil), technologically dynamic countries with their own diversified multinationals (Korea) or in countries located near to core country markets (Mexico). Apart from Mexico, there is no Third World country adjacent to a core country. In Europe, the nearest comparison has been Spain, which the multinationals (GM, Ford, VW, Peugeot, Renault) have identified as the low-cost producer of small cars for the European market. Third World countries may be able to maintain assembly operations but a genuine development of an export-oriented industry seems difficult, particularly for small countries with small markets. Even for large markets, such as India and China, future growth in vehicle production will be limited unless exports can rapidly increase. At present, however, the world motor vehicle industry is characterized by spatial retrenchment, increasing its concentration in the industrial market economies of North America, Europe and Japan. In global terms, the Third World seems set to be a marginal producer of cars, at least into the foreseeable future.

4 The transformation of the Japanese motor vehicle industry and its role in the world: industrial restructuring and technical evolution

Yasuo Miyakawa

In 1980, the year after the second oil crisis hit the world economy, Japan became the world's leading motor vehicle producer. The industry in the United States, in particular, suffered great damage from the energy shortage since it had traditionally manufactured large-sized cars, and in 1980, the US passed a special law granting government money to bail out Chrysler from its financial crisis. The restructuring of the US motor vehicle industry affected the Japanese industry as their government agreed to implement a self-control policy in exporting motor vehicles to the US. Further, in 1980, the president of the UAW (United States Union of Automobile Workers) made a strong request to Japanese companies to construct their factories in the US. In 1980, Honda, a leading motor vehicle company in Japan, announced the construction of its first car factory in the United States. Following Honda, many Japanese companies began to expand their manufacturing facilities in the United States. The international development of the Japanese motor vehicle industry, in turn, has exerted a great influence on the structural and locational pattern of the entire industry in the world.

The rapid growth of the Japanese motor vehicle industry has attracted much attention, but despite this growing interest in the industry, and in Japan itself, few are aware of the historical and geographical background for the development of the industry in Japan, and how it has evolved in the highly competitive world market, originally dominated by advanced European and American motor vehicle firms. This chapter examines the growth and transformation of the Japanese motor vehicle industry, focusing on its restructuring, and on the rapid development of technology and manufacturing know-hows in the industry.

THE DEVELOPMENT OF THE JAPANESE MOTOR VEHICLE INDUSTRY BEFORE THE SECOND WORLD WAR

In 1853, the US Commodore Matthew Perry arrived at Uraga at the mouth of the Edo Bay. Edo, today's Tokyo, was then the centre of administration of the Tokugawa Shogunate. The arrival of the American naval fleet gave the final blow to Japan's over 200-year-old seclusion. The 1854 Treaty of Amity with the United States was followed by a series of similar unequal treaties concluded with other countries. In 1860, the small fishing village of Yokohama, located between Uraga and Edo, was opened as an international trade port, and a foreign settlement council was established here. Thereupon, Yokohama became the centre of foreign trade and one of the most important settlements for foreigners in Japan. As for the development of Japanese modern industries, Yokohama played a significant role as a hinge between Japanese manufacturing areas and foreign countries, the US and Europe, in particular. In the Meiji Restoration of 1868, the national capital was relocated from Kyoto to Tokyo (renamed from Edo). In 1872, the first Japanese railway was opened between Tokyo and Yokohama, connecting the two closely linked areas.

The first motor vehicle was imported to Japan by a foreign trader in 1897 in Yokohama, where later in 1901, the first importing agency was established. The manufacture of motor vehicles in Japan was developed first in Tokyo by the Japanese company, Tokyo Motor Vehicle Manufacturing in 1904, only a year after the establishment of Ford Motors in the United States. Tokyo was an important incubator of modern industries in Japan. In Tokyo there were several government-owned plants, such as the Akabane Works, Koishikawa Arsenal, Tsukiji Navy Works, where pioneering engineers gathered to copy modern Western industrial products and technologies.

In the early 1900s, Osaka emerged as the second centre of motor vehicle manufacturing in Japan. In 1911, the Osaka Army Arsenal began manufacturing army trucks there. When the First World War broke out in 1914 the demand for army trucks increased. In 1916, Kawasaki Vehicles (a subsidiary company of Kawasaki Shipbuilding) also started manufacturing army trucks in Kobe, an important international trade port in the Osaka metropolitan area. Further, Mitsubishi Shipbuilding in Kobe entered into the motor vehicle industry by manufacturing passenger cars modelled after Fiat.

The industrial policy of the Japanese Army played an important role in the growth of the motor vehicle industry in Japan. In 1918, the Japanese government passed the Law of Aid for Military Vehicles and the Army established the Army Military Vehicle Force. Under the law, the Osaka Army Arsenal sent orders of army trucks to Kawasaki Shipbuilding and Mitsubishi Shipbuilding as well as to Hatsudoko Seizo (today's Daihatsu). Both Mitsubishi Shipbuilding and Kawasaki Shipbuilding established separate divisions within their companies for the manufacture of motor vehicles, as well as divisions for aircraft manufacturing. After the First World War, the Kubota Iron Works (today's Kubota) established the Jitsuyo Motor Vehicle (later merged into Nissan) in Osaka in 1919, most of whose skilled workers were retirees of the Osaka Army Arsenal. Thus, the Osaka metropolitan area emerged as one of the most important areas for the motor vehicle industry in Japan (Fig. 4.1). Indeed, in terms of industrial output in Japan, Osaka stayed at the top until 1936.

Figure 4.1 The major motor vehicle manufacturing centres of Japan

The 1920s was a decade of great change in the history of the Japanese motor vehicle industry. In 1923, the Great Kanto Earthquake hit the Tokyo metropolitan area and the motor vehicle companies in this area suffered great damage. After the earthquake, in 1924 the Department of Trams in the Tokyo Municipal Government issued an order for 800 T-type Ford cars to establish a Department of Bus Transportation. Through this trade, Ford, which had intended to establish an Asian branch factory in Shanghai, realized the importance of the Japanese market, and chose Yokohama as its Asian base in 1925.

The establishment of Japan Ford gave a great stimulus to the development of the Japanese motor vehicle industry. The Ministry of Commerce and Industry established a special committee on the development of domestic motor vehicles in 1926 and the Ministry of Home Affairs permitted the driving of small cars (less than 350 cc) without a driver's licence. General Motors, a rival of Ford, also entered the Japanese market. The Osaka municipal government took an active interest in introducing foreign motor vehicle companies into the area, with GM as its first choice, to rival the expansion of the Tokyo metropolitan area. In 1927, GM established Japan General Motors in Osaka. This rapid development of foreign assemblers caused considerable damage to the domestic motor vehicle companies in Japan, and several were forced to close down. By 1929 the big three foreign companies manufactured 29,338 cars compared to only 437 by domestic companies whilst 5,018 were imported (Fig. 4.2).

Envisioning the development of the domestic motor vehicle industry as an important national policy, the Ministry of Commerce and Industry formed a committee in 1929 to formulate a policy, and the Ministry of Railways formed a research committee to look into motor vehicle traffic. The Army also feared the demise of Japanese motor vehicle companies under pressure from foreign companies; it saw such an example in the case of Germany where a domestic motor vehicle company was taken over by GM in 1929. In order to develop an indigenous motor vehicle industry, the ministries and the Army supported the recovery of existing Japanese-owned motor vehicle companies. At the same time, they promoted the establishment of new domestic companies which could compete against foreign companies. It was largely due to these government policies implemented after the World Depression, that Toyota came into existence in the Nagoya metropolitan area, located between Tokyo and Osaka. This was to become the core of the motor vehicle industry in Japan (Fig. 4.1). In 1929, the Toyoda Automatic Loom Works, the predecessor of Toyota,

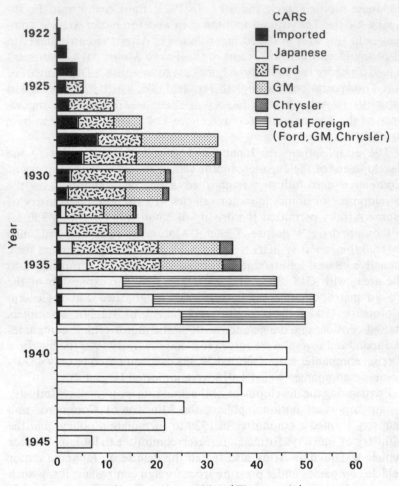

Figure 4.2   Japanese car output, 1922–45

started the manufacture of motor vehicles using royalties paid by Platt Brothers of the United Kingdom. The Toyoda Automatic Loom Works was established in 1923 at Kariya on the south-eastern fringe of the Nagoya metropolitan area by Toyoda Spinning and Weaving (founded 1897 at Nagoya).

Nagoya was a castle town traditionally associated with a large timber and wood-processing industry and the clock industry. These laid the foundations for the development of a textile machinery industry, and then a vehicle manufacturing industry in this area. The agglomeration of existing industries attracted new ventures to this area: Nippon Sharyo Seizo Kaisha, a vehicle manufacturing company was established in Nagoya in 1895, and in 1907, the Atsuta Weapon Manufacturing Works of Tokyo Arsenal was established at a site adjacent to Nippon Sharyo Seizo. This later started the manufacture of aircraft engines and the assembling of aircraft in 1917. The Nagoya metropolitan area gradually developed into the centre of the aircraft industry in Japan.

Toyota was established in 1937 in Koromo, on the eastern fringe of the Nagoya metropolitan area. This economically depressed town, which had suffered from the decline of the silk industry, attracted Toyota Motors by providing a large site at a lower price than the other rival towns (Kariya, Ookaka and Higashiura) in the area. It had good transport connections by means of private railway lines and was therefore able to offer Toyota easy access to the agglomeration of component industries in Kariya which had been developed by the motor vehicle division, established in 1933, within the Toyoda Automatic Loom Works. Thus, Toyota could take advantage of these locational merits within the local metropolitan area. On the other hand, in terms of access to vital information, it faced a problem of isolation from the two large metropolitan areas of Tokyo and Osaka.

Toyota was able to overcome the problem of isolation by obtaining vital information from some friends of the founder, Kichiro Toyoda (son of Sakichi Toyota). This information – which helped Toyota to become one of the three major companies in Japan – concerned the decision of large financial groups (Mitsui, Mitsubishi, etc.) not to enter the industry, the passing of the Act for Development of the Motor Vehicle Industry in 1936, and the future control over the production of Ford and GM by the Ministry of Commerce and Industry and the Army.

As for technological development, Toyota again faced the problem of isolation and needed to catch up with Tokyo and Osaka, especially the Tokyo metropolitan area where Ford had already developed its subcontractors, such as Nissan. In order to meet this need, Kichiro Toyoda founded a motor vehicle industry research and development institute at Shibaura, Tokyo in 1937. Among the researchers and advisers of this institute there were many young distinguished researchers and associate professors of local universities, and excellent engineers from existing companies.

When assembling the first passenger car, Toyota employed, copied and improved on the excellent components which Ford, GM and Chrysler had already developed. As in the case of Nissan (established in 1933 at Yokohama), Toyota learned the mass-production system from Ford by sending its engineers to work with Ford. While acquiring Western technology, Toyota endeavoured to strengthen its own research ability; in 1940 it established the Toyoda Science and Chemical Institute in Tokyo for the development of basic research.

The sales know-how of General Motors was traditionally incubated in Osaka, the centre of Japan's economy and trade, whereas the actual sales activities, both advertisement and mass-sales, were based in Tokyo. Toyota converted Pacific Motors, a GM sales agency in Tokyo, to its own agency, and many other GM sales agencies later became Toyota's subsidiary agencies, with many staff transferring to Toyota.

In the 1930s the Japanese government and the Army put pressure on Ford and GM to develop the domestic motor vehicle industry. In 1934, the Army formed the Domestic Motor Vehicle Model Committee to manufacture domestically designed cars, and put an end to the expansion of the Ford factory at Yokohama. Facing protectionism in the Army, GM attempted to make cooperative arrangements with Nissan, which had factories both in Osaka and Yokohama, but this operation ended in failure. In 1936 the Japanese government passed the Motor Vehicle Industry Development Act. The Ministry of Commerce and Industry limited the assembly of motor vehicles by Ford and GM. Further, the Ministry of Finance increased the import tariff for motor vehicles from 50 per cent to 70 per cent, and for engines from 35 per cent to 60 per cent. In order to retain competitive operations under these circumstances, Ford attempted to make cooperative arrangements with Nissan. As in the case of GM, this ended in failure because of heavy pressure from the Army. Under these protective policies, the Japanese motor vehicle industry developed not only domestically, but also overseas, first in China. This overseas expansion of the Japanese motor vehicle industry took place at the same time as the expansion of Japanese military force in Asia. After China, factories were built in Korea and Taiwan, and later in Singapore and Jakarta.

As the military increased its control over politics, foreign companies in Japan faced a crisis. In 1939, when the Military Motor Vehicle Act was passed, Ford and GM were forced to close their factories in Japan, despite their efforts to survive by means of cooperative operations with Toyota or Nissan. Under the Act, only cars with military or government use could be manufactured. Thereupon, the Japanese motor vehicle industry directed itself towards the war economy, with the construction of many factories to manufacture army trucks, including the Hino works in Tokyo in 1942.

RAPID GROWTH AND RESTRUCTURING OF THE JAPANESE MOTOR VEHICLE INDUSTRY, 1945–70

After the Second World War, the Japanese motor vehicle industry was depressed and did not recover until after 1950, when the Korean War broke out, and created a substantial demand for motor vehicles. The General Headquarters (GHQ) of the Supreme Commander for the Allied Powers gradually permitted the manufacture of trucks by Nissan, Diesel Motors and Toyota because of its own need for replacements, although it prohibited the manufacture of military goods. When the Labour Union Law was enacted in 1945, workers formed labour unions and often went on strikes under the post-War economic depression. A series of financial austerity programmes by the GHQ, particularly the Dodge Line announced in 1949 (super-balanced budget, anti-inflation measures, establishment of single exchange rate, etc.) caused deep economic depression. As a result, most motor vehicle companies reduced their labour force. This caused long strikes, such as the 1950s strikes in Nissan, Isuzu (Diesel) and Toyota.

By overcoming the post-War economic crisis and union antagonism, and successfully responding to Korean War orders, Toyota surpassed Nissan and Isuzu. Toyota sent orders for car bodies to the Nakanihon Heavy Industry (formerly Mitsubishi Aircraft, today's Mitsubishi) in Nagoya, and also recruited top engineers from the Aichi Aircraft Industry (today's Aichi Machine Industry, a subsidiary of Nissan). Toyota owed its financial recovery primarily to one man: M. Takanashi (former president of Tokyo Tokyopet), the manager of the Bank of Japan's Nagoya Branch, who suggested the separation of the sales division and the manufacturing division of Toyota. As a result, Toyota Motor Sales (in Nagoya city) and Toyota Motor Manufacturing (in Koromo town) came into existence.

In 1951, the San Francisco Peace Treaty and the Japan–US Security Treaty were signed, symbolizing Japan's rejoining of the international economy. At the same time, Toyota started the manufacture of passenger cars. In 1952, the Ministry of Industry and Trade announced an industrial policy for the development of the domestic motor vehicle industry. Under the Amended Law for Introduction of Foreign Capital (enacted in 1951), Nissan, unlike Toyota, decided to make arrangements for technological cooperation with Austin in the United Kingdom in 1952 to overcome initial technological weaknesses.

Other agreements included Isuzu Motors with Rootes in the UK, and Hino with Renault in France. From a global viewpoint, the expansion of European companies in Japan can be explained as a result of the re-organization of European motor vehicle industries caused by the expansion of the American 'big three', viz. GM, Ford and Chrysler in Europe. In competition with these American companies, European companies were impelled to develop their markets by means of cooperation with Japanese companies.

As the Japanese companies progressed technically, they gradually began to expand again in the international market. In 1952, Nissan started technological cooperation with Taiwan's YeuLoong Motor, and Toyota started to export to Brazil. In response to this trend of internationalization, in 1953 Nissan and Isuzu constructed factories to manufacture Austin cars and Rootes cars, respectively. Toyota constructed a technical research centre adjacent to its head office in Koromo city (today's Toyota city) in 1954.

In 1955, the year when the government formulated a 5-year plan for economic self-dependency, the Ministry of International Trade and Industry (MITI) announced a programme for the development of domestic popular passenger cars. This caused passenger car makers to compete with each other by decreasing car prices and thus promoted the rationalization of manufacturing; Toyota Manufacturing received loans from the World Bank in 1956, and in the same year it assembled its first popular passenger car. The development of assembly factories caused the agglomeration of automobile parts factories. This trend of agglomeration accelerated under the implementation of three types of policies: the policy of passenger car companies, the industrial policy of the Small Business Agency of the MITI, and the industrialization policy of each municipal government. A good example of this was the establishment of the Arakawa Auto Body (today's ARAKO) in 1956 on land leased by Toyota in line with the ordinance issued in 1954.

In 1957 Toyota established United States Toyota at Los Angeles, and started its exports to that country in 1958. The economy of the US slackened and Toyota, which lacked the technology for manufacturing high-speed driving cars, failed in its first venture in the US. To improve on its technology and to develop the domestic market first, Toyota constructed the first Asian factory specializing in manufacturing passenger cars at Motomachi in Toyota city. Motomachi was near the location already planned for an interchange on the Tomei Highway, the major route between Komaki and Tokyo opened in 1969. In this year, Nissan stopped manufacturing Austin cars and started developing its own original cars.

In the 1960s, as the development of the Japanese economy accelerated, the motor vehicle industry became increasingly competitive. In 1960, the Cabinet adopted a liberalization policy for trade and exchange, a decision that resulted in the activation of sales and research efforts by Japanese companies. Furthermore, the Japanese companies endeavoured to increase exports, particularly to the United States. Honda and Nissan established sales companies in the United States in 1959 and 1960 respectively. European car sales also increased considerably in the US market from 270,000 in 1957 to 340,000 in 1958. In order to compete with these imports, American companies started the manufacture of compact cars in 1959. The share of compact cars in the US market amounted to 35 per cent of newly registered cars.

Under the governmental plan for the development of domestic popular cars (announced in 1955), new motor vehicle companies emerged in Japan: Suzuki in 1955, Fuji Heavy Industry in 1958, New Mitsubishi Heavy Industry (the predecessor of Mitsubishi) in 1960, and Toyokogyo (the predecessor of Mazda) in 1960. As a result, sales activities in the Japanese market became very competitive. In order to survive in the keen competition, motor vehicle companies were compelled to invest heavily in technological development.

Toyokogyo made a contract with the German firm NSU to develop the rotary engine in 1960. In the same year, Toyota relocated its research and development institute from Tokyo to Nagoya, and enlarged the institute to make the Toyota Central Research and Development Laboratories. The efforts by Japanese companies in sales and technological development thus raised the Japanese motor vehicle industry to an important position in the world. In 1960, Japan surpassed Canada in terms of the number of manufactured motor vehicles. The Canadian government immediately announced restrictions on the imports of Japanese products. As the exports from Japan began to cause trade friction, Japanese manufacturers were urged to be highly competitive by increasing productivity.

In order to increase productivity, Japanese companies began to construct large-scale factories. Following Toyota, Nissan constructed a large factory with a test course for passenger cars at Oppama in Yokosuka city on the south-western fringe of the Tokyo metropolitan area in 1961. Some other companies constructed large factories in the Tokyo metropolitan area: Isuzu at Fujisawa (in 1962), Prince (later merged with Nissan) at Murayama (in 1962) and Hino at Hamura (1963).

The other factor affecting world industrial structure during this decade was the economic growth of developing countries. In response to the increase of exports of Japanese motor vehicles to these countries, they began to tighten their industrial policies for the development of their domestic motor vehicle industries. Consequently, Japanese firms were compelled to establish local companies for the assembly of Japanese cars in these countries. Daihatsu constructed a 'knock-down' (KD) assembly plant in Pakistan in 1961. In this year, Japan surpassed Italy and the USSR in terms of the number of assembled cars. Toyota and Nissan established their overseas subsidiaries in many developing countries including Toyota Thailand and Nissan Chile in 1962. Following Nissan and Toyota, Toyokogyo started its export of KD parts to South Africa in 1963; it also established a technical centre at its head factory in Hiroshima to compete with Nissan and Toyota. In order to develop exports Japanese car companies began to employ ships specially designed for the transportation of motor vehicles. By 1964, Japan had surpassed France in terms of the number of cars manufactured.

In 1965, the Japanese government decided to liberalize imports of passenger cars, which gave a great stimulus to the re-organization of Japan's motor vehicle industry. Isuzu cancelled the technological cooperation with Rootes Motors, which was taken over by Chrysler in this year. Nissan constructed the Zama factory, and employed ships specially designed for the export of cars in 1965, and then merged with Prince in 1966. To compete with Nissan, Toyota constructed an engine factory at Kamigo in Toyota city in 1965 and another factory with a huge test course for the manufacturing of expensive cars at Higashifuji on the eastern fringe of Shizuka Prefecture in 1966. Toyota decided to start a joint business with Hino in 1966, a move which stimulated the development of Hino's overseas activities in New Zealand, Greece, Panama and Thailand. In 1967, Toyota made cooperative arrangements with Daihatsu. Hence, Toyota, with its headquarters of production in the Nagoya area, obtained two other production bases in Tokyo (Hino) and Osaka (Daihatsu).

Led by the competitive race among the major car companies, the Japanese motor vehicle industry continued to thrive; Japan's car production surpassed that of the UK in 1966 and then that of West Germany in 1967 (Fig. 4.3). In response to the rapid growth of Japan, the first Japan–US Motor Vehicle Conference was held in 1967, at which the US car companies asked for liberalization of capital transactions. In 1968, Japan surpassed the United States and Italy in terms of the number of exported cars; Japan's rising role in the world motor vehicle industry was confirmed.

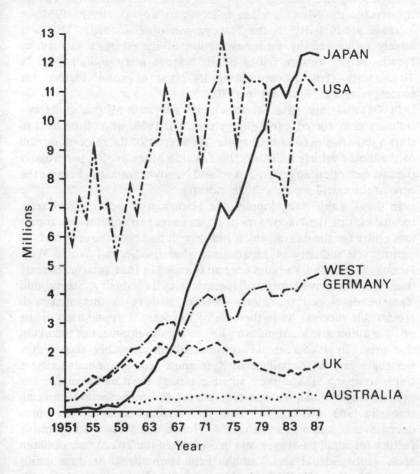

Figure 4.3 Car production in Japan and other countries, 1951–87

In 1968, the Foreign Capital Investment Committee in Japan decided to liberalize the introduction of technologies and a series of liberalization policies implemented by the government under pressure, particularly from the United States, accelerated the re-organization of the Japanese motor vehicle industry. Many car companies entered into joint business: Nissan with Fuji Heavy Industry and Mitsubishi Heavy Industry with Isuzu in 1968. Nissan relocated its head office from Yokohama to Tokyo to cope with the trend of internationalization. Toyota developed a branch office in Tokyo and promoted the construction of a small car factory of Hino at Hamura in Tokyo. While strengthening the strategy for the Tokyo metropolitan area, Toyota constructed the Miyoshi plant adjacent to Toyota city in 1968, to increase productivity in the Nagoya metropolitan area. This was largely influenced by the construction of the Shizuka factory by Honda on the western fringe of the Nagoya metropolitan area. In Toyota city, Toyota constructed its latest assembly factory for passenger cars at Tsutsumi in 1970.

In Okazaki city adjacent to Toyota city, the Mitsubishi Heavy Industry constructed a technology centre in 1969, when it decided to start a joint business with Chrysler. As a result of the re-organization of the motor vehicle industry, the Tokaido Megalopolis, particularly the two metropolitan areas, Tokyo and Nagoya, gradually became the core of the world motor vehicle industry.

In the Tokaido Megalopolis, the Hamamatsu metropolitan area, located east of the Nagoya metropolitan area, emerged as an important centre for the motor vehicle industry. It had been the centre of the motor cycle industry in Japan since after the Second World War. Honda, Suzuki and Yamaha were all founded in Hamamatsu. Largely thanks to the development of the motor cycle industry, Suzuki and Yamaha developed the motor vehicle industry in this area with remarkable success. As in the case of Toyota, the foundation of the existing automatic loom industry helped the development of Suzuki in this area. In 1965, Suzuki constructed an assembly factory for passenger cars at the village of Kamimura near Hamamatsu city, a single-company village like a single-company town of Toyota.

Following Suzuki, Honda also started the manufacture of small trucks in 1963, the year in which both Nissan and Toyokogyo produced over a million cars. In 1964, Honda constructed an assembly factory for small passenger cars in Sayama in the Tokyo metropolitan area, whilst Suzuki and Yamaha kept Hamamatsu as their major production area. In 1965, Toyota sent an order to Yamaha for the manufacture of Toyota's sports car, the 2000GT, because of the high technology and economy of the Hamamatsu agglomeration. Suzuki constructed the Iwata factory in the eastern part of this metropolitan area in 1967, whilst Honda constructed a factory at Suzuka on the western fringe of the Nagoya metropolitan area. Further, Suzuki constructed Osuga factory and Kosai factory in 1970, and Yamaha constructed its own Iwata factory in the Hamamatsu metropolitan area.

In sum, the 1960s was a thriving but transitional decade for the Japanese motor vehicle industry; the rapid growth of the industry could not have taken place without the fundamental restructuring which was largely promoted by strong pressure from the big three of the United States. Furthermore, it was noteworthy that the Japanese motor vehicle industry acquired technological cooperation from European car companies who themselves had faced strong competition from the big three in the European market.

As for the consequences of the restructuring of the Japanese motor vehicle industry during this decade, three important changes should be pointed out. First, the restructuring of the motor vehicle industry affected the spatial system of Japanese metropolitan areas. With car companies increasingly engaging in joint business, two kinds of linkages appeared, closely connecting the three major metropolitan areas: Hino–Toyota–Daihatu (Toyota group) and Fuji–Nissan–Aichi Machine Industry–Nissan Shatai (Nissan group). Second, in the Tokaido Megalopolis, in addition to the three large metropolitan areas, the Hamamatsu metropolitan area became the fourth core of the Japanese motor vehicle industry, although this gradually merged into the Nagoya metropolitan area because of the development of a new linkage between Yamaha and Toyota. Furthermore, Honda and Suzuki, originating in Hamamatsu metropolitan area, constructed factories in the Nagoya metropolitan area; Honda at Suzuka on the western fringe and Suzuki at Toyokawa on the eastern fringe of the area. Consequently the integrated Nagoya–Hamamatsu metropolitan area has become the largest centre of the Japanese motor vehicle industry.

Third, within each metropolitan area, single-company towns have developed. The most remarkable among these was the city of Koromo, renamed Toyota in 1959, the year when Toyota constructed the first assembly factory in Asia for manufacturing only passenger cars. As Toyota developed and constructed engine and assembly factories and a new recreational centre, the city of Toyota amalgamated with surrounding towns and a village.

The development of the Japanese motor vehicle industry since the Second World War has been remarkable. But as the exports of Japanese cars continued to increase in the world market trade friction began to emerge.

GLOBALIZATION OF JAPAN'S MOTOR VEHICLE INDUSTRY AND THE CHANGING INTERNATIONAL STRUCTURE OF THE MOTOR VEHICLE INDUSTRY

In 1971, the Japanese Cabinet adopted the policy of liberalizing capital transactions for the motor industry. Under this policy, foreign companies were able to expand in Japan by investing in joint business with Japanese companies: Chrysler with Mitsubishi (1971), GM with

Isuzu (1971), and Ford with Toyokogyo (1979). These 'big three' had already established their own industrial system in Europe by the late 1960s so they turned to the Asian market for their next target area; by then Japan had already become the third largest market in the world after North America and Western Europe. This interest of the big three in Japan matched the need of the three Japanese companies which were faced with keen competition from two Japanese oligopolies, Toyota and Nissan. These two developed remarkably during the high economic growth phase while Isuzu lost its ground considerably. Although Isuzu was the oldest Japanese motor vehicle company, its output of 1971 (135,709) was less than that of Honda's (308,578). Another old company, Mitsubishi (a part of Mitsubishi Heavy Industry until 1971), also lost its position after the Second World War, being surpassed by Toyota, Nissan and Toyokogyo. By restructuring the production system through joint business with Chrysler, Mitsubishi (output 484,226) hoped to catch up with Toyokogyo (output 501,080). In other words, these three companies, each of whose output was less than one-third of Nissan's (1,591,490) and Toyota (1,955,030), intended to survive by making cooperative arrangements with the three US multinational enterprises that were bigger than Toyota and Nissan.

In 1972, Isuzu established its Tochigi factory and Toyokogyo constructed its second factory, Ujina, specializing in the manufacture of passenger cars. As the number of cars on roads rapidly increased, environmental pollution became a serious problem and the development of anti-pollution measures became an urgent requirement in designing cars. Honda had already started selling its anti-pollution technology (CVCC) to Toyota and had passed the test under the 1970 Air Pollution Protection Act. This technology was then transferred to Ford, Chrysler and General Motors in 1973.

In 1973, the yen floated and the oil crisis hit the world market. Immediately Japan suffered a severe economic depression. The government legislated the National Livelihood Emergency Measures Law and the Oil Supply–Demand Adjustment Law. Japanese motor vehicle companies coped well with the oil crisis by developing original technologies for manufacturing energy-efficient cars; for example, Toyota's engine automatic stopping system (EASS) and Nissan's fuel control system (manufactured by the Nippon Electronic Appliance, a joint company by Nissan, Diesel Kiki and Bosch in 1973). While other countries lagged behind Japan in the development of energy-efficient cars, Japanese companies increased their output. Toyota's Corolla became the world best seller of 1973. Several new plants were established during this period; Shiga Engine Plant of Daihatsu (in 1974) and a design centre of Toyokogyo at Hiroshima, for example. Following GM Japan (established in 1970), Ford was re-established in 1974 to develop its production base in Japan.

Each of the three Japanese motor vehicle oligopolies established a large foundation in 1974 to perform a social role; the Toyota Foundation to develop international collaboration, the Nissan Science Promotion Foundation to develop basic science, and Honda's International Transport and Safety Academy to research car accidents. The establishment of these foundations greatly raised their social status as leading companies in a successful industry. In particular, it helped Honda to expand, and subsequently catch up on Toyokogyo and Mitsubishi.

The US government passed the Energy Policy and Conservation Act in 1975 which increased the demand for small-sized cars in the market. Japanese motor vehicle companies were able to make an immediate response to this growing demand, largely thanks to the accumulation of energy-saving know-how and technology. As a result, Japan increased its export share of production from 38.6 per cent in 1975 to 54.0 per cent in 1980, the year in which it became the world's leading producer.

In 1975, the United States Environment Protection Agency authorized strict control over exhaust gas from motor vehicles in California, a main market for exported Japanese cars. To cope with the regulation, Toyota constructed a plant for the manufacture of exhaust emission control equipment at Shimoyama in Miyoshi near Toyota city. Nissan constructed an engine factory at Kanda in the northern part of the Kyushu Island. In 1976, the Japanese government announced an unprecedentedly strict reinforcement plan of exhaust emission control in Japan; however, the government mitigated the control for imported cars to some degree because of strong complaints from the US and European companies, who maintained that the control was a barrier to exports to Japan.

In 1976 the Japanese government passed the Vibration Control Law and decided to increase car tax. Facing a managerial crisis, Toyokogyo had to accept a series of rationalization plans submitted by Sumitomo Bank in 1977. In order to survive in the highly competitive domestic market, Toyokogyo was compelled to activate its overseas business; it established a sales agency in France in 1975, the year in which Japan surpassed France in terms of exported passenger cars. In 1976, it resumed the export of passenger cars to the US.

In 1977, the President of the United States announced the National

Energy Plan and a bill was passed prohibiting the sale and manu-facture of cars with energy efficiency below the standard. The anti-pollution measures taken by the United States further stimulated commercial demand for Japanese cars with high energy efficiency. Consequently, the imports of Japanese cars both in American and European markets rapidly increased. The increase of imports of Japanese cars caused serious politico-economic problems, and Britain asked Japanese companies to limit their share in the UK market to under 10 per cent, whereas France requested them to keep to under 3 per cent.

In response to the increasing trade friction, Japanese car companies endeavoured to further rationalize their production system. At the same time, they started feasibility studies for constructing factories in the United States and in Europe. Following Honda's decision to con-struct a factory in Ohio in 1977, Nissan started a feasibility study for a factory in the US in 1978. Stimulated by these companies, Toyota con-structed its first coastal factory, at Kinuura port near Nagoya and Toyota city, for manufacturing components. In 1978, the Japanese government abolished import tax for cars, an action which gave a strong negotiating position in international trade contracts.

In 1979, the Japanese government passed the Lower Energy Con-sumption Law and issued an order for the closing of petrol stations on Sundays and holidays. Furthermore, the government tightened control over exhaust emission. Thus, a series of requirements imposed on the motor vehicle industry after the second oil crisis encouraged the industry to rationalize its production, transportation and sales system. Toyota started the operation of its first coastal assembly factory Tahara, located next to Toyohashi, a local urban centre between Hamamatsu and Toyota city. Daihatsu, which developed a prototype electric car, constructed an export base at Kobe port in 1979. Isuzu constructed a test course at Tomakomai, a huge coastal industrial area in Hokkaido.

About this time Japanese car companies began to increase their overseas operations. Isuzu established a joint company with GM in the Philippines. In Australia, Mitsubishi invested in the reconstruction of Australia Chrysler. This symbolized the fact that the Japanese motor vehicle industry had become a leading power in the Pacific Rim Region. Another symbolic case was found in the joint business con-tracted between Ford and Toyokogyo (in 1979); although Toyokogyo was considered as a depression-stricken company at the time of con-tract, it gradually became a second important company for Ford in the Pacific Rim Region, surpassing Ford Australia.

The Japanese motor vehicle companies increased overseas manufacturing by constructing plants outside of Japan, a fundamental change in strategy after the second oil crisis. The companies targeted both the United States and Europe for their overseas operations. Honda constructed the Ohio factory in the US, while it signed a contract of technological cooperation with British Leyland and started assembling Honda's small passenger cars at Leyland's Cowley, Oxford factory in the UK.

Following Honda, Nissan invested in Motor Iberica in 1980. In this year, Honda announced the construction of an assembly factory for passenger cars in the US. Honda's decision was made under strong political pressure from the US government and the US Union of Automobile Workers (UAW), whose chairman made a direct request in Japan to the presidents of Japanese car companies for the construction of assembly factories in the United States. At the same time, the UAW and Ford requested the International Trade Committee to restrict the import of Japanese cars to the United States. Following Honda, Nissan established the Nissan Motor Manufacturing Corporation USA at Smyrna, in Tennessee. It further established ARNA near Naples in 1980, when the EC asked Japanese car companies to put a self-restriction on the export of Japanese cars to Europe.

The self-control of exports by Japanese companies began in 1981. The upper annual limit for the export to the US for the following three years was set at 1,680,000. Then, the export to Canada was set at less than 110 per cent of 1980's export, while the export to France was set at less than 3 per cent of total imports of France. The EC Commission continued to make Japanese car companies observe the self-restriction measure on exports. At this time, the big three in the United States suffered deficits and tried to control the import of Japanese cars whilst at the same time allowing their Japanese partners to establish their own sales companies in the US in 1981. As a result, America Isuzu, North America Mazda and United States Mitsubishi Motor Sales were established.

In 1982, GM started to negotiate with Toyota for a joint business. To construct global strategies as a world company and to compete with other multinational companies, Toyota Motor Manufacturing and Toyota Motor Sales amalgamated to become Toyota Motor in 1982. The negotiations between GM and Toyota gave a great stimulus to Honda, which in this year started the operation of an overseas manufacturing factory in Ohio, the first for a Japanese company. Honda had started exporting to the United States in 1970, and after the second oil crisis its export of small cars increased remarkably. By

1981, exports to the US amounted to 370,000 (4.3 per cent of the total sales in the US). However, the self-control imposed on the export of Japanese cars to the US was implemented in this year. This put an end to the rapid increase in Honda's exports to the US. Instead, Honda decided to construct a passenger car factory in the US to maintain the 500,000+ sales level for passenger cars to its 1,000+ sales outlets. America Honda (established in 1959) had already come out at the top for selling motorcycles in the US, with 39.2 per cent of total sales in 1979, the year in which it started the operation of the Ohio factory for manufacturing motorcycles. Its profits in 1981 reached $400 million, enough to construct the passenger car plant. In other words, Honda was in a more advantageous position than Toyota and Nissan, in terms of previous experience, as well as capital stock, accumulated from manufacturing and selling motorcycles. The Ohio plant is able to manufacture cars competitive with the price of imported Japanese cars, including transportation costs. Further, it enjoyed the agglo-meration economies of the motor vehicle industry in the Detroit area and succeeded in reducing traditional conflict between workers and employers.

In 1982, Nissan's exports to the United States were limited to 456,000 (Honda's to 348,000 and Toyota's to 517,000). In 1983, the Nissan Motor America Sales and Finance Corporation began a joint business with the CAC to develop its share in the market by employing the instalment system. Nissan Motor Manufacturing was established in 1980 in Tennessee, beginning with the manufacture of trucks in 1983 followed by small passenger cars in 1985. Several factors acceler-ated this operation: the bill of local contents in 1982, the operation of Honda in Ohio, and the announcement of the joint business between GM and Toyota to manufacture small passenger cars at the site of the GM factory in California. In 1984, the joint venture, New United Motor Manufacturing Inc. (NUMMI) was established and it started manufacturing small passenger cars within a year. Notwithstanding the local production at the three Japanese car factories, in 1984 the United States government asked the Japanese government to prolong the self-control of exports (with the annual upper limit set at 1,850,000), which stimulated further inward investment. Following the establishment of Nissan Research and Development in Michigan in 1983, Honda established Honda Research of America in California, and then in 1984 announced the construction of a passenger car factory in Ontario, Canada.

Despite the recovery of the big three, the Japanese government, concerned about trade friction, decided to continue the self-control policy in exporting cars to the US, with the upper limit set at 2,300,000. GM announced the establishment of a subsidiary company for small passenger cars. This was a major factor in the establishment of a Mazda plant in 1985, using one of Ford's factories, near Detroit. This facility, in turn, accelerated the construction of Mitsubishi's factory, and furthermore influenced the final decision of Isuzu to set up a base in the US in 1985, Mitsubishi signed a contract for a joint venture with Chrysler in the US, while Isuzu established the Isuzu Technical Center of America.

As the Japanese car companies increased their production in the US, Japanese autopart companies were encouraged to construct factories there as well. They faced considerable politico-economic pressure both from the US government and from individual states to localize their production system in the US. Further, the Japanese car companies, to which the autopart companies supplied their products, used the just-in-time supply system. Honda and Honda group's autopart companies established Berma, a subsidiary components company in Ohio (in 1981) and another subsidiary autoparts company, the KTH Parts Industry, for manufacturing pressed parts in Ohio (in 1985). In 1985 Honda surpassed American Motors in terms of the number of manufactured cars. Honda further decided to construct an engine factory in Ohio.

Nippon Denso, established its first car air-conditioner factory in California in 1971, followed in 1975 by a sales agency in Michigan. When the NUMMI was established, Nippon Denso constructed an integrated factory for manufacturing autoparts in Los Angeles, while signing a contract for technological cooperation with GM. In 1984, Honda encouraged Nippon Denso Manufacturing to establish a works in Michigan, to manufacture radiators and air conditioners, to supply Toyota, Honda, Mitsubishi, Mazda, GM and Ford. In 1985, the Nippon Denso Technical Centre and Nippon Denso America (for the United States and Canada) was established.

Japanese motor vehicle companies expanded their operations in North America. In Canada, Toyota established Canadian Auto Parts in British Columbia in 1985, and Canada gradually became an important subcentre for the Japanese motor vehicle industry. Mexico was another important subcentre, where Nissan had already established Mexico Nissan in 1961 and started exporting transmissions (in 1985) and E-type engines (in 1986) to Nissan Motor Manufacturing USA.

Following Honda (in 1984), Toyota established a factory in Ontario, Canada. Furthermore, Suzuki, which had already begun a joint business with GM in Japan (in 1981), constructed a small car factory with GM in Ontario in 1986. This decision by Suzuki gave a great stimulus to Daihatsu, a rival of Suzuki in the market for small-sized motor vehicles; Daihatsu decided to construct a factory in Quebec in 1987.

In the US, Toyota established a plant in 1986 in Kentucky, paying due regard to the locus of the state and to the state incentives. Honda doubled its sales and production in the US, and Nissan started a joint business with VW in Mexico to compete with Toyota in the US.

Japanese car companies not only located manufacturing in the US but also the research, development and design stages of the industry. Fuji Heavy Industry built Subaru Research and Design, whilst Mazda constructed the Ann Arbor Research and Development Center in 1986. Fuji Heavy Industry and Isuzu decided to establish a joint venture, Subaru–Isuzu Automotive at Lafayette, Indiana, in 1987, although they belonged to two different manufacturing groups in Japan, viz. Nissan–Fuji and GM–Isuzu. The operation of the joint venture began in 1989. In 1989, the self-control of exports was expected to remain at the present level (upper limit of 2,300,000), although the export of passenger cars from the United States to Japan had already started in 1988.

In response to the increase of production of Japanese cars in the US (about 1.2 million in 1989), the US motor vehicle industry experienced another phase of restructuring. In 1988, VW closed one of its factories. The autoparts industry in the US has been revitalized under the strict requirements of Japanese car companies. In order to meet these requirements, American autoparts companies began to establish new factories, such as LOF (glass) and Jonson Control (sheet) in Kentucky, adjacent to Japanese car factories. In 1988, Nissan signed the contract for manufacturing multi-purpose cars at Ford's truck factory in Ohio, the operation of which began in 1990.

On the other hand, the Japanese car companies themselves are trying to develop high-quality cars which attract consumers in foreign countries. In consequence, all over the world there can be observed a global system of the Japanese motor vehicle industry, operating in the entire range of manufacturing, sales, research and development, design and management.

In Europe, Honda started manufacturing the first Japanese passenger cars at BL's Cowley factory in the UK in 1981, the year in which the European Commission requested Japanese car companies to restrict their exports to the EC market. BL decided to employ Honda's latest technologies to revitalize its own manufacturing systems; amongst the five biggest Japanese car companies, Honda was the smallest but most active company in the EC market. Honda intended to introduce its technology for manufacturing high-quality cars with over 1800 cc engine capacity. These cars, manufactured by Honda in the UK, became treated as UK cars by the Italian government in 1982. In 1983, the European Commission authorized an indirect control policy on the import of Japanese motor vehicles. Under these adverse circumstances, Honda decided to sign a contract for a joint business with BL to develop high-quality passenger cars with large engine capacity.

Following Honda, Nissan started the operation of ARNA's assembly factory (in Italy) for small passenger cars in 1983. This factory was closed in 1988, the year in which Alfa Romeo was taken over by Fiat. In 1983, Toyota invested in Lotus, a UK firm which was taken over by GM in 1986.

In 1984, Nissan announced its decision to construct a passenger car factory at Washington, Tyne and Wear in North-East England. It had started feasibility studies in 1981 by when it had already achieved fifth position (5.9 per cent share) in the UK market. Because of this initial advantage in the UK market, Nissan decided to construct a factory in the UK rather than in other potential countries such as West Germany, Belgium and Austria. From its overseas experiences at Motor Iberica in Spain and at ARNA in Italy, Nissan paid particular regard to local labour conditions, quality of components, regional policy for foreign investment and structural changes in the motor vehicle industry of each country. Among the fifty-five proposed sites, Nissan finally narrowed the choice down to three (Shotton, Humberside and Washington) in 1984. Of the three sites, Washington was not far from a port and was able to provide an 800-acre site, which was close to a New Town located in a Special Development Area. Nippon Seiko already had a successful operation in this area. Nissan made the final decision to construct a factory at Washington in 1985, and started the operation of the factory in 1986. In 1987, it doubled its original production goal, to 200,000 for 1992, and it established the European Design Centre in 1988. In 1989, Nissan Motor Europe was finally established as an integrated management company to strengthen Nissan's manufacturing system in Europe.

The establishment of Nissan Motor Manufacturing (UK) accelerated joint business for developing new cars among major Japanese and European car companies: Honda and BL for XX (1984) and Mitsubishi and Benz for commercial vehicles (in 1985). In 1986, GM took over Lotus; as a result, Lotus cancelled the joint business with Toyota and signed a new contract with Isuzu. Isuzu and GM established IBC Vehicles (small vans) in the UK in 1987.

In 1987, Toyota contracted with VW at Hanover for the assembly of Toyota's cars. With its overseas experiences in negotiating with VW (West Germany) and Salvador Caetano (Portugal), Toyota decided, in 1989, to construct an assembly factory in the UK. Out of thirty proposed sites, Toyota chose Burnaston, near Derby in the Midlands, the home of Rolls Royce aero engines, although it would not be granted a subsidy from the UK government, because Derby was not located in an assisted region. To compete with Nissan in the EC market, Toyota needed to establish a strong sales system and a comprehensive cooperation system with European car companies. Following Nissan and Honda, Toyota decided to construct an engine factory at Shotton in north-east Wales as it turned out to be difficult to contract with Renault for a joint venture for manufacturing engines before 1992.

Honda decided to construct an engine factory at Swindon, where Honda UK Manufacturing had been established in 1985 on a former Vickers aircraft site with good road communications. In 1989, Honda also decided to invest in the Rover group (formerly BL, renamed in 1986), which had been taken over by British Aerospace in 1988. Rover is expected to hold a 20 per cent share of Honda UK, while its assembly factory at Swindon is planned to be managed by Honda. As a result, Honda became competitive with Nissan and Toyota in the EC market, with Rover's sales agents added to Honda's sales system. Furthermore, Honda gains access to BAe's high technology.

The expansion of Honda exerted a great influence on Mazda, the third largest Japanese car company in the EC market. In 1989, Mazda decided to send orders to Ford for the assembly of its passenger cars, instead of taking the risk of constructing its own factory in the EC.

In Japan, Honda constructed a new factory at Haga in Tochigi Prefecture. Mazda constructed a new factory at Houfu in Yamaghachi Prefecture. After the second oil crisis, Honda bought this site (249 ha), where it constructed a test course in 1979. Honda endeavoured to improve on its technology and to develop high-quality and high-technology passenger cars targeted at the domestic market. In 1982, the Honda Racing Corporation was established to develop the company image as a high-speed car company. It re-entered Formula One racing in 1983, the year in which it surpassed Mitsubishi in terms of the number of cars manufacturd. In 1984, Honda transferred its production line for light commercial cars from Suzuka factory to Yachiyo Kogyo's factory near Suzuka in order to increase production at Suzuka factory. Then, it started a new channel of sales. In 1985, Honda located its head office at Aoyama (in Tokyo) a new fashion centre of Japan, to compete with the image of Nissan, whose head office is at Ginza, the old central business district and shopping centre. As a result of technological development, Honda succeeded in the development of the first four-wheel steering system in the world in 1986. In the same year, it constructed Maoka Autoparts factory in Tochigi and surpassed Mazda in output. In 1987, Honda became the third largest motor vehicle company in Japan and constructed an engine factory for light passenger cars within Kumamoto factory (established in 1976 for motorcycles). In 1988, Honda decided to construct its third assembly factory at Suzuka and to build its third factory at Haga, in addition to Sayama in Saitama Prefecture and Suzuka in Mie Prefecture. At this factory, Honda first developed sports cars.

Mazda (former Toyokogyo) started its reconstruction in 1979, when it began a joint business with Ford. In 1980, it established the Toyo Sales and Finance (today's Mazda Credit) and increased its domestic sales, together with its export. In 1982, it started the operation of an engine factory (at Ujina) and a passenger assembly factory (at Houfu), both in Yamaguchi Prefecture along the Inland Sea. With the high ratio (68.5 per cent) of exports to its total output, Toyokogyo endeavoured to increase domestic sales and to decrease the high export ratio (65.5 per cent in 1982) by creating new sales channels to sell both Toyokogyo and Ford cars. To compete with Honda, Toyokogyo further established the Mazda Speed Co. Ltd in 1983, when Honda re-entered Formula One racing. In 1984, Toyokogyo was renamed Mazda and established the Mazda Foundation. Despite the endeavour to decrease export share, Mazda's exports increased remarkably reaching 70.1 per cent in 1985, compared to Isuzu (69.4 per cent), Honda (59.6 per cent), Nissan (57.4 per cent), Mitsubishi (55.1 per cent), and Toyota (54.0 per cent). Hence, Mazda suffered great damage from the rapid rise of the yen in 1985. It was surpassed by Honda (in 1987) in terms of the number of manufactured cars. Mazda decided to restructure its global production system by entering upon a joint business with Ford. In 1987, Mazda established the Research and Development Laboratory at Yokohama in the Tokyo metropolitan area to compete with other car companies in technology and design. In 1988, Mazda developed a reconstruction plan and contracted with Fiat and Citroën for the sales of these imported cars. As a result, two sales channels were established for them in 1989. In the same year, Mazda began to reconstruct its system for purchasing components from its subsidiaries and subcontractors and decided to construct its second Hofu factory for passenger cars.

In 1989 Nissan decided to expand the passenger car assembly line at the Kanda factory in the northern part of Kyushu whilst relocating its truck line to the Hiratsuka factory of Nissan SHATAI (Nissan's subsidiary for assembling trucks, passenger cars and sports cars). Kanda was originally constructed for assembling trucks in 1977. However, the self-control of exports started in 1981, and the Tennessee factory in the US began manufacturing the same type of trucks as ones manufactured at the Kyushu factory. Thus, Nissan was compelled to decrease the manufacturing of trucks and to increase the manufacturing of high-quality cars. To develop a high-quality and high-technology car, Nissan established a technical centre in 1981 at Atsugi, Kanagawa Prefecture, a centre of research and development activities in Japan. It then constructed the Kurihama branch of Yokohama factory in 1982.

With the rapid rise of the yen, Japanese car companies have had to develop the domestic market instead of overseas ones. Since 1986, the share of exports to total production has decreased. In 1987, it became less than 50 per cent. Facing keen competition in the domestic market, the Japanese car companies are now required to develop high-quality, high-technology cars to meet the demands of a new market led by relatively young customers. Furthermore, the price for this new type of car has decreased due to the abolition of the commodity tax as a result of levying consumption tax in 1989. Mitsubishi decided to develop new high-quality, high-technology cars in the Nagoya metropolitan area in 1989, to compete with the increasing imports of European cars. European companies are endeavouring to increase their share in the Japanese market by establishing new sales channels with Japanese car companies, together with their own sales channels (Mazda−Fiat and Citroën, Mitsubishi−Benz, Isuzu−Opel, and Fuji−Volvo).

In addition to the Teiho factory in Toyota city for the manufacture of machinery and robots (constructed in 1986), Toyota constructed the Hirose factory in Toyota city for the manufacture of electronic devices and microelectronic parts including special integrated circuits in 1989. At the same time Toyota announced the construction of a huge technology centre with a test track at Shimoyama adjacent to Toyota city.

CONCLUSION

The globalization of Japan's motor vehicle industry has thus caused restructuring, developing it into a truly worldwide industry. At present, the industry faces the risk of catastrophic changes in the highly competitive markets of the world. While American, European and Japanese car companies still dominate as world major powers, Asian car companies, particularly those in South Korea (which cooperate with Mitsubishi and with Mazda) and Taiwan (which cooperate with Toyota and Nissan) are now exerting an influence on the world industrial system. In response to the growth of the Asian market, Japanese car companies increasingly make efforts to improve their production and sales system in the Asian market. Furthermore, they have begun to venture into new business fields, a trend which can be discerned in the construction of Kasugai factory for prefabricated houses in the Nagoya metropolitan area in 1987. Consequently, Japan has become a central part of the core of the global industrial system of the motor vehicle industry of the world, not only in manufacturing and sales but also in technology and management.

5 The impact of Japanese investment in the United States

James M. Rubenstein

Japanese motor vehicle firms have invested heavily in the United States in recent years. The increasing involvement in the US market has come from both the final assemblers of motor vehicles and the suppliers of motor vehicle parts. This chapter examines some of the significant impacts on the American motor vehicle industry resulting from the Japanese investment. Four elements of Japanese investment in the US motor vehicle industry are discussed:

1 the impact on the US motor vehicle market;
2 the impact on production strategies adopted by American companies;
3 the impact on the location of motor vehicle plants within the United States; and
4 the impact on communities where Japanese plants have located.

IMPACT ON THE US MOTOR VEHICLE MARKET

Japanese motor vehicle firms have penetrated the US market in three waves. During the first era, primarily the 1970s, Japanese manufacturers exported an increasing number of vehicles to the United States. During the second era, primarily the first half of the 1980s, several Japanese manufacturers decided to construct assembly plants in the United States. During the third era, beginning in the late 1980s, Japanese parts suppliers increased investment in the United States. Each of these three waves of investment is discussed in more detail.

Exports to the United States

Vehicles produced by foreign manufacturers first made inroads in the US market during the late 1950s. Imports rose from 1 per cent of total

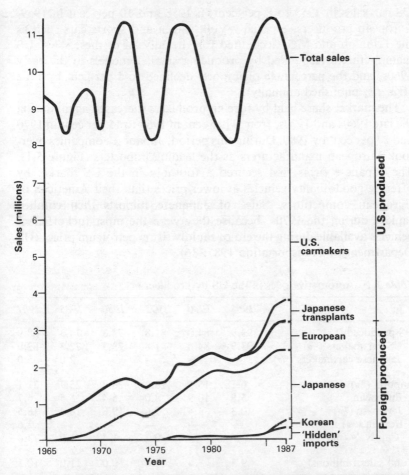

Figure 5.1 US car sales, 1965–87. US car sales reached highs of over 11 million in the early 1970s, late 1970s and mid-1980s, and lows of approximately 8 million in the mid-1970s and early 1980s. The low levels were aftershocks from the two periods of petroleum shortages, associated with the 1973 OPEC boycott and the 1979 Iran revolution. Each time that the US market recovered, however, the peak level of sales achieved by US car makers has progressively declined (dotted line). The area below the heavy black line represents total foreign car sales in the US. European companies accounted for nearly all foreign car sales in 1965 but failed to increase their market share during the 1970s and 1980s. By the 1980s Japanese firms had captured the overwhelming percentage of foreign car sales in the US. During the 1980s, two new foreign produced groups appeared, first the 'hidden' or 'captive' imports, brought to the States by US car makers, and more recently Korean models. In addition, Japanese plants in the US began to carve out a significant percentage of the US-produced market

Sources: MVMA (1988) and *Ward's Automotive Yearbook*

US car sales in 1955 to 8 per cent in 1958 and 10 per cent in 1959. European producers, especially Volkswagen and sports cars such as the Triumph and MG, accounted for virtually all of these sales. US manufacturers responded by producing smaller models in the early 1960s, and the percentage of imports declined to 5 per cent by 1962 (*Ward's*, published annually).

The market share held by foreign producers increased again during the late 1960s and 1970s, from 9 per cent in 1967 to 15 per cent in 1970 and 27 per cent by 1980. During this period, Japanese companies overtook European manufacturers as the leading importers (Figure 5.1). The Japanese firms first secured a foothold in the US market by offering good-quality vehicles at lower prices than their American or European competitors. Sales of Japanese imports then climbed rapidly during the 1970s, because they were the most fuel-efficient vehicles available during the era of rapidly rising petroleum prices (US Department of Transportation 1981: 36).

Table 5.1   Automotive sales in the US by producer

	1965	*1970*	*1975*	*1980*	*1985*	*1987*
US-produced (%)	93.9	84.8	81.8	73.3	74.3	68.9
US car makers (%)	93.9	84.8	81.8	73.3	72.3	62.9
Japanese car makers (%)	—	—	—	—	2.0	6.0
Imports (%)	6.1	15.3	18.2	26.7	25.7	31.1
European (%)	5.8	10.9	8.0	5.4	5.5	6.7
Japanese (%)	0.3	4.4	9.6	19.8	18.4	18.5
Korean (%)	—	—	—	—	—	2.6
'Captive'*a* (%)	—	—	0.7	1.4	1.9	3.4
Total sales (millions)	9.3	8.4	8.6	9.0	11.0	10.3

Source: Motor Vehicle Manufactureres of America (1988); *Ward's Automotive Yearbook*, 1976 and 1988

*a*Imported by US car makers

The first wave of foreign car sales in the US, during the 1960s, came from European car makers, especially Volkswagen. Japanese cars first penetrated the US market only in the late 1960s, yet captured nearly 20 per cent of the market by 1980. Imports have continued to expand their market share in the United States during the 1980s, primarily by US and Korean car makers. The 'captive' cars imported by US producers are built primarily in Japan, Korea and Mexico

During the 1980s, the share of the US market held by Japanese firms no longer increased. This market stagnation resulted from a 1981 agreement between US and Japanese officials to limit import of Japanese cars to 1.68 million, or 22 per cent of the US market (Sobel

1984: 298). US companies urged the imposition of the quota to prevent further erosion of their market share. In 1985, the limits were raised to 2.3 million vehicles (Table 5.1).

The main impact of the quota was to increase profits for Japanese producers. Because demand for Japanese cars in the United States exceeded supply, Japanese firms could import their most expensive models and sell them at relatively high mark-ups. The principal beneficiaries were the largest Japanese manufacturers, especially Toyota, Nissan and Honda, because the Japanese government allocated import limits to each company on the basis of their share of the US market in the 1970s.

Assembly plants in the United States

In view of the widespread concern in the United States with the growth in imported vehicles, Japanese producers concluded in the early 1980s that the most effective means to further increase their market share was to build assembly plants in the United States. Honda, the first Japanese producer to construct an assembly plant in the United States, began to sell vehicles produced at its Ohio plant in 1982. In 1989, Honda built a second plant a few miles west of its first one.

Table 5.2 Japanese-owned or operated assembly plants in the US

	Production start-up	Production capacity	Number of employees
Honda	1982	500,000	4,800
Nissan	1983	220,000	3,200
NUMMI (Toyota and GM joint venture)	1984	250,000	2,500
Mazda	1987	240,000	3,500
Toyota	1988	200,000	3,500
Diamond-Star Motors (Mitsubishi and Chrysler joint venture)	1988	240,000	2,900
Subaru/Isuzu	1989	120,000	1,700
Total	—	1,770,000	22,100

Source: Rehder (1988: 53)

During the 1980s, Japanese car makers increased their American sales primarily through construction of assembly plants in the US. In 1987, sales from the first four Japanese plants reached 619,000 cars, but when all seven plants reached full operation in the early 1990s, nearly 2 million cars could be produced, creating the prospect of a substantial overcapacity in US assembly plant production capability

Nissan opened its Tennessee plant for the production of light trucks in 1983 and for passenger cars two years later. Mazda began to produce vehicles in 1987 at a Michigan plant originally built by Ford. In 1988, Toyota opened an assembly plant in Kentucky and Mitsubishi and Chrysler jointly opened an assembly plant in Illinois under the name of Diamond-Star Motors. Subaru and Isuzu jointly opened a plant in Indiana one year later (Table 5.2).

In addition to these six plants, Toyota and General Motors jointly established the New United Motor Manufacturing Inc. (NUMMI) at a former GM plant in California. NUMMI began to produce cars for General Motors in 1984 and for Toyota in 1986.

The seven Japanese assembly plants in the United States are currently capable of producing approximately 2 million vehicles, and if sales are justified, several firms anticipate expanding capacity. More than 20,000 people are employed at the seven assembly plants.

Parts suppliers in the United States

The third wave of Japanese investment in the United States is by manufacturers of motor vehicle parts. In the late 1980s, Japanese parts suppliers followed the strategy previously adopted by the Japanese car makers: having first penetrated the US market by importing, manufacturers further expanded their market share by constructing plants in the United States.

As recently as the 1970s, foreign parts producers accounted for less than 10 per cent of the US market. Virtually all of these imported parts entered the United States already attached to fully assembled vehicles, primarily German-made Volkswagens during the 1960s and Japanese-made cars beginning in the 1970s.

Although the US market for foreign-assembled vehicles remained relatively constant during the 1980s, sales of imported parts increased by more than 20 per cent per year. By 1988, the percentage of foreign-made parts reached approximately one-third, and the figure is expected to exceed one-half in the early 1990s (Uchitelle 1987: D1).

By 1984, approximately fifty Japanese parts suppliers had constructed plants in the United States; four years later, the figure had risen to over 150, although rapid growth has made accurate figures difficult to obtain. Approximately one-third of these plants employ less than 100 persons, while only 8 per cent have more than 500 employees. Median size is approximately 115 workers (Table 5.3).

Japanese-owned firms are not always easy to identify, because their American operations are usually known by English names, such as

Stanley Electric, Midwest Mold and Pioneer Electric, or by initials such as AP Technoglass, TS Trim, and KTH Parts. The best source of information about Japanese plants in the United States comes from economic development offices operated by each of the fifty states.

Table 5.3 Employment at Japanese parts suppliers in the US

Number of employees	Percentage
1– 99	37
100–199	30
200–499	24
500–999	6
1000 and above	2
N = 115, Median = 115	

Source: Computed from survey results

Producers of motor vehicle parts can be divided into two groups, according to their main customers. One group, known as 'original equipment manufacturers' (OEMs), sells parts intended for assembly in new cars. OEMs in turn can be either independently owned companies or subsidiaries of the large car makers. The other group, which makes replacement parts designed for sale to individual motor vehicle owners, is called the aftermarket.

Although the aftermarket accounts for two-thirds of the total parts sales in the US, more than three-quarters of Japanese parts are sold in the OEM sector. Sales of new car parts by Japanese firms amounted to $19,000 million in 1987, more than one-fourth of the total US OEM market of $70,000 million that year. Japanese aftermarket sales totalled $7,000 million, 5 per cent of the $130,000 million US total in that sector (Brown 1988).

Most of the parts produced at Japanese-owned plants were sold to the seven Japanese-owned or -operated assembly plants in the United States. To ensure rapid delivery of parts to their US assembly plants, the Japanese car makers strongly urged their major suppliers to build factories in the United States. In some cases, parts manufacturers have been required to construct US plants if they wished to continue as suppliers to Japanese car makers. Other parts suppliers are subsidiaries of the Japanese car makers; Honda, for example, has built a plant in Anna, Ohio, to supply engines to its assembly plant in Marysville, Ohio.

Japanese plants built in the United States are more likely than American firms to produce body parts, such as glass, seats and trim, as well as electronics, such as radios, starters and wiring. Compared to US suppliers, a smaller percentage of Japanese firms in the United States make chassis parts, such as brakes, tyres and wheels, or drive train parts, such as transmissions, clutches and axles (Table 5.4).

Table 5.4 Products manufactured by Japanese parts suppliers in the US

	Percentage of production	
	Japanese plants in US	US-owned plants
Raw materials (die castings, stampings, steel, tubing, vinyl, plastics)	18	14
Chassis components (frames, engine mounts, brakes, springs, steering gear, tyres, wheels)	18	25
Drive train (transmission, axle, clutch, shaft, differential)	8	16
Body assembly (sheet metal, bumpers, seats, paints, glass, wipers, moulding, carpets, hinges)	28	15
Engines (camshaft, cylinder head, manifold, piston, tappets, valves, carburettors)	6	11
Electrical and electronics (alternators, batteries, clock, condenser, air conditioner, lights, instruments, radio, relays, switches, wire harnesses)	17	11
Exhaust and emission (air pump, catalytic converter, muffler)	5	5
Other (bearings, bushings, fasteners, gaskets, petrol, anti-freeze, hardware, screws, cables, zippers)	1	3

Source: Adapted from Kamath and Wilson (1983: p. 29) and compiled from survey results

Japanese-owned plants in the US are more likely than American-owned plants to produce body and electrical parts for car makers and less likely to produce chassis, drive trains and engines. Japanese assembly plants prefer to obtain high-value parts requiring skilled labour from Japanese suppliers located either in the US or in Japan, rather than from US-owned suppliers

US car makers spent approximately $2,000 million on foreign parts in 1987. Approximately one-half of all parts imported by US car makers came from Japan, one quarter from Mexico, and one-sixth from West Germany. Suppliers in Brazil, France, the United Kingdom,

South Korea and Taiwan sold most of the other imported parts. Purchases of Japanese parts by US car makers thus amounted to approximately $1,000 million in 1987, or 5 per cent of all parts sold in the United States by Japanese firms (Table 5.5).

Table 5.5   US market for new car parts, 1987

	Sales ($ million)	Percentage of total OEM market
US-owned suppliers	48,000	69
Subsidiaries of car makers	30,000	43
Independently owned suppliers	18,000	26
Japanese-owned suppliers	19,000	27
Subsidiaries of car makers	4,000	6
Independently owned suppliers	15,000	21
Other suppliers	2,000	3
Subsidiaries of car makers	1,000	1
Independently owned suppliers	1,000	1
Total	70,000	100

Source: Adapted from *The Economist*, 23 May, 1987, p. 72

Japanese-owned suppliers have captured more than one-quarter of the US OEM market. Most US suppliers are subsidiaries of the big three car makers, primarily General Motors, while most Japanese suppliers are independent of that country's large car makers. Japanese suppliers have captured only 5 per cent of the US aftermarket, but that figure is expected to rise during the 1990s

To some extent, Japanese parts suppliers are likely to further expand their market share in the United States during the 1990s by increasing sales to US car makers. However, in view of the large number of Japanese vehicles now owned by Americans, most of the increasing sales are expected to be in the aftermarket.

IMPACT ON ORGANIZATION OF US MOTOR VEHICLE INDUSTRY

Since the 1920s, three firms have dominated production of motor vehicles in the United States: General Motors Corporation (GM), the Ford Motor Company, and the Chrysler Corporation, known collectively as the 'big three'. As recently as 1967, prior to the growth in Japanese sales, the big three accounted for nearly 90 per cent of all US sales. GM controlled 50 per cent of the US market, Ford 22 per cent, and Chrysler 16 per cent. Twenty years later, following the Japanese invasion, only two-thirds of the cars sold in the United States were manufactured by the big three. GM's market share declined to 37 per cent, while Ford accounted for 20 per cent and Chrysler 11 per cent of US sales.

To compete with the Japanese invasion, US car makers and parts suppliers have adopted a number of strategies, including construction of new plants and closure of old ones, cooperation with Japanese producers and adoption of Japanese production methods. This section examines these major restructuring strategies.

Plant openings and closures

In 1979, the big three operated 43 car-assembly plants in the United States, including 22 by General Motors, 13 by Ford, and 7 by Chrysler (one of which was operated by American Motors prior to its 1987 merger with Chrysler). During the 1980s, the big three closed eleven of these assembly plants; General Motors and Ford were responsible for closing four plants each, while Chrysler closed the other three (Table 5.6). Three other plants ceased production of cars but were kept open for truck production; two plants were converted by Ford and one by GM. Another General Motors plant was turned over to NUMMI, the company's joint venture with Toyota (Rubenstein 1986; 289; 1987: 362; 1988b: 16).

Table 5.6   US car assembly plants

	Open as of 1979	1979–89 Closed	1979–89 Opened	Open as of 1989
General Motors	22[a]	5[b]	6	23[a]
Ford	14	6[c]	0	8
Chrysler	7[d]	3[d]	1	5
Japanese	0	0	6	6
Volkswagen	0	1	1	0
Total	43	14	14	42

[a] Including plant transferred to NUMMI (joint venture with Toyota)

[b] Including one converted from car to truck production

[c] Including two converted from car to truck production

[d] Including one plant inherited from merger with American Motors

Source: Adapted from *Ward's Automotive Yearbook*, published annually

During the 1980s, US car makers have opened 7 new car assembly plants, closed 11, and converted 3 from car to truck production

The big three opened seven assembly plants during the 1980s, one by Chrysler and the remainder by GM. Three of the new plants were built within a few miles of recently closed facilities, while the remaining four were placed in communities not traditionally associated with automotive production. Finally, Volkswagen opened and then closed an assembly plant in the United States during the period. Thus, at the end of the 1980s, forty-two car-assembly plants remained in the country, only one less than a decade earlier, but now five were Japanese-owned, two were joint US–Japanese ventures, and only thirty-five were operated exclusively by the big three.

Cooperation between US and Japanese firms

The second major impact of the Japanese invasion on the organization of the US motor vehicle industry is increased cooperation. At the same time they are competing to sell their products, Japanese and US motor vehicle companies are working together in several ways. First, US car makers have invested in Japanese firms. Second, US and Japanese firms have initiated several joint ventures. Third, both US and Japanese car makers increasingly purchase parts produced by suppliers in the other country.

US investment in Japan

US motor vehicle producers have acquired minority shares in several Japanese manufacturers. General Motors owns more than 40 per cent of Isuzu and 5 per cent of Suzuki, while Ford and Chrysler hold approximately one-quarter of Mazda and Mitsubishi, respectively (Holusha 1988a).

The major benefit to US manufacturers has been the ability to import cars produced by these companies to supplement their domestically produced models. These imports have been largely hidden from American consumers, because the vehicles carry American names. Since the 1970s, Chrysler has marketed a car made by Mitsubishi as one of its Dodge models, called the Colt. Ford imports a car made by Mazda as one of its Mercury models, called the Tracer. To further complicate the relationship, the Tracer is actually assembled in Hermosillo, Mexico, from Mazda components produced in South Korea, as well as in Japan. General Motors imports cars from both Suzuki and Isuzu that carry American names.

The level of these so-called 'captive' imports had been limited for a number of years because of the quota on total Japanese imports.

Under the quota system, the Japanese Ministry of Trade and Industry (MITI) each year decided how many vehicles each company could import. Allocations were originally based on the share of the American market held by each firm prior to instituting quotas, favouring the early entrants into the American market, primarily Toyota, Nissan and Honda, but in the late 1980s, MITI allowed the other major producers to expand their imports. The principal beneficiaries of this re-allocation were US car makers, who could increase their 'hidden' imports through their partially owned Japanese partners.

Joint ventures

A number of US and Japanese firms have cooperated to produce motor vehicles in the United States. The Japanese have entered joint ventures to help insulate them from future trade barriers and currency fluctuations. American companies have decided that they are unable to produce smaller cars that can compete with the Japanese in quality and price.

NUMMI, the first joint venture, produced one model each for Toyota and General Motors at a plant GM had closed in Fremont, California. GM entered the agreement in order to observe Japanese management and production methods. Toyota felt pressure to invest quickly in the United States in order to remain competitive with Honda and Nissan, which at the time were already producing vehicles at their US plants. Diamond-Star Motors, the joint venture between Chrysler and Mitsubishi, assembles cars for both companies in Normal, Illinois, while Mazda builds Fords at its Flat Rock, Michigan, assembly plant. The American and Japanese cars built at the joint-venture plants are mechanically identical but have somewhat different appearances. Ford has also undertaken a joint venture with Nissan to build a mini-van at a Ford truck-assembly plant. As a result, Ford is working with a competitor of Mazda, which is one-quarter owned by Ford. Thus, joint ventures are creating an increasingly complex web of interrelationships among the major producers (Holusha 1988b).

Joint ventures have become common among suppliers as well. Approximately 20 per cent of the Japanese parts suppliers in the United States have been built as joint ventures with US firms. Japanese firms have also entered into joint ventures with Canadian, British and German firms.

The long-term prospects for the joint-venture plants are unclear. The basic problem is that the Japanese and American cars assembled at a particular joint-venture plant compete against each other in the US market. What happens to the plant if the product of one of the partners is no longer viable?

The NUMMI plant was the first to experience this problem, because sales of General Motors' car, the Chevrolet Nova, proved disappointing. Consumers preferred the Toyota version, even though it sold for $2,000 more than the GM model. 'Nova' proved to be an unsuccessful choice for the car's name because Americans associated it with a poorly designed model marketed during the 1960s and 1970s. According to consumer surveys, virtually all Nova buyers knew that their car was in reality a Toyota, but few Toyota buyers recognized that the Nova was a twin to their car (Chethik 1988). In 1988, General Motors decided not to market its NUMMI car as a Chevrolet model and began to call it the Geo Prizm instead. The company's 'captive' imports from Suzuki and Isuzu, also previously marketed as Chevrolets, were sold as Geos as well (Holusha 1988a, b).

Purchasing parts from the other country

Cooperation between US and Japanese firms has also increased through relationships between producers and parts suppliers. On the one hand, Japanese producers have increased purchases from suppliers based in the United States, while at the same time US producers have increased purchases from overseas suppliers. These apparently contradictory trends are occurring for the same reasons: better quality at lower prices.

Japanese producers have been sensitive to maximizing domestic content, but the issue has not been raised in the United States to the same extent as in Europe and Canada. Honda, the first Japanese assembly plant in the United States, surpassed 60 per cent domestic content by 1989 and was publicly committed to achieving 75 per cent by 1991. The company has run advertisements in the *Wall Street Journal* showing the location (although not the names) of its large number of US suppliers (*Wall Street Journal* 1988). The domestic content percentage exceeds 50 per cent at the other Japanese assembly plants operating in the United States (Brown 1988).

The Japanese assembly plants in the United States have pledged to achieve high percentages of domestic content partly in exchange for generous subsidies from state and local governments. However, the most significant economic factor underlying the willingness of Japanese firms to buy American products was the sharp increase in the value of the yen compared to the dollar in the late 1980s. American suppliers primarily provide Japanese car makers with bulky, low-value products which require less skill to manufacture, such as carpets, glass, tyres, exhaust systems and audio equipment.

For the high-value components, requiring relatively skilled labour, such as engines, transaxles, suspension systems and brakes, Japanese car makers prefer to deal with familiar Japanese suppliers who are strongly encouraged to build plants in the United States (Brown 1988). In essence, Japanese car makers tell these 'captive' firms that if they wish to continue as suppliers they must begin production in the United States. US parts suppliers complain that Japanese purchasing agents do not give them a fair chance to compete. However, Japanese car makers respond that rejected US firms do not meet their precise specifications and are unlikely to make the necessary modifications (*New York Times* 1988).

While most Japanese parts manufacturers built plants in the United States to supply the Japanese-operated assembly plants, a number have signed contracts with US car makers as well. For example, Nippondenso sells Ford heaters, blowers and electric radiator fans (Brown 1988), and Nihon Radiator sells air conditioners to General Motors (*The Economist* 1987). At American-owned assembly plants, foreign-produced parts account for less than 10 per cent of the content, but the percentage is increasing (Table 5.7).

Outsourcing

Traditionally, the large US car makers, especially General Motors and Ford, manufactured most of their own parts. For example, General Motors operates some of the largest foundries in the United States, while Ford's Rouge Steel plant in Dearborn, Michigan, is the nation's largest integrated steel mill. The large car makers also transformed formerly independent parts suppliers, such as Delco, Packard Electric and Harrison Radiator, into captive subsidiaries. Parts produced by subsidiaries account for approximately two-thirds of the average GM car and half of Ford's vehicles (Vartan 1986).

The availability of parts from subsidiaries has been considered a source of strength and a major factor in the long-term market dominance enjoyed by GM and Ford in the United States. In contrast, Chrysler's dependence on outside suppliers for two-thirds of its parts has been regarded as an indicator of the company's weakness. However, during the 1980s Chrysler turned the dependency into an asset, because independent suppliers, including many Japanese ones, could produce parts at a lower cost than the subsidiaries owned by GM and

Ford. As a result, Chrysler's cost per vehicle dropped from the highest to the lowest of the big three.

Table 5.7 Domestic content at US assembly plants, 1987

	Percentage of parts produced in US
US-owned assembly plants	
Chrysler	91–98[a]
Ford	86–99[a]
GM	94–99[a]
Japanese-owned assembly plants	
Honda	60
Mazda	50
Nissan	
Cars	63
Trucks	56
Subaru/Isuzu	50[b]
Toyota	60[b]
Joint ventures	
NUMMI	
General Motors	60
Toyota	50
Diamond-Star (Chrysler/Mitsubishi)	55[b]

[a] Varies by model.
[b] Anticipated.

Source: Brown (1988)

Japanese car makers have pledged to buy most of their parts from suppliers in the United States. However, a large percentage of this domestic content is in fact in the hands of Japanese-owned suppliers who have followed the assembly plants to the US.

To reduce their costs per vehicle, GM and Ford increased their purchase of parts from independent companies, a practice known as 'outsourcing'. Subsidiaries no longer enjoy guaranteed contracts to supply parts to the parent company but must compete with independently owned suppliers. GM's Delco subsidiary, for example, is no longer the sole supplier of the company's radios. Subsidiaries, in turn, are now free to compete with independent firms to supply car makers other than the parent company (Rubenstein 1988a: 294; Roberts 1987).

Adoption of Japanese production methods

US car makers have adopted a number of Japanese production methods, especially the 'kanban' or just-in-time system of producer–

supplier relationships. The best-known characteristic of the just-in-time system is delivery of components from suppliers to assemblers on very short notice. However, the just-in-time system involves several other changes in the traditional relationships between US motor vehicle producers and their parts suppliers (Rubenstein 1988a: 293–5).

Tiers of suppliers

The first impact of the just-in-time system is a reduction in the number of direct suppliers to assembly plants. The Japanese assembly plants in the United States generally have only 100–200 direct suppliers, compared to approximately 1,000 for the big three assembly plants. The US-owned car makers have reduced the number of direct suppliers by adopting a 'tier' system or hierarchy of suppliers. Under the 'tier' system, producers sign contracts with a handful of parts manufacturers, who are known as 'first-tier' suppliers. The 'first-tier' suppliers in turn obtain needed inputs from 'second-tier' suppliers, some of whom previously sold directly to the car makers. The hierarchy of suppliers then continues to other tiers.

Cooperation in research

The second impact of just-in-time is greater cooperation between car makers and first-tier suppliers. Traditionally, producers designed the parts they needed themselves and invited suppliers to manufacture the parts in conformance with precise specifications. Most design and engineering information concerning the motor vehicle remained confidential. Now, the big three share previously proprietary information concerning design and engineering of their motor vehicles. In exchange, suppliers bear some of the risks and financial burdens of the design process (Afriat *et al.* 1987: 44).

Concern for quality

The third impact of just-in-time is greater concern with the quality of parts. The big three traditionally were more concerned with purchasing the least expensive rather than the highest quality parts. Each year, GM, Ford and Chrysler invited suppliers to bid for the manufacture of particular parts. Because contracts were awarded annually, an unsuccessful supplier one year could receive a contract the next year by submitting a lower bid.

In recent years, the producers have begun to select suppliers on the basis of their ability to produce high-quality parts. To assure the availability of high-quality parts, US car makers now give long-term contracts to their suppliers. Armed with the assurance of long-term contracts, suppliers have more incentive to invest in new facilities and bear the financial risks involved in the design and engineering of high-quality parts (Brown 1988).

Modules

Traditionally, American car makers purchased detached parts from suppliers. Now, first-tier suppliers are more likely to provide car makers with modules, such as seats, instrument panels and steering columns, rather than individual parts. For example, producers now obtain seats from first-tier suppliers rather than separate shipments of metal frames, foam and cloth.

Reduced inventory

The fifth impact of just-in-time is reduced inventory of parts. Producers demand that first-tier suppliers deliver parts directly to the assembly plants when they are actually needed rather than to distribution centres located in Michigan. First-tier suppliers may receive as little as 2 hours' notice that particular components are needed.

IMPACT ON DISTRIBUTION OF MOTOR VEHICLE INDUSTRY WITHIN THE US

The opening of six Japanese-owned assembly plants and more than 150 parts producers has altered the industrial landscape of the United States. Nearly all of these plants have clustered in the Midwest, the country's old heavy manufacturing belt. The Midwest lost much of its industrial base in the 1960s and 1970s, but the new Japanese-owned motor vehicle plants played a major role in arresting further decline during the 1980s. However, these firms have generally not selected specific communities in the Midwest traditionally associated with motor vehicle production. As a result, a complex pattern of industrial growth and further decline has emerged within the region.

Distribution of Japanese assembly plants

The distribution of Japanese assembly plants differs from the pattern which had predominated in the United States for more than sixty years.

In the early years of the twentieth century, the automotive industry concentrated in southern Michigan, and by 1910, 80 per cent of all motor vehicles were produced in that state (*Automobile Quarterly* 1971: 139; May 1975: 333–4). However, in 1914, the largest producer, Ford, began to assemble motor vehicles at branch assembly plants located near consumers in the north-east, south and west. General Motors also adopted the strategy of assembling its more popular products at branch assembly plants population concentrations (Boas 1961: 226–7; Hurley 1959: 4).

Locations near coastal population concentrations were preferred, because the large producers calculated that the cost of shipping finished motor vehicles from branch assembly plants to consumers was less from coastal locations than from Michigan (Hurley 1959: 5; White 1971: 41). The percentage of motor vehicles assembled in Michigan dropped to around 40 per cent, primarily the more expensive, less popular models. The trend of building branch assembly plants at coastal locations continued after the Second World War (Fig. 5.2); between 1945 and 1965, 11 of 15 new assembly plants were in coastal locations (Hurley 1959: 9).

In contrast, all six of the Japanese-owned plants have been built in Midwestern states. The six plants are located in adjacent states, Honda in Ohio, Nissan in Tennessee, Mazda in Michigan, Toyota in Kentucky, Mitsubishi in Illinois, and Subaru/Isuzu in Indiana (Fig. 5.3). It is no coincidence that each Japanese-owned assembly plant is located in a different Midwestern state. While firms used similar logic in selecting Midwestern sites they carefully avoided locating in any states already chosen by a competitor. This policy enabled each firm to establish unique relationships with state and local governments and to avoid existing concentrations of motor vehicle workers.

Honda, the first Japanese car maker to build an assembly plant in the United States, began the pattern by locating in Ohio rather than Michigan, the state most closely identified with the industry. The choice followed aggressive wooing by Ohio's governor, one of the first local government officials to visit Japan in search of industrial investment. Nissan, the second Japanese car maker to build an assembly plant in the United States made a bold choice, because rural Tennessee is several hundred miles south of the motor vehicle industry's traditional core area. The company selected a state where trade unions are weak and the cost of labour is lower than further north.

Mazda's location in Michigan was influenced by the fact that Ford, which owns one-quarter of Mazda, had a redundant plant there. Toyota, the fourth Japanese firm to decide to build in the United

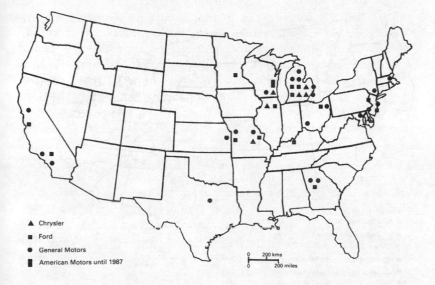

Figure 5.2 US assembly plants, 1979. From 1914 until the late 1970s the distribution of assembly plants within the US had remained relatively unchanged. Approximately 40 per cent of national production was concentrated in southern Michigan, the industry's historic core region. However, most of the newer plants were placed near population concentrations in the north-east, south and west. These branch assembly plants were designed to deliver more popular models to nearby customers
Source: Adapted from *Ward's Automotive Yearbook* (1980)

States, made a logical selection given the location of the first three plants. Kentucky was the only state between Michigan and Tennessee without a Japanese-owned assembly plant. Mitsubishi and Chrysler then located their joint assembly plant in Illinois, midway between Chicago and St Louis, two metropolitan areas with Chrysler assembly plants. By the time the Subaru/Isuzu plant was announced, the locational pattern had become clear, and the choice of Indiana was predictable, because it was the only state in the region without a Japanese assembly plant.

Every new assembly plant built by US car makers in the 1980s has also been located in the Midwest. Three plants in Michigan and one in Missouri replaced older facilities which were closed, while three others were located in Oklahoma, Kentucky and Tennessee (Rubenstein 1986: 288; 1988b: 13).

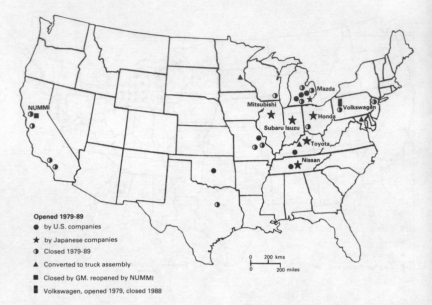

Figure 5.3 US assembly plants, 1989. During the 1980s, every new assembly plant built in the US was located in the Midwest, in contrast to the long-term pattern shown in Fig. 5.2. Seven new assembly plants were built by American companies and six by Japanese companies. Volkswagen opened and then closed an assembly plant during the period
Source: Adapted from *Ward's Automotive Yearbook* (1988)

Distribution of suppliers

Historically, nearly 90 per cent of the OEM suppliers clustered in the automotive industry's core area of southern Michigan, northern Ohio and northern Indiana (Alexander and Gibson 1979: 279; Henrickson 1951: 1). By the late 1980s, less than two-thirds of the nation's suppliers remained in the region (Glasmeier and McCluskey 1987: 147–8). However, relatively little is known about the current spatial distribution of parts suppliers in the United States, in part because of the large number of firms involved and in part because of difficulty in using secondary data sources to distinguish between OEM and after-market suppliers. It is not clear to what extent the decline in the Midwest is due to relocation of OEM suppliers or of aftermarket suppliers to the south, west and Mexico (Fig. 5.4).

In contrast to the trend away from the Midwest by American

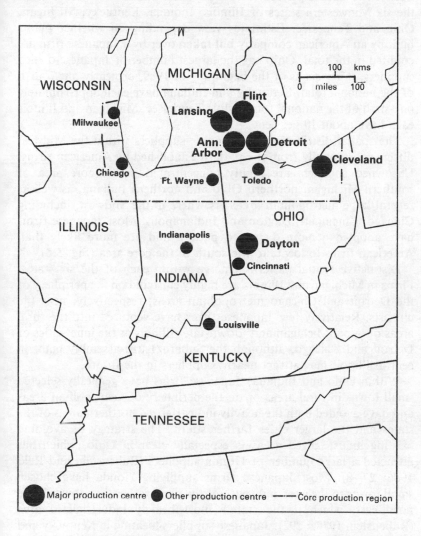

Figure 5.4 US parts-producing centres. In contrast to assembly plants, US parts producers remained highly clustered in the Midwest until the 1970s. Most parts suppliers were concentrated in southern Michigan or in several nearby cities with access to the Great Lakes. The major concentration of suppliers outside the core region was Dayton, Ohio, which had nine parts plants owned by General Motors

Source: Adapted from US Department of Commerce, Bureau of the Census, County Business Patterns (1982)

companies, Japanese firms have overwhelmingly preferred the region. Between 75 and 90 per cent of the Japanese plants have been built in the six Midwestern states of Illinois, Indiana, Kentucky, Michigan, Ohio and Tennessee. Estimates vary depending on whether plants built by an American company but taken over by a Japanese firm are counted in the total. Ohio has the largest number of Japanese-owned suppliers, thirty-six as of the beginning of 1989, or nearly one-fourth of the national total. Kentucky and Indiana have each approximately one-sixth of the national total, while Tennessee, Michigan and Illinois each have about 10 per cent.

The spatial distribution of Japanese suppliers within the Midwest differs substantially from the pattern established by American firms. US-owned suppliers are highly concentrated in the core area of southern Michigan, northern Ohio and northern Indiana, as well as several large metropolitan areas elsewhere in the Midwest, including Chicago, Cincinnati, Dayton and Indianapolis. Most Japanese firms have adopted a more dispersed pattern and are more likely than American firms to locate to the south of the core area (Fig. 5.5).

Distinctive spatial patterns emerge within each of the six states. Firms in Michigan and Illinois are highly clustered on the periphery of the Detroit and Chicago metropolitan areas, respectively, near the airports. Relatively few Japanese firms have ventured into the rural areas of upper Michigan and 'downstate' Illinois or the inner cities of Detroit and Chicago, although the Subaru/Isuzu assembly plant in central Illinois may attract nearby suppliers in the future.

Within Ohio and Indiana, Japanese firms have generally selected small towns in rural areas or on the periphery of metropolitan areas and have avoided both the heavily industrialized northern areas of the states and the larger cities farther south. The strategy of avoiding existing industrialized areas is especially clear in Ohio, which has attracted a large number of Honda suppliers (Rubenstein and Reid 1986: 27–8). Most Japanese firms supplying Honda have chosen small towns to the west and south of the plant rather than towards the north-east, which is the state's most heavily industrialized area (Rubenstein 1988a: 292). Japanese suppliers locating in Kentucky and Tennessee are closely tied to the major interstate highways. These two states are less industrialized than those farther north and face problems providing adequate infrastructure for industrial needs in their more remote areas.

Japanese suppliers rarely select a community that already has a Japanese firm. As the only Japanese presence in the community, the firm is better able to establish a unique working relationship with local officials and citizens and avoid competing with other firms for labour and financial benefits.

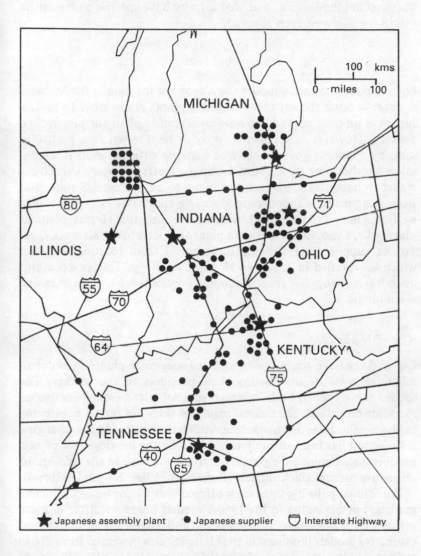

Figure 5.5 Japanese suppliers, 1989. Japanese suppliers have clustered in the Midwest but have selected sites farther south than the industry's traditional core region. Ohio has the largest number of Japanese suppliers, while Michigan ranks only sixth

Reasons for distribution

To explain the spatial distribution of Japanese motor vehicle firms in the United States, two scales must be examined. First, why are firms clustered in the Midwest, and second, why have specific communities within the Midwest been selected?

Suppliers

For a Japanese-owned supplier the reason for locating in the Midwest is clear: because the Japanese assembly plants are nearby. In part, a Japanese supplier needs to be near an assembly plant for just-in-time delivery. However, a supplier is likely to be directed to a particular state by Japanese government and banking officials even if it considers another state to be optimal. Japanese officials perceive each car maker to have staked an exclusive claim to a different US state, and steer a car maker's suppliers to the same state. For example, southwestern Ohio lies within 90 minutes of both the Honda plant at Marysville, Ohio, and the Toyota plant at Georgetown, Kentucky, yet Toyota suppliers are strongly discouraged from locating in Ohio, which is regarded in Japan as Honda's territory. This practice also discourages a supplier from arranging contracts with more than one assembly plant.

Assembly plants

Car makers have traditionally situated assembly plants in order to minimize costs of distributing their products to the market. The sudden preference by both Japanese- and American-owned companies for Midwest rather than coastal locations does not reflect a lessening in the importance of this locational factor. Instead, the changing distribution has been strongly influenced by the development of new production techniques, especially a sharp increase in the number of distinctive motor vehicle models (Rubenstein 1986: 291–2; 1988b: 14).

Traditionally the big three each offered only a handful of distinctive models, but beginning in the 1960s, models began to differ in more substantial ways, such as size, body and engine. The number of distinctive models produced in the United States increased from 216 in 1955 to 348 in 1965 and to 370 in 1967 (White 1971: 203). US-owned branch assembly plants which formerly produced models for regional markets were converted into specialized plants assembling one or two models for national distribution. Similarly, the Japanese-owned US assembly plants have been located in the Midwest in order to minimize the costs of distributing their models throughout the country.

The selection of specific plant sites within the Midwest has been influenced in part by proximity to good transport links. Most sites are near one of three major interstate highways: I-70, which runs east—west, and I-65 and I-75, which run north—south. I-75 between Michigan and Tennessee has attracted so many Japanese parts suppliers that it is now frequently referred to as the Kanban Highway. Also attracting Japanese plants are I-24, I-71 and I-74. Most shipments are by truck, but the assembly plants also utilize the rail service, and all six are located on main or secondary main lines.

Along the preferred interstate highways corridors, Japanese firms have generally selected plant sites in small towns. The median population of the six communities selected for assembly plants is approximately 10,000 inhabitants; the median for suppliers is also approximately 10,000.

The selection by Japanese car makers of small towns on the urban periphery reflects in part a widespread phenomenon of industrial dispersal, fuelled by lower land prices and ease of assembling large tracts of land. Japanese firms often purchase a parcel far larger than necessary to build the plant, because the cost of land is much lower in the United States than in Japan.

Japanese firms also choose rural sites in order to avoid existing concentrations of industrial workers in general and automotive industry workers in particular. According to a Mitsubishi official, 'The rule of thumb we have been using in our site selection process is to avoid going right into the heart of existing heavily automotive industrial regions' (Jensen 1986). This avoidance stems primarily from the automotive industry's long history of labour unrest (Hurley 1959: 8). General Motors and Chrysler agreed to recognize the United Auto Workers union in 1937 only after years of violent confrontations, and Ford resisted bargaining with the union for another decade. After the Second World War, strikes frequently crippled the automotive industry. The union's strategy was to strike against the big three car maker considered most vulnerable while permitting the other two to operate; the contract eventually signed by the targeted company was taken to the other two car makers. Three years later, when the contracts expired again, the union would initiate the process against another car maker.

Japanese firms recognized that the auto union's strength was concentrated in the industry's core area. By locating plants elsewhere, Japanese firms were better able to institute new work rules and to block the union's organizing attempts (Green and Schor 1988). Japanese assembly plants with unions include the two joint ventures with US car makers – Diamond-Star and NUMMI – plus Mazda, which produces cars for Ford and is the only Japanese assembly plant located in the industry's core region, where union support is strongest. Few Japanese suppliers are unionized. Although Japanese officials vehemently deny the allegation, American black leaders claim that the plants have been deliberately located in areas with few minorities (Buckley 1988: 56–7; Schlesinger 1988).

IMPACT OF JAPANESE INVESTMENT ON COMMUNITIES

The arrival of a Japanese plant in a small Midwestern town is a major event. Typically, the Japanese plant becomes the community's largest employer and stimulates the local service economy. The change is most dramatic in towns like Marysville, Ohio, and Smyrna, Tennessee, which contained only a few thousand inhabitants prior to construction of Japanese assembly plants. However, even a parts manufacturer employing 100 people makes a major impact on a small town.

A Japanese firm looking for a site in the United States normally makes its initial contact with state economic development agencies, rather than with local or federal government officials. Most states maintain offices in Tokyo and send trade delegations to woo potential transplants. State officials are also instrumental in identifying a short list of suitable communities for the representatives of the Japanese firm to visit. At this stage, local government officials are not informed that their community is being considered, but rumours are flying: a Japanese firm may wish to visit a potential site without attracting publicity, but it is impossible for a group of camera-toting foreigners driving a limousine to explore a small Midwestern town in secret.

Financial incentives

State economic development officials take the lead in putting together a package of incentives to entice the Japanese firm. In the early 1980s, Honda extracted $30 million from the state of Ohio, primarily for construction of new highways. As competition among states became more intense, the level of subsidies increased. By the late 1980s, the states of Illinois and Indiana each allocated $86 million to attract Mitsubishi and Subaru/Isuzu, respectively. Illinois' $86 million package included $40 million for worker training, $10 million for site acquisition and grading, $13 million for new water and sewer lines, and $20 million for highway improvements (Holusha 1987; Pastor 1988).

Suppliers also work with state officials, although the level of support is lower than for assembly plants. For example, to attract an electronics subsidiary of Mitsubishi, employing 250 workers, Ohio provided $1.5 million in loans and grants for water and sewer improvements, parking and accessories to the factory building.

Local governments also make financial contributions to attract Japanese firms. In the case of Mitsubishi's electronics subsidiary, the city of Mason, Ohio, a city of less than 10,000 inhabitants, provided $100,000 for the company to construct either sewers or roads, whichever it preferred. In addition, for fifteen years the company pays local property tax (rates) only on the value of the unimproved land, a subsidy which city officials estimate to be worth $4 million. Nonetheless, Mitsubishi will still pay nearly $500,000 annually in local taxes, far more than the value of the subsidies.

Community attitudes

While financial incentives are expected, they are rarely the most critical factor in the site selection process. Instead, the Japanese place a high priority on assessing attitudes of residents and local government officials towards the prospect of a Japanese-owned plant becoming the community's largest employer.

Japanese firms assess attitudes in part by distributing questionnaires to officials in communities being considered. These questionnaires are frequently elaborate, as long as twenty pages, and do not reveal the name of the company. Local officials find many of the questions difficult and time-consuming to answer, such as documenting all unions operating in the area and recalling all incidents of labour unrest. Some questions relate to governmental jurisdictions outside the control of the respondent.

Japanese firms also assess community attitudes by interviewing local officials. Representatives of the firm do not reveal the name of their company to local officials at their initial meeting. Japanese representatives do not indicate their positions in the corporate hierarchy, nor which representatives understand English. Economic issues, such as taxes, grants, loans and infrastructure improvements are not discussed at the first meeting. Instead, local government officials are questioned about their families, hobbies, recreational interests and other aspects of their personal lives.

Assessing local attitudes is critical to Japanese firms in part because they want to receive a friendly reception in the selected community (Clayton 1987). Older Americans may remember the Second World War and do not want the Japanese running the community's largest business. Defenders of small-town life may oppose a plant that would require the community to expand.

Japanese firms consider local attitudes primarily to determine acceptance of Japanese-style management techniques. In contrast to US-owned assembly plants, which have as many as eighty job classifications, Japanese plants have teams of up to ten workers performing a wide variety of tasks, such as inspecting, housekeeping, changing tools and dyes, and filling out forms. Members of the team rotate responsibilities. The Japanese plants also practise levelling policies, such as elimination of special parking spaces and dining rooms for top management, common uniforms with first-name tags, group exercises and open offices. Workers are taught the company's philosophy, because understanding and accepting it are considered essential to the firm's success (Rehder 1988: 57–8).

Evidence concerning the acceptance of Japanese management techniques in the United States is mixed. An apparent success is the NUMMI plant in Fremont, California. When operated by General Motors, the plant compiled one of the industry's worst records with regard to productivity, product quality, absenteeism, drug usage and sabotage of equipment (Holusha 1988a). In 1983, General Motors turned over management of the plant to Toyota officials, who agreed to hire from among the laid-off workers and to pay them the prevailing industry wage and benefit scales. In exchange the United Auto Workers agreed to accept Toyota's production system with flexible work rules and broad job classifications. Significantly, NUMMI did not rehire former plant managers. The hiring process included a three-day pre-employment assessment programme based on Toyota's values, philosophy and system. Workers were flown to Japan for three weeks of on-the-job training at Toyota's Takaoka plant. Today, the plant is one of the nation's most productive, and its products are considered by the leading consumer magazines to be the best-built cars sold by General Motors in the United States (Rehder *et al.* 1985: 37).

On the other hand, workers at other US plants organized according to Japanese management principles report increased pressure and stress. Problems have been especially severe at Nissan's assembly plant in Smyrna, Tennessee. Some employees claim that Nissan has increased the speed of the assembly line on several occasions, resulting in a high incidence of health problems. Nissan has allegedly fired sick and injured workers, as well as those complaining about plant conditions. Other employees may be 'working hurt' and hiding ailments in order to keep their jobs.

The landscape of small Midwest towns has changed as a result of Japanese automotive industry investment. On the one hand, local supermarkets stock octopus and seaweed, sashimi restaurants have been established, and local video rental stores carry samurai films. On the other hand, Japanese workers have learned to shop in American-style supermarkets, engage in small talk at cocktail parties, and learn to appreciate country-and-western music. Several communities have established Saturday schools to keep the children of Japanese workers at the same educational level as those back home (Buckley 1988: 57; Wilkerson 1987).

CONCLUSION

American and Japanese car makers have spun a complex web of joint ventures, innovative products and modernized production techniques in the United States. They have constructed new plants and discarded old ones at a pace not seen since the infancy of the automotive industry. They have been instrumental in revitalizing a depressed region of the country, although new investment has not been uniformly distributed within the Midwest.

However, the construction of six assembly plants and more than 150 parts manufacturers in the United States by Japanese firms has created substantial excess capacity in the production of motor vehicles and component parts. Total output of all US assembly plants now exceeds consumer demand by between one-third and one-half, and the US market is unlikely to expand enough to accommodate the increased output. The current situation will change, but it is unclear whether Japanese firms will cohabit with American car makers or displace them.

One possibility is that Japanese firms will expand their sales in the United States at the expense of the big three. However, none of the big three appears to be a likely loser. General Motors has already seen its share of the US market decline from one-half to one-third since the Japanese invasion began in the 1960s, yet the nation's largest car maker retains a substantial core of long-time loyal consumers. GM lost much of its small car business, but Japanese car makers do not offer the range of products, especially large middle-priced models, which appeal to current GM buyers.

Ford has replaced GM as the most profitable US car maker in recent years by offering models consumers find attractive. Some erosion of its market share is possible if Ford's future models are less appealing. As the smallest of the big three, Chrysler may appear most vulnerable to the Japanese, and a loss of sales could threaten the survival of the company. However, the US government already saved Chrysler from bankruptcy with loan guarantees in 1979 (US Department of Transportation 1982: 22) and is likely to feel compelled to do the same again, if necessary (US Department of Transportation 1981: 7).

The other possibility is that Japanese firms will retain their current market share by selling Americans US-built rather than Japanese-built cars. Japanese firms would then have to seek other markets for their domestically produced models, perhaps in Asia. Alternatively, the Japanese may export some of their American-built cars to Europe.

6 Nothing new about Nissan?

Philip Garrahan and Paul Stewart

The North-East of England has been undergoing an intensified process of de-industrialization in the last ten years. Against a profile of industrial restructuring, company closures and escalating unemployment, the Nissan investment invites analysis of the other side of this experience of decline. The region has lost its employment base in mining, shipbuilding, heavy engineering, and other long-established sectors of manufacturing. Yet, it has gained a car industry. The topic we address is whether this recently introduced car industry represents fundamental change in the region's political economy, and if so of what kind? It is important to stress that many associated developments are only now becoming evident. Not the least of these is the phenomenon of other extensive Japanese investment in the region. In mid-1989 there are around two dozen Japanese companies with regional or local interests in the North-East, compared with only one a decade ago. Some of these, but by no means all, have a direct commercial link with Nissan. We deal only tangentially with this broader phenomenon and, since the focus is on Nissan directly as a force for change, the empirical evidence on which we draw is related solely to the car industry.

While the research on which this chapter is based was being conducted, coincidentally similar studies were being undertaken in the United States. In one of these (Hill *et al.* 1989), there is an account of a research method based upon 'qualitative, open-ended interviews with strategic informants', who were identified by a variety of means. These included: the authors' past knowledge of the local area, 'sifting through the written record of events contained in hundreds of newspaper articles, organizational records and government publications; through the use of snowball interviewing techniques whereby one strategic informant leads to another; and, in a couple of instances, through chance encounters'. This research method was employed to to study the impact of the Mazda plant in Flat Rock, Michigan and it is paralleled by our approach to the analysis of Nissan's development in Sunderland. Those with whom we have made contact include local government officers and elected councillors, Members of Parliament, the local media, local development corporations, trade unions, manufacturing workers and company managers. As with the Mazda study, by mutual agreement we do not identify any one of our interviewees when reporting on this research. For the purposes of this chapter, we are examining changes in industrial attitudes and practices brought about at Nissan. We are assessing the impact Nissan has had, as it is experienced and interpreted by our interviewees. The data collected from the interviews are therefore of a qualitative kind.

GLOBAL TRENDS AND LOCAL EFFECTS

On a worldwide basis, Nissan manufactures 2.6 million vehicles per annum, of which 1.8 million are made in Japan. The investment in the UK is a continuation of a corporate plan to extend production outside of Japan itself, and this strategy has led Nissan into making vehicles in Australia, Mexico, the US, Spain and elsewhere, as well as in the UK. In some instances, as with Motor Iberica in Spain, joint ventures or takeovers were the basis for the investment. In its two major foreign excursions, however, Nissan has opted for the development of 'greenfield' sites. The first of these was in Smyrna, in Tennessee, and this was followed within a few years by the choice of Sunderland for the site of the company's first major manufacturing platform in Europe. As with the Smyrna plant, that in Sunderland has the capacity to produce in excess of 250,000 cars a year. Whether it could, or will, produce many more than that is likely to result from a balance of forces, most notably arising from Nissan's success in exporting to the member states of the European Community. In any event, the Sunderland development is a highly significant element of the Nissan strategy to become and remain a world leader in the car industry.

Site clearance for the Nissan plant in the North-East of England began in July 1984 and the foundation stone was laid in November of the same year. The first part of the factory was ready for occupation in December 1985, and the official opening ceremony conducted by Mrs Thatcher took place in September 1986. The initial workforce numbered fewer than 500, with production aimed at 24,000 cars in the first year. These cars were assembled from kits imported from Nissan's factories in Japan. Sunderland is situated in an area of high unemployment, and the first 500 jobs advertised by the company attracted 25,000 applications.

Output at the Sunderland plant was 55,000 Nissan Bluebirds in 1988, and this is planned to double by 1991. Additionally, the company has announced production of another model in the Nissan Micra range, which will add a further 100,000 cars by 1992. With production of these two models therefore expected to add up to 200,000 cars a year, or more, by 1992, total investment in the plant will exceed £600 million.

The investment has come in two main phases. In the first of these, the British government contributed £105 million towards the £350 million development costs (Trade and Industry Committee of the House of Commons, Minutes of Evidence, 15 January 1986, p. 42). This state subsidy came in the form of regional development and selective financial assistance grants, which might be attracted to the second phase of the development also. Overall, there are about two dozen Japanese companies in the Northern Region of England (out of a total of 280 foreign companies in the Region), and Nissan is presently the largest of the Japanese firms in terms of investment cost, output and size of workforce.

A major conclusion from the North American experience of inward investment by Japanese car manufacturers is the speed with which events have happened. It has become commonplace to note the accelerating impact of Japanese vehicle production in the context of global shares. Of less obvious consequence to European observers has been the impact within the North American domestic economy of new Japanese car firms. The scale of investment by Japanese car companies in the US during the last decade suggests developments likely to have an effect in the UK and Western Europe. In particular, attention can be drawn to: the spatial location of vehicle assemblers and their related components' suppliers; and the trend towards joint ventures consequent on the effect that competition from Japanese 'transplants' has had on the Big Three US car companies (Cox and Mair 1988; see also Chapter 5). It is evident that such features will not be repeated in their entirety in the UK, but the one which is central to our current concern is the impact of Japanese management styles on local communities and workforces. This does not automatically lead to straight intra-company comparison: for example, in the Nissan plant in Smyrna there is no independent labour organization as the State of Tennessee's right to work statutes effectively prevent the collective organization of workers. However, the Mazda plant in Flat Rock has union recognition and is in an area of Michigan with a tradition of strong labour organization in the heavy industries located there for the last 150 years. So, while direct comparison between the two Nissan plants (Smyrna and Sunderland) is not straightforward, the Mazda development together with others in North America offer some guidelines for the research.

While offering pointers for comparative research, the North American experience also poses interesting questions about future international movement by Japanese capital in the car industry. We should not expect that this investment has reached the limit of its global dispersion just because Japanese car firms are opening factories in Britain. With the integrated market planned after 1992 by the Community in the West of Europe, there may follow developments in the car industries in the East of Europe. After the speed of investment into North America, and then Britain, can we now expect Japanese companies to be looking for the next possible major area of world growth, and could this be in the Eastern European countries in the age of '*glasnost*'? This is not a rhetorical question: the implications of internationalized production are already with us since Nissan cars to be sold in British or other European Community markets can be made wholly or in part either in Japan, or in the US, or in Britain. Arguments about 'local content' are proving to be superficial, since evidently Nissan can lay claim to over three-quarters 'local content' while still importing high value-added components such as the power train. Some commentators in the US have already forecast Nissan products from Sunderland being exported not just to Western European countries, but also to North American ones. Changes in exchange rates, disruptions in national economies leading to falling demand, or worsening industrial relations, can now all be met by a globally flexible production system. The reality of a global company responding to the changing conditions of domestic demand and international trading is already with us.

These points are made to draw attention to the uncertainties at a time when there is a natural temptation (particularly strong in the North-East) to regard Nissan as a panacea to regional economic problems. In an area of high unemployment and de-industrialization like the North-East, the arrival of Nissan as a world manufacturing leader was met only with congratulation and forecasts of better things to come (Crowther and Garrahan 1988). However, the applause at local good fortune for employment in Sunderland should not eclipse the words of caution for the medium- to long-term future. In this respect, the Nissan development is not a break with the recent past but a mark of continuity. As Massey (1984) and others have noted, declining regions made great efforts to keep their economies relatively 'open' in the 1960s precisely to attract new inward investment.

The experience of having won the approval of this inward investment in the 1960s was mixed, but its effects were mainly twofold: first, regions like the North-East experienced the uncertainties of the 'branch plant economy', where there was restricted local ownership of companies. With the recession of the 1970s many factories new to the region were cut back or closed as their mostly UK- and North American-based multinational parent companies responded to the altered market conditions. Second, the spatial division of company activities resulted in the depressed regions largely attracting skilled/unskilled assembly work. The higher order/added-value jobs did not come to places like Sunderland. The fact that Nissan is currently searching for a site for its research and design centre somewhere outside of the North-East testifies that little has changed. And if the car market in the next decade is as volatile as it has been in the last decade, who is to say with certain confidence that the Nissan factory's planned expansion in Sunderland will be sustained?

The final issue to consider in this section is the degree to which the state plays a role in promoting a particular kind of economic restructuring. In September 1988 Lord Young, the Secretary of State for Trade and Industry, drove Nissan's 100,000th Bluebird model off the production line for the benefit of the assembled media cameras. In this publicity gesture Lord Young cemented the relationship between the Nissan company and the Conservative government. The coincidence of this event with the impending closure of the shipbuilding industry in Sunderland did not escape critical attention, however. In November 1988 the government announced a 'rescue package' for Sunderland following its decision to implement the closure of North East Shipbuilders Limited. But the notion of rescuing the local economy had been the talk earlier when Nissan announced its decision to build a car plant in Sunderland in 1984. These events are not unrelated, and it is significant that the rhetoric of government policy on both occasions called for the necessity of dragging the local economy into a period of modernization. In this rhetoric, modernization means a change away from state-subsidized, public sector and highly unionized economic activity, and towards an enterprise culture generating small firms/high technology employment.

While Nissan is unequivocally a private multinational, the state-subsidy of Nissan's investment in Sunderland is over one-third of the £350 million cost of the first phase. Far from being a privately led recovery exercise in the local economy, this has all the characteristics of shared risk taking between capital and the state typical of the previous period of inward investment from multinational companies. There thus seems little evidence from this case that industrial regeneration depends on the unleashing of market forces in a manner consistent with the thinking behind the enterprise culture. The refusal to subsidize shipbuilding, while underwriting Nissan's investment, thus constitutes an overtly ideological state policy regarding the future direction of the North-East's political economy. A further measure of the ideological environment concerns the government's anti-union policies. In the 1960s Labour and Conservative governments acted in corporate unison to attract foreign investment to declining industrial regions like the North-East. Then, as now, the prospect of new employment found ready approval. However, a new feature in present circumstances is the record of Conservative legislation in the 1980s restricting trade union activity. The signing of a single-union deal with the AEU has led to AEU plant membership of less than one in five of Nissan's workforce, with the union thus being effectively marginalized.

So far, we have briefly alluded to some of the questions raised by state-led restructuring of a local economy. Overall, there is nothing new about Nissan as a multinational company investing in a context of high unemployment with explicit government assistance. The major discontinuity is the recasting of the corporate model to exclude multi-union participation along the lines exercised in the 1960s. In essence, the state's role in stimulating the restructuring process is a direct one, both in terms of financial support for inward investment and in terms of employment legislation restricting the role of independent trade unions. The local response to change and the experience of working in the 'modernized' industrial base are areas of concern to which we now turn. While our empirical focus is on the Nissan car company, the broader aim is to characterize the changing political economy of an area previously fretted over as in economic decline, and now fêted as leading by example in the matters of enterprise and initiative.

NOTHING NEW ABOUT NISSAN?

The draft introduction to the development plan of the Tyne and Wear Urban Development Corporation described Sunderland as the 'advanced manufacturing capital of the north of England'. The jewel in the crown of this reputation is the Nissan car company, whose industrial philosophy is represented as based on the triad of 'Flexibility,

Teamwork, and Quality'. In his book, 'The Road to Nissan' the personnel director of Nissan, Peter Wickens (1987) outlines the well-publicized claims of the Japanese approach. A renaissance of sensible management allied with a new style of worker and of work organization is the anticipated bedrock for increased productivity and hightened competitiveness. The belief that Japanese production methods could be transferred to the UK was significant in influencing the investment and having come this far along the road, the company target is to be 'Number One in Europe'.

It is very much part of our study to discover whether the Nissan philosophy can in fact bear the test of close examination. One associated interpretation is that Japanese companies can close the door on the old, conflictual industrial relations between management and workers in the British car industry. The novelty of the Japanese approach is contained in the promise that opposition and intractability need not be part of industrial relations any longer. Indeed, in the US the packaging of this promise led many workers to conclude that it offered a better route if not to industrial democracy itself, then at least to an improved quality of working life for employees of Japanese companies. Worker participation was to be achieved by replacing individual ambition with team spirit, and the emphasis on quality over all else would restore the worker's sense of a personal investment in keeping standards of production high.

The social relations of production are thus foregrounded by the company which, on seizing the initiative, has posed major issues of investigation. If the organization of work at Nissan is effectively different, then positive feedback should emerge from such features as recruitment and training policy, the flexibility of the employee, the integration of workers in decisions made about them by management, and the satisfactory resolution of industrial disputes by the company council. In the discussion which follows, these concerns are set against the contemporary debate about the alleged epoch of 'post-Fordism'.

THE SOCIAL AND POLITICAL DIMENSIONS OF COMMITMENT AT WORK

It is in this context then, that the question of the social character of work organization in Nissan becomes significant. The claims made by commentators about its uniqueness are varied and more or less sophisticated (Wickens 1987; CAITS 1986). What is required therefore is some understanding of the ways in which the shopfloor works, and the kinds of conceptual devices that can be used to make sense of these workings.

Although one should not make general claims on the basis of one industrial locale and environment, it is important that knowledge of the way Nissan 'works' is set against recent attempts to explain the social and political physiognomy of Japanese inward investment to the UK, and the socio-economic patterns which Japanese investment is supposed to herald. The discussion of Japanization (Pollert 1988a,b; Wilkinson and Oliver 1988; Turnbull 1990) would seem to be approximate to, although be in no sense entirely commensurate with, what those predicting a post-Fordist social environment have in mind when they consider recent changes in social and technical production cycles (Murray 1985, 1988, 1989; Clarke 1988; and for a rather different evaluation, Jessop *et al*. 1988). Japanization may not be how they envisage post-Fordism occurring *per se*, but what appears to have the potential for a new phase of capitalist expansion is really an imposition of extra-national forms of subordination from the core, in this case, Japanese capital. This is a critical point to make. The parameters of post-Fordism are very broad, and its exponents hail from different theoretical and political locations. What they all have in common, however, are four core assumptions: that post-Fordism is technologically progressive; that it ushers in the potential for even greater expansion of the capitalist mode of production; that it establishes the possibility of more human-centred forms of work; and that the old Fordist era has been, or is about to be, terminated.

In this context, what some call Japanese production methods and social relations, may either be imported with the bearer (as in the present example of Nissan in the UK), or they may be adapted to cut against the torpor of Fordism (Ford UK in 1988 attempted to introduce an extensive JIT management system). But either way, the point has to be recognized that these production relations are imposed. There are many sides to this point, and because it is not obviously clear what this imposition means in the case of Nissan, it may be worth pointing out that what is central to these 'new' working methods is a reconstitution of social control. In the end, it would probably matter little what these working practices are called. The question is whether they enhance the scope of human creativity and decision-making. What is pre-eminently wrong with the concept of post-Fordism is its apriorism. It will be of more use to discover what is truly unique but at the same time to see how links to past continuities of social and economic forms of subordination are recreated. Our contention is that Nissan's novel working practices articulate social and technological subordination at work in ways which only super-ficially and rhetorically go beyond the social and political context of Fordism. To this extent, post-Fordism, and its exponents, would need to demonstrate that decentralized production; individual commitment to work; core–periphery differentiation; small group work tasks, overcome the most intractable problem that is Fordism, namely, class conflict and domination in the process of production. In this case, the issue becomes not whether Fordism or post-Fordism is the operative conceptual device for making sense of new forms of work (which for sure are being created), but rather how are different paths to the same goal – social subordination at work – achieved (Clarke 1988, hints at this).

What has happened to ensure the prominence of this neo-Fordist mode of work organization and social control that we call Japanization? CAITS (1986) has noted that common to all forms of Japanization are at least three imperatives:

1 reduction of union influence;
2 new technology systems; and
3 employee motivation for the company

In addition these depend upon:

1 close subcontracting relationships;
2 absence of autonomous and proactive union representation;
3 abolition of demarcation; and
4 restructuring of work organization

Wickens (1987) sums up the management success in achieving each of these four, under the slogan 'Quality, Flexibility, Teamwork'.

Since we are sceptical about the meaning of the latter, we would expect an ellision between the successful implementation of a range of organizational strategies, and a rhetoric of fulfilment – if you say it often enough, and describe existing patterns as having met this triadic criteria of success, it is easy to convince outsiders and lay-people that the 'Nissan-way' (Japanization, post-Fordism, etc.) has succeeded. However, what we want to concentrate on is the way in which a system described as having achieved the kind of corporate consensus Wickens believes exists is actually made to work for those involved in its implementation on the shop floor. Following on from this, we want to question the credibility of union policies (described as 'new realist') which take all this as given, and then desirable without any critical appreciation of the inherently debilitating character of these adopted work practices variously described as Japanese and/or post-Fordist.

Our research findings indicate both the importance of this organizational rhetoric in the implementation of managerial control strategies, and in the operation of some of these for 'manufacturing staff', i.e. line-workers, including team leaders and supervisors.

What we want to argue is that not only does the implementation of Japanese production methods (just-in-time systems) at Nissan not suggest the end of Fordism *per se* but rather the combination of these Fordist modes of subordination with alternative forms of technical and social organization. These alternative forms concentrate on the transfer and sublimation of power out of the technical cycle. Paradoxically they still exist in the technical cycle of production to a greater degree than in 'Fordism' *par excellence*. However, emphasis is placed on securing this subordination in terms of what we call self-subordination, and which Gramsci terms 'consent' (Gramsci 1971). This emphasis upon the social character of employee self-subordination builds a set of social and cultural practices around a tight technical system which some define as 'management by stress' or MBS (Slaughter 1987; Slaughter and Parker 1989).

Thus, in contrast to traditional Fordist structures of subordination, the 'Nissan-way' merely reconstitutes relations of domination and subordination, in some ways more pernicious and disempowering than those traditionally associated with Fordist production scenarios. When we say 'sublimate power', we mean that the confrontational, hierarchical and coercive power normally associated with Fordist production is in theory and appearance reversed. Emphasis is placed on individualizing the relationship between worker and production system. When Nissan talk about this, they describe this relationship as a system of 'total quality control' (TQC) (Nissan 1988). TQC depends upon individual competition between operatives who are 'made aware of their own individual contribution to the overall philosophy' (Nissan 1988: 9).

This is epitomized especially, though not only, by the 'neighbour watch' system, but it is also reinforced by the importance which the TQC philosophy attributes to the 'vehicle evaluation system' (VES). These act to monitor, via a process of self-evaluation, and peer surveillance, worker activity. The coveted roles of team leader and supervisor serve as the eyes and ears of management on the line. Team leaders, whose role is comparable to that of charge-hand, act as both line-workers and management intermediaries. But unlike charge-hands in a traditional Fordist mode of organization, their relationship to line-workers constitutes a form of paternalism untempered by the usual kind of restraint provided by a resolute union structure offering an alternative vision of the work organization, and the importance of the work tasks. Even if what unions sometimes offer is another form of paternalism, its centre of inspiration, and the sense of identity proffered lies elsewhere. It does not in fact lie in a company-inspired individualism, where line-workers are both united for the company, and by the same token, and for the same reason, divided by it, but a corporate independence where competitive individualism has to be continually won by management, and is never assured.

Indeed the interesting point is how much our respondents openly expressed feelings of dissatisfaction with the absence of any alternative for making their feelings known. This antipathy was directed as much at the AEU as it was at Nissan. Indeed given the publicity about Nissan's consensual way, and the fawning of the local media, we have been constantly surprised by the degree of scepticism expressed by line-workers up to and including team leaders, and one of the supervisors we interviewed.

If we can reveal the existence of at least some cracks and gaps in the Nissan-consensual-way, and if it is obvious that the shop floor needs some relieving alternative source of definition, then the source of the AEU's business unionism seems even more obscure. Yet this latter commitment reveals a very real misperception of the social and technical environment enshrined in the neo-Fordist modes of work organization. For if, as Wilkinson and Oliver (1988) perspicaciously demonstrate, Japanization, and what others term post-Fordist production cycles are more, not less, bound by tight social and political imperatives that are an indispensable part of JIT systems, then the work organization is subject to even more acute problems of technical and social insecurity. This latter provides the key to the reason why alternative loci of power must, as the *sine qua non* of the system's functioning, be eschewed such that independent forms of social organization in the factory are denied. This does not mean, following Forster and Woolfson (1989), that Japanese production cycles/neo-Fordism are not technically progressive. What is questionable is whether production based on human-centred need would require a work methodology of flexibility that jettisoned quality, teamwork and flexibility on the shop floor's terms.

As Wilkinson and Oliver's research illustrates, alternative sources of power have to be very difficult to achieve even when the trade-off for union control is a very high degree of enhanced power. However, this potential remains only dangerous for the down-side of the system since it is part of the system's inherent operation to ensure the exclusion of internal threats (organized shopfloor dissent) where the corporate or class power of external agencies (trade unions) exist only as social and economic shibboleths (collection of union dues at source; absence of prime responsibility for the expression of collective identity).

What we are arguing is that even though the system is conflictual for sure, there is no sociological reason why a collective (let alone organized collective) response will inevitably appear. New realism/ business unionism begins from the misconception that individual discomfiture with the work organization reflects an individual's cognitive dissonance, rather than seeing this as an expression of the ways in which the system's socially subordinating stresses and strains (the tight cycles imposed on work routines by JIT) are reflected in line-worker antipathy and dissent.

The problem for individuals on the shop floor is that the individualized collective experience of line-workers merely serves to reinforce a consensual company ideology, organizational preference, and the company's definition of social experience. This is notwithstanding what Wilkinson and Oliver call 'power capacity', unless power alternatives in the form of oppositional corporate organizations can, or are willing to demonstrate their wish, let alone ability, to pursue individual grievances in a collective fashion.

This is why the individualizing of labour, the competitiveness of work, and the relative importance of individualized peer assessment are so important. Since quality, teamwork and flexibility are vital for any system, the Nissan management's definitions of these, as enshrined in its very organizational culture, and the technical organization of the production process, both of which are defied by the AEU's new realism/business unionism, are the only definitions of quality, teamwork and flexibility available.

CONCLUSION

The main feature of the contemporary debate about the North-East's car industry is that it is a force for change. Nissan is regarded as a new lead to be followed, but we argue that this does not necessarily engage the car industry in taking a new direction. It is clear from our research that Nissan's working methods, whilst indicating some variance with the experience of line-workers in so-called traditional Fordist organizations, do not significantly transform the attitudes of employees to work. The explanation for this variance lies less in the work routines than with extra-technical factors which are rooted in company ideology and Japanese production practices (just-in-time). Even then attitudes are less than fulsome, since however one interprets assembly-line work, it is still, as one of our interviewees described it, 'boring, tedious, and mind-numbing'. However, it is also clear that individual misgivings about a particular work methodology only attain collective and oppositional expression, where and when alternative definitions of the work place exist. At Nissan they do not.

7 Motor components: locational issues in an international industry

David Froggatt

INTRODUCTION: SETTING THE THEME

The motor vehicle industry is organized, to an increasingly high degree, on a global and transnational basis, not only in marketing terms but also in terms of corporate structures and strategies, finance, product design and development and manufacture.

While the growth of vehicle industries in newly-industrializing countries is an important current development, in the major industrialized countries the motor industry is mature.

These two broad features of the industry mean that the main dynamics of change in its structure are generated by technical development and competitive forces rather than market growth. And both these dynamic forces express themselves transnationally rather than within the confines of national boundaries.

In turn, these considerations imply that the main locational issue in the motor components industry centres on 'which country(ies)' rather than site location within a particular country.

These are very broad generalizations. This chapter attempts to point out some of the specific factors and trends which are reshaping the structure of the motor components industry and, in particular, their possible locational implications. The focus of attention is West Europe, where transnational forces are most powerful and clearly observable, though many of the factors identified apply in the Americas, in the Far East and indeed on a global scale.

SOME BASIC FEATURES OF THE MOTOR COMPONENTS INDUSTRY

Diversity of products and materials

The wide diversity of products and materials making up the industry is well illustrated by the British Standard Industrial Classification where the 'Motor Vehicle Parts' Activity Heading (No. 3530) itself consists only of parts 'wholly or mainly of metal'. Electrical parts and those made of asbestos and its substitutes, glass, rubber or plastics are all classified (and not separately specified as motor components) under the relevant materials industry, while gasket sets are classified under 'Precision components for engines and machinery not elsewhere specified'.

The emphasis on reducing weight is tending to reduce the proportion of metals in vehicles and widen still further the range of other materials used.

Company structure

The company structure of the motor components industry is fragmented. It has been estimated that in the UK there are around 2,000 makers of components, but that 100 firms account for about 80 per cent of output and 20 for 40 per cent of the value of the vehicle builders' purchases of components. Moreover, the industry's company structure is obscured by the fact that several of the larger suppliers are subsidiaries of diversified firms with substantial non-automotive interests. Motor component manufacture may also be 'hidden' within factory establishments classified, on the 'dominant activity' principle, to industries with no apparent automotive connection.

Original equipment and the aftermarket

The motor components market consists of two distinct, though connected, sectors. Components are supplied as original equipment (OE) for new vehicles and also as replacement parts in the aftermarket. The OE sector itself contains an element of replacement business in that vehicle builders have spares distribution operations; components supplied into the replacement sector by this route are known as OE spares.

The proportion of sales accounted for by each of the two market sectors varies widely from component to component. For 'wearing' components, such as brake linings and pads and bearings, and for certain items which require fairly regular replacement, such as filters, plugs, gaskets and seals, the aftermarket can account for 50 per cent or more of the total supply. For 'hard parts', such as power train components, the proportion supplied for replacement purposes – to engine rebuilders, for example – may be less than 20 per cent.

The OE supply chain

Many components for OE are supplied not to final vehicle assembly plants but to plants manufacturing subassemblies and systems (e.g. engines, braking systems, gearboxes, clutch assemblies). Subassembly plants are owned and operated both by independents and by the vehicle builders themselves. In the latter case the subassembly operations may be an integral part of a final vehicle assembly site but are often housed on physically separate sites.

Independent subassembly suppliers are particularly important in braking systems and within the transmission system, but also feature in other segments such as diesel engines for heavy vehicles. Where subassemblies are made by independents it is nevertheless usual for the vehicle builder to specify the supplier of at least the more critical components of the subassembly.

In-house component manufacture

The major vehicle assemblers themselves also supply a substantial proportion of the component parts of vehicles from in-house manufacture. While much of this is concerned with body shells, engine blocks and other heavy castings, it also extends to smaller and lighter components – for engines and transmission systems, for example. Overall, it is estimated that 25–50 per cent by value of the parts for new cars are supplied from in-house manufacture. The proportion varies amongst assemblers. Generally, European vehicle assemblers are towards the lower end of the range (with the British very much so), while producers in North America are generally towards the upper end. It is significant that the proportion of in-house supply is generally falling as vehicle assemblers turn increasingly to outside component suppliers.

Certain broad inferences may be drawn from a consideration of these basic features of the motor components industry:

1 Because of its diverse product and company structure, it is difficult to define, classify and measure the motor components industry as such. This applies to its location pattern as to other structural features.

2 With the exception of components manufactured in-house by vehicle assemblers themselves, the location pattern of the industry tends to be quite dispersed. For a wide range of components (especially those with a large aftermarket) proximity to vehicle assembly plants, or to separate subassembly plants, has been a less dominant consideration than might be supposed.

FORCES OF CHANGE

The motor components industry has been subject over recent years to many significant changes, which still have a long way to run. Among the driving forces of change are the following:

Increasing technical sophistication of motor vehicles

Motor vehicles have become much more sophisticated technically in recent years. Greater demands are being placed upon motor vehicle assemblers and component suppliers in terms of:

1 higher standards of vehicle performance;
2 higher safety standards;
3 improved fuel economy;
4 better emission control, meeting higher environmental standards; and
5 greater driver/passenger comfort.

In meeting these requirements, a strong theme is the development of lighter components and of electronic management and control devices for the engine, gearbox, braking, suspension and other systems within the vehicle. Multi-valve engines, turbocharging and catalytic converters are other developments directed towards the same ends.

Trend towards systems rather than individual parts

There is growing demand for self-contained 'subsystems' (or mini subassemblies) rather than individual parts. This trend reduces vehicle assembly costs, and, like the move to more sophisticated technical requirements, increases the added value in the components sector. Again, the incorporation of electronics is often a key element in new subsystems.

Reduction of in-house components supply by vehicle assemblers

The incidence of in-house components supply by the major vehicle assemblers is tending to fall (see above). There are many reasons for this trend, including the economies that may be derived from more tightly focused specialization in terms of development and manufacturing costs and capital expenditures. The increasingly high degree of specialized technical input required in almost all parts of the vehicle (see above) is an important underlying factor.

Closer involvement of component suppliers in vehicle/engine development

A corollary of the three factors already considered is that vehicle assemblers are seeking earlier and deeper involvement from component suppliers in the design and development of vehicles and engines. While price will always be a key consideration, the competitive focus for many components is shifting towards the ability of suppliers to contribute to the development process through their innovative and intellectual input, their response to demands for prototype production and their general technical support. Typically, the development process for components for new vehicle or engine models extends over 2–3 years or more. The components supplier must therefore be able to make a lengthy advance commitment of human, technical and financial resources in order to gain 'Day 1' supply contracts on the new model.

Higher quality assurance standards

Greater demands are also being made of component suppliers in terms of quality assurance, supported by statistical verification, to exacting customer standards. Zero defect supply targets are being set more widely.

Less multi-sourcing of components

In consequence of the greater inputs required from components suppliers, the incidence of multi-sourcing of components by the original equipment manufacturers (OEMs) is declining. Where a minimum of two component suppliers on an initial contract for a new vehicle model or engine used to be a norm, this is now tending to break down to a maximum of two and, in many cases, to just a single source.

Supply contracts are therefore tending to become fewer in number, but larger in the quantities and values involved and longer in duration. Second or third sources may still be brought in, especially during the later stages of the life of a particular component specification. But, for the leading players in the motor components industry, gaining 'preferred supplier' status with the major OEMs and winning initial contracts as the primary supplier are the vital considerations.

Delivery performance

Delivery performance standards have become tighter in terms of both frequency and punctuality. The wider adoption of 'just-in-time' manufacturing systems in the motor vehicle industry is raising components delivery standards still higher.

Transnational sourcing and supply

The ever-increasing internationalization of corporate organizations, design and development, production and marketing in the motor vehicle industry has crucially important implications for the component supplier. This is an especially vital factor in Europe, where no single country has a large enough vehicle production base to support, on its own, front-rank components suppliers. All the volume assemblers have plants, licensees or limited technical or production alliances with other companies in several countries, so that variants of a core range of vehicles and engines may be sourced cost-effectively for the international market. More than ever, the major OEMs are seeking close relationships with components suppliers who have not only proven technical competence but also an international presence. The advent of the 'Single Market' in the EC by the end of 1992 will strengthen still further the transnational linkages in the European motor industry.

EFFECTS ON THE STRUCTURE AND LOCATION OF THE MOTOR COMPONENTS INDUSTRY

The motors of change that have been identified have two broad and interrelated implications for the structure of the components industry. First, at least in the OE sector, the trend is towards fewer, larger components firms, with an increasingly strong technological orientation. Second, there is ever stronger emphasis, as a necessary condition of success for motor components firms, upon international organization and operations. These two factors together mean that a substantial and growing proportion of the OE market for motor components (as for assembled vehicles) is supplied by multinational firms. (This point needs to be remembered when assessing the relative strength of different countries as motor components suppliers; it is simplistic to measure this purely in terms of physical exports and imports or of output within the boundaries of each country.)

There are, in any case, limits to what can be achieved internationally by way of direct exports of motor components. Local content rules and import barriers are obvious constraints, though these are of declining significance within Europe now that Spain has an established motor vehicle industry and is a member of the EC along with Portugal and Greece. Nevertheless, there remains some natural bias to source from local suppliers regardless of any actual import barriers there may be.

But, above all, in an increasing number of cases, a physical presence is required of the components supplier in those countries where the major vehicle assemblers are themselves located. This is not simply a case of a manufacturing presence. Close links with the design and development engineering centres of the multinational vehicle companies are vital to winning component supply contracts. Similar links must also be maintained with purchasing functions, which may be centrally coordinated throughout Europe or even globally. While these linkages may be sustained and serviced across national boundaries, there are drawbacks in this situation – including language problems – which can result in competitive disadvantages.

An important, if obvious, aspect of this issue concerns internal sourcing arrangements of the multinationals for subassemblies and systems manufactured in-house. Many components are supplied to physically separate subassembly plants rather than to the point of final vehicle assembly. Thus, for example, it is significant to an engine components supplier that General Motors produces its European engines only in West Germany and Austria; and that Ford's new generation of car engines for the 1990s – the Zeta – will be sourced predominantly from the UK for all its European car assembly plants – hence the large expansion programme recently announced for the Bridgend engine facility.

Yet the components needs of the vehicle and engine builders may still be served by means of export, particularly where a supplier has a clear technical competitive edge. In the case of some components, it is not unknown for OEM customers to source on a particular plant (rather than a company), to meet their requirements in the different countries in which they operate.

The specific locational response of the European motor components industry to the various technical and commercial trends that have been identified has been expressed during the 1980s more in terms of site closures and relative shifts amongst countries in production volumes than in terms of new production sites. (An exception to this generality is Spain, where volume vehicle production has developed relatively recently in a framework of local content and import regulations.)

A major reason why comparatively few new motor components sites have emerged is that, at least until the last year or two, there has been surplus capacity in much of the motor vehicle industry. Thus, the European components industry has been restructured to a large extent by merger, acquisition and strategic alliance. This process has frequently taken place across national boundaries – a feature reinforced by the growing need for motor components suppliers to demonstrate a truly international presence. A restructuring process of this kind can be carried through more quickly and effectively by amalgamations and alliances between companies already established in one or more national markets, than by greenfield developments. Moreover, the need for additional capacity on greenfield sites has been reduced by productivity improvements arising from the installation of new machinery and manufacturing techniques, allowing greater volumes to be produced in the same factory space.

There are now at least four factors which suggest that more new greenfield sites might be established by motor components suppliers in Europe in the next few years:

1 *Capacity constraints.* Capacity constraints are now appearing in some sectors of the European motor vehicle and components industry.
2 *More out-sourcing by OEMs.* As indicated earlier, OEMs are tending to source more of their components requirements from outside suppliers as they contract their in-house components activities.
3 *'Just-in-time' systems.* OEMs in Europe are gradually introducing 'just-in-time' manufacturing systems. In some circumstances, components suppliers may be able to service these systems through the maintenance of buffer or consignment stocks held at or close to the customers' plants. However, manufacturing plants for certain components at least will increasingly need to be established in closer proximity to vehicle or subsystem assembly plants.
4 *Japanese 'transplants'.* The likely establishment of vehicle and engine assembly plants in Europe by Japanese companies will lead to a net increase in demand for locally supplied components. In

addition, these plants are likely to be organized on quite stringent 'just-in-time' principles, thus reinforcing the need for new components supply sites close to vehicle assembly plants.

5 *Lack of suitable acquisition candidates*. The increasing sophistication and higher added value of the motor components required by OEMs has led to a diminishing number of suitable candidates for acquisition by components manufacturers attempting to reinforce or extend existing high technology positions. European companies wishing to extend geographically their manufacturing bases, or US or Japanese companies seeking a European presence might well choose to establish greenfield operations rather than acquire an existing company which does not have the potential to meet the technical standards required.

As indicated in 4 and 5 above, Japanese transplants should give rise to new greenfield sites for components manufacture, often located close to these vehicle and/or engine assembly plants. Some of these new components plants are likely to be established by Japanese suppliers, reflecting their relationships with the respective vehicle manufacturers in Japan. But indigenous suppliers are also likely to benefit – both independently and in joint ventures with Japanese components suppliers. There have already been a few examples in the UK of the acquisition of local motor components companies by their Japanese counterparts. This mixture of responses in the components sector to Japanese penetration of the European motor vehicles industry will probably continue, but it is too early to discern any clear patterns.

FACTORS AFFECTING SHIFTS IN THE INTRA-EUROPEAN PATTERN OF THE MOTOR COMPONENTS INDUSTRY

As inferred in the introduction to this chapter, the main locational issue in the European motor components industry concerns relative shifts in the supply-source pattern between individual European countries. It is almost a truism that these shifts are generated predominantly by changes in the sourcing policies of the vehicle assemblers, which are, to an ever higher degree, arranged transnationally.

To analyse the relative importance of the many factors which influence the European OEMs' sourcing policies is a complex exercise well beyond the scope of this chapter. Attention has been focused largely and deliberately upon the more technical, structural and organizational factors affecting the motor vehicle assembly and components industry because these are too easily overlooked in broad-brush debates on the industrial competitiveness of individual countries and their ability to attract new investment in competition with one another. Moreover, several of the current technical and structural trends in the industry are powerful forces which can be key factors in specific sourcing decisions.

Yet, at the same time, the European vehicles market is highly price competitive and the OEMs are under constant pressure to meet consumer demands for improved performance, safety, comfort, fuel economy and a cleaner environment at minimum extra cost. This pressure is passed on to components suppliers and is reinforced by the buying power of the major OEMs. Thus, cost and price considerations remain of great importance in sourcing decisions, relating to both assembled vehicles and components supply.

Differences between national cost bases must therefore exert a considerable influence on sourcing patterns. Significant differences certainly exist. Payroll costs in the car assembly industry vary widely within Europe. Taking the period 1984–7 in order to modify the effects of exchange rate movements, payroll costs per employee/hour in West Germany were the highest in Europe. As percentages of German rates, those in Belgium and the Netherlands were in the 80–90 per cent range; Italy and France 70–75 per cent; the UK less than 60 per cent; and Spain 50 per cent. It is, however, difficult to make valid international comparisons of total production costs per unit of output, largely because differences in levels of productivity (as opposed to changes in the rate of productivity) are notoriously hard to measure. Such differences certainly appear to narrow the competitive gaps between countries, though they do not totally close them.

A further factor complicates attempts to analyse sourcing decisions in terms of pure comparative costs. The vehicle assembler is also interested in less tangible factors which might influence not only long-run costs of production but also continuity of supply. The strength and militancy of trade unions and the labour relations climate in general are factors which have had a demonstrable effect on recent European location decisions in the motor industry.

It should also be emphasized that comparative cost analyses are essentially macroeconomic. An implication of this is that in countries with a relatively low cost base but also a low overall productivity rating, individual plants which manage to attain the highest international standards of productivity might well have a significant competitive advantage in international markets. In the motor components industry, additional competitive edge may often be gained through technical superiority – a factor of increasing importance, as stressed earlier. Thus, European OEMs have considerable scope to adjust their sourcing patterns to secure overall cost benefits, while the most efficient components suppliers in lower cost locations have competitive potential to exploit.

Finally, exchange rates are a factor in the industry's responses to cost and other supply-side differences between countries. Unlike labour cost structures and productivity, exchange rates are subject to short- and medium-term fluctuation as well as to long-term movements. They are thus a volatile factor in international cost comparisons. The exchange rate has been especially important to British-based suppliers of internationally traded goods. Since sterling is still a widely traded international currency and was not part of the Exchange Rate Mechanism of the European Monetary System until October 1990, it fluctuated more widely against other major European currencies than the latter have against each other.

The effects of exchange rate movements on motor industry sourcing patterns are not, however, clear-cut or easily distinguishable. The time factor is a major complication. The development lead time on OE components contracts can be 2–3 years and new contracts may themselves run for several years, albeit subject to performance and to price variation. Thus, while exchange rate fluctuations can affect the profitability of on-going contracts to the components supplier, the influence of exchange rates on sourcing patterns is exerted only over time and more on the basis of sustained trend movements in rates than short-term variations. Moreover, the key consideration in the context of sourcing decisions is not so much movements in nominal exchange rates, but rather in real exchange rates – that is, nominal rates adjusted for relative rates of cost/price inflation in the countries concerned.

The fall of the pound sterling against the deutschmark from DM3.54 at the end of 1985 to DM2.85 a year later, at a time when labour costs per unit of output in UK manufacturing industry were stable, provides a good example of a quite decisive shift in nominal and real exchange rates. There is little doubt that this shift played a part in decisions taken in 1987 by several European vehicle assemblers to source more finished vehicles and components in the UK.

An extension of this example also illustrates how fickle the exchange rate factor can be. From DM2.85 at the end of 1986, the pound rose again to DM2.96 at end-1987 and into a range of DM3.15–3.30 in 1988 and the early part of 1989 (since when it has slipped back below DM3.00). It was noticeable that in 1988 UK imports of cars sourced from the multinationals' plants in continental Europe climbed back again, although factors other than the exchange rate were also involved

– for example, the high level of UK car demand and a strike at Ford UK early in 1988.

OE components sourcing was probably not much affected by sterling's strength in 1988 and early 1989. Product specification and supply contracts, neither of which can be varied in the short term, are considerations here. More fundamentally, UK industry itself fore-stalled the potential effects of the pound's rise in 1988 by increasing productivity strongly, and so holding down unit costs. Nevertheless, the trend towards greater components sourcing in the UK remains vulnerable to long-term sterling exchange rate movements in relation to trends in unit costs.

CONCLUSIONS

The transnational organization of the motor industry in Europe makes the components market potentially sensitive to comparative costs. Consequently, some interesting questions of international location arise.

However, apart from long-term shifts in the balance of components production between different European countries, broadly in line with the relative expansion or contraction of final vehicle assembly in those countries, recent changes in the location pattern of the components sector have been less dramatic than might have been expected. The existence of surplus capacity in the industry and the scope for cross-border mergers constitute one reason why more new components locations have not yet emerged.

Time factors also complicate attempts to establish the balance of factors currently influencing locational change. Lengthy new model development and components supply contract periods help to explain why, for example, exchange rate movements apparently fail to exert a stronger and more direct influence on locational change.

More generally, components sourcing decisions are often the out-come of a trade-off between economic and technical factors, or between relative prices and the unique technical input which each components supplier can provide. Technical considerations and their effects on buyer–seller relationships are increasingly important and a powerful force for change in the structure and location of the motor components industry.

Several of the factors that have been identified as influencing current and likely future changes in the structure of the European motor components industry point to the need for major components producing firms to have a multi-country presence. This often, though not always, necessitates control of a production unit in each (or most) of the main vehicle producing countries. Conversely, intra-national location has become a less significant issue. For lighter, non-bodywork components, the importance of proximity to vehicle assembly plants and of industrial linkages leading to concentrations of components producers has probably never been quite as great as conventional wisdom might have suggested. The relevance of these considerations has diminished further over the last three decades with the dispersion of vehicle assembly operations away from original locations, with improved road transport systems, and with changing technical factors in both manufacture and product requirements.

It is an interesting proposition that the spread of 'just-in-time' manufacturing systems in Europe – which will be hastened by Japanese vehicle assembly 'transplants' – might lead to a revival of the 'concentration' concept, with new clusters of components suppliers forming around major vehicle assembly sites. Such trends are, however, likely to be limited in terms of the range of components involved because of the sheer diversity of the components industry, the demands of components sourcing patterns across the motor vehicle industry as a whole, and the alternative means available of satisfying the varying requirements of the range of manufacturing and procurement systems covered by the 'just-in-time' label.

8 Vertical integration or disintegration? The case of the UK car parts industry

Ash Amin and Ian Smith

A decade ago, the motor components industry could still be considered a jewel in the crown of British manufacturing industry. It employed over 150,000 workers (Table 8.1), it covered over 60 per cent of total domestic demand in the industry, and it contributed over £700 million (at 1980 prices) to the manufacturing trade balance

Table 8.1 The British motor vehicle parts[a] industry: selected indicators (1980 prices)

	Employment	Gross output	Productivity (gross output per capita)	Net capital expenditure
	(£000)	*(£m)*	*(£000)*	*(£m)*
1979[b]	157.0	3075.9	19.6	235.4
1980	146.5	2629.8	17.9	132.5
1981	121.3	2181.3	18.0	93.0
1982	108.0	1997.0	18.5	54.6
1983	102.6	2036.8	19.9	44.0
1984	98.1	2062.1	21.0	63.2
1985	97.4	2175.3	22.3	73.9
1986	92.2	2098.2	22.8	88.7
1987	91.1	2155.5	23.7	87.1
Percentage annual average change				
1979–83	− 10.0	− 9.5	0.6	− 33.6
1983–7	− 2.9	+ 1.5	4.5	19.7

Source: Calculated from HMSO, *Report on the census of production* (various years)

[a]Most non-electrical components, including: KD sets for vehicles, chassis frames, sheet metal, bumpers, exhausts, springs, oil filters, carburettors, engine components, gearboxes, radiators, steering gears, axles, wheels, brakes, clutches, shock absorbers, seats, safety belts, locks, other metal parts and accessories

[b]Figures prior to 1979 not separated from those referring to the motor vehicle industry

(Table 8.2). This is no longer the case. By the mid-1980s, the industry had lost over a third of its workforce (Table 8.1), it held less than 40 per cent of a smaller domestic market (down from about £2.5 million in 1979 to £1.8 million in 1983) and, despite its efforts to maintain its past export vigour, its once healthy trade balance was looking more and more jaundiced (Table 8.2). Such was the sense of alarm about its future, that the Parliamentary Trade and Industry Select Committee launched an investigation into the nature and causes of the crisis in the industry. This long and thorough inquiry led to the publication of a weighty document in 1987, a document which offered few easy solutions (HMSO 1987).

Table 8.2   The British motor vehicle parts[a] market (1980 prices)

	Total UK market (£m)	Of which imports[b] (£m)	(%)	Total sales of UK firms (£m)	Of which exports[b] (£m)	(%)	Balance of trade (£m)	Export/ import ratio
1974	2519	412	16	3534	1426	40	1014	3.46
1975	2180	422	19	3199	1439	45	1017	3.41
1976	2418	462	19	3387	1431	42	969	3.10
1977	2171	571	26	3023	1421	47	850	2.49
1978	2447	613	25	3169	1335	42	722	2.18
1979	2298	935	41	3021	1657	55	722	1.77
1980	1699	691	41	2539	1531	60	840	2.22
1981	1474	740	50	2179	1444	66	704	1.95
1982	1528	908	59	1952	1332	68	424	1.47
1983	1799	1108	61	2005	1314	66	206	1.19
1984	1815	1162	64	2097	1443	69	281	1.24
1985	1941	1302	67	2159	1520	70	218	1.17
1986	2080	1450	70	2092	1463	70	13	1.01
1987	2336	1693	72	2141	1498	70	−195	0.88
1988[c]	2468	1566	63	2152	1251	58	−314	0.80

Source: Calculated from HMSO, *Business Monitor*, PQ 381.1 and PQ 3530 (various years)

[a] See note [a], Table 8.1

[b] Based on producer price index for home sales in the passenger car industry. Indices for overseas trade in the vehicle and vehicle parts industries not available, therefore deflated values of imports and exports not strictly accurate

[c] New system of product classification introduced in January 1988, therefore there may be some discontinuity with previous years

From the Select Committee Inquiry, as well as many other independent and press reports, could be gleaned a number of conflicting positions on the causes of decline. Disgruntled components manufacturers complained about an overpriced pound sterling, which made exports too expensive and imports too cheap. They also complained of the inhibiting effect on investment of high interest rates. Most important, however, was their dismay with the British vehicle manufacturers who were blamed for running down output, reducing local content, squeezing UK suppliers on price, and eating into the lucrative aftermarket for replacement parts (CAITS 1983; EIU 1983; Jones 1985; Monopolies and Mergers Commission 1985). In turn, the vehicle makers attacked, in most cases unfairly, the independent component manufacturers for not being competitive on price, quality and delivery in comparison to overseas suppliers, and for complacency with regard to developing export potential as well as overseas capacity.

More recently, the debate on the reasons for the industry's decline has given way to a new set of questions concerning the threats and opportunities which face this supposedly smaller but restructured industry (West Midlands Industrial Development Association 1989; Tomkins 1989). The assumption is that the worst is now over and that the industry is poised to take advantage of the upturn in particularly car manufacture in Britain. The increase in recent years of car output in the UK by Ford, the market leader, the raised local content of Talbot and GM Vauxhall cars produced in British factories, and the decision of Nissan, Toyota and Honda to produce cars in the UK, are seen as factors which could provide a significant boost to the British components industry (Done 1989).

To a large degree, this is speculation drawn in isolation of recent aggregate performance indicators. They reveal that it is the export performance of the components industry which has kept steady in the course of the late 1980s, rather than its share of the domestic market (Table 8.2). The 1.5 per cent annual average growth in output during the late 1980s (Table 8.2) is not, therefore, the result of any great improvement in winning domestic orders. UK component manufacturers may not have been the major beneficiaries of the improved demand for components within the domestic economy, which in 1988, peaked to a record value £2.5 billion (1980 prices). Notwithstanding, the significant improvement in productivity (4.5 per cent per annum) and capital investment (19.7 per cent per annum) between 1983 and 1987 (Table 8.1), employment in the industry has continued to shrink (2.9 per cent per annum), and sales have continued to hover, in real terms, around the £2 billion mark – a figure which is at least 30 per cent lower than the average for the mid–late 1970s (Table 8.2). Imports have continued to soar, curtailing the market share of UK-based manufacturers to between 30 and 35 per cent. In 1987 and 1988, for the first time in recent history, the industry registered a trade deficit of respectively £195 million and £314 million (Table 8.2). This can hardly be described as an indicator of 'good times' (Tomkins 1989) in the British components industry.

In this chapter we examine the process of restructuring within the industry and some of the key pressures which it has faced in recent years. The coverage of the chapter is partial, to the extent that it does not address developments affecting the commercial vehicle components industry or the replacement equipment market. The focus, then, is on the original equipment market for the car industry, that is, components purchased or produced by car manufacturers. The chapter also does not endeavour to cover or apportion importance between all the causes of decline in the industry, nor does it examine the effects of the process of restructuring on different types of components manufacturers (e.g. assemblers, large independents, large specialists, small independents, etc.). This is because we have addressed these questions elsewhere (Amin and Smith 1990a,b).

The chapter, instead, examines in some detail the damaging effects of two aspects of restructuring in the car assembly and components industry, which, in our assessment, are the most important challenges facing the sector. The first relates to the effects of the internationalization and 'quasi' vertical integration of the activities of the major corporations of the UK car assembly industry. We argue that the combination of international integration of both cars and in-house components production, with the increased power of the assemblers in the supply market for components, has severely restricted the opportunities for independent components manufacture in the UK. The second major development, which has serious implications in terms of local ownership and control is the delivery, in recent years, of the industry into the hands of the international oligopoly within components manufacture. Through the study of different product markets – engine components, shock absorbers, brake and clutch linings – the second half of the chapter illustrates how, as a result of intense inward investment and takeover activity in the 1980s, this industry, once dominated by small and independent domestic firms, is now controlled by a handful of international corporations, few of which are of British origin.

THE IMPACT OF RESTRUCTURING IN THE CAR ASSEMBLY INDUSTRY

In a decade or so, a number of changes have occurred in the structure of the domestic car industry and components purchasing arrangements. Notwithstanding, the potential benefits of one of these changes, namely the decision by Japanese car makers (Nissan, Honda and Toyota) to open three car factories in Britain, it is argued below that the overall effect of these changes on the components industry has been negative.

Perhaps the most significant development, in terms of market opportunities for domestic components suppliers, has been the gradual run down of car production in the UK since the mid-1970s. This has occurred in the context of rising, rather than declining, demand for cars in the domestic market. After a sharp fall in demand in the immediate aftermath of the 1974 oil crisis, from about 1.7 million cars in 1973 to under 1.2 million cars in 1975, the UK market for new cars has risen steadily to reach a record peak of around 2.2 million cars in 1988 (Table 8.3). It is not, therefore, a shortage in the level of demand for cars, but rather a shortage in the number of cars produced in Britain, which has been responsible for reducing the domestic market for original equipment.

Table 8.3 The UK car market – production and demand (millions)

	New registrations	Imports	UK car output	Exports
1973	1.66	0.45	1.74	0.63
1974	1.26	0.35	1.53	0.57
1975	1.19	0.39	1.44	0.53
1976	1.28	0.49	1.33	0.55
1977	1.32	0.60	1.28	0.59
1978	1.59	0.78	1.23	0.49
1979	1.71	0.96	1.08	0.37
1980	1.51	0.86	0.97	0.31
1981	1.48	0.82	0.96	0.30
1982	1.55	0.90	0.88	0.23
1983	1.79	1.00	1.05	0.23
1984	1.75	1.00	0.91	0.20
1985	1.83	1.07	1.05	0.22
1986	1.88	1.07	1.02	0.18
1987	2.01	1.04	1.13	0.22
1988	2.22	1.25	1.23	0.24

Source: Society of Motor Manufacturers and Traders, the *UK Motor Vehicle Industry* (various years)

Owing to rising import penetration from a level of around 33 per cent of the domestic market in the early 1970s to an average of about 57 per cent in the late 1980s (Table 8.4), and owing also to the 60 per cent reduction in the quantity of exports during the same period

(Table 8.3), UK car output has dropped from a level of well over 1.5 million cars in the early 1970s to around the one million mark during the 1980s (Table 8.3). Car output has increased since 1987, but this has been due largely to an increase in the final assembly, rather than the full production of cars by Peugeot-Talbot cars as well as, since 1988, of Nissan cars. The UK, therefore, has gone from being a sizeable manufacturer of cars which once dominated the domestic markets and exported over a third of its output, to a significantly smaller actor in both the domestic and export markets. The significance of this development on the car components industry is not difficult to infer. It has caused a decline in the volume of demand for original equipment from components makers, which, in turn, has put severe pressure on survival prospects in export markets, owing to the loss of cost-reducing scale opportunities.

Table 8.4 Import penetration in the UK new car market (per cent)

	All imports	Tied imports[a]
1975	33.0	2.5
1976	37.5	7.5
1977	45.0	12.0
1978	49.5	14.5
1979	56.0	19.5
1980	56.5	24.0
1981	55.5	22.0
1982	57.0	24.0
1983	57.0	25.0
1984	57.5	23.5
1985	58.5	23.5
1986	57.0	19.5
1987	51.5	16.0
1988	56.5	20.0

Source: Society of Motor Manufacturers and Traders, *The UK Motor Vehicle Industry* (various years)

[a]Imports by companies based in the UK – Ford, Peugeot-Talbot and Vauxhall (GM). Imports of Nissan excluded, since UK productive capacity not fully realized

The assemblers have squeezed the British components makers also in another important way, which is related to the strategy of Ford, General Motors and Peugeot-Talbot to integrate their production and components purchasing network on a European basis. Before Britain's entry into the EC, manufacturers, irrespective of their ownership, sourced all of their cars sold in Britain from local factories, and these cars were also built almost entirely from British components

(Rhys 1979). This is no longer the case. Progressively, the above mentioned multinationals have chosen to integrate their European facilities in order to rationalize capacity and derive plant-based scale economies through either task or car model specialization (Maxcy 1981; UNCTC 1983; Shepherd *et al.* 1985). This had the effect of raising the import of cars built in European factories, which are then sold in the domestic market as 'British' cars. By the mid-1980s, the 'tied-imports' of Ford, General Motors and Peugeot-Talbot from Europe amounted to no less than a quarter of the total number of new cars sold in Britain (Table 8.4). The import of such a large volume of cars (441,000 in 1988), accounting for 58 per cent of Peugeot-Talbot sales, 39 per cent of General Motors sales and 43 per cent of Ford sales in the UK, has removed a sizeable market opportunity from British components makers. The cars of particularly Peugeot-Talbot and General Motors sourced from European factories have a very low content of British-made parts since the UK is a small source base within their global operations.

Another, more direct cause of reduced demand for British original equipment is that the local content of cars made within Britain itself has dropped since the early 1970s, when the use of imported parts was negligible. The only exceptions are Rover and Jaguar, who, notwithstanding their efforts in the 1980s to purchase cheaper and better quality components from European sources, still continue to purchase 87 per cent, by value, of their externally sourced parts and materials from British-based suppliers (*Financial Times* 15 May 1987; HMSO 1987). The paradox, however, is that the bigger of these two British-owned companies, Rover, which accounts for about 40 per cent of British car output, now faces a very difficult future. The company, which held over 30 per cent of the UK car market in the mid-1970s, has progressively lost its market share, reaching a trough of 15 per cent in 1987 and 1988. It now faces direct competition also from the Japanese multinationals setting up in Britain, who are likely to erode Rover's market share in the years to come, unless Honda is allowed to purchase the company from British Aerospace. This will deal a severe blow to that 40 per cent or so of the car components industry which Rover currently keeps afloat, especially in the West Midlands (Bessant *et al.* 1984).

The question regarding the local content of cars built by the old established multinationals in Britain is quite different. They have also posed a serious threat to British component makers, but not because of problems related to survival in the market-place. Instead, the reduction in local content is very much the result of a strategy pursued after the oil crisis and membership of the EC, to rationalize sourcing requirements. The key new development has been the integration of components supply on a Europe-wide basis for individual plants, as a means of reaping the benefits of scale economies, avoiding unnecessary sourcing duplication and obtaining best practice from preferred suppliers (CIS 1978; Beynon 1984).

The significance of this development in terms of the local purchase of components has varied between the three companies, in proportion to each one's scale of-car production in Britain. The local content of General Motors and Peugeot-Talbot cars is dismal. In comparison to the 1960s, the UK operations of both companies amount to little more than the final assembly of major parts and subassemblies imported from Europe. This explains why, despite their recent attempts to gain credibility as 'British' manufacturers, neither one buys more than an estimated 30−35 per cent by value of its externally sourced materials and components from local suppliers. Together, the two companies are responsible for about a fifth of the 2.2 million cars sold in Britain every year, and yet the net benefit which they have brought to the components industry is drawn from the 30−35 per cent of local content built into the mere 240,000 cars assembled in British factories.

On the whole, British suppliers have been penalized by the integration of production and purchasing on a European basis by the two companies: a process of restructuring which has seen a run-down in the size and status (in terms of local content) of British operations. Although in the last two years, both have claimed to have raised UK car output in response to rising market share, this change amounts to little in comparison to the situation before the mid-1970s. More importantly, raised 'local content' has tended to signify simply greater final assembly, or, especially in the case of Peugeot-Talbot, increased purchases from its traditional major continental suppliers who have opened new facilities in Britain. The benefits to British suppliers appear to have been negligible. This danger of bringing only final assembly to Britain could also apply to the new engine plant which General Motors plans to build at Ellesmere Port in the North-West.

Ford, too, has integrated its car production system on a European basis, but owing to its strong commitment, at least until hitherto, to maintaining both a high level of car output and the full car production cycle within Britain, this integration has had less deleterious consequences on the components industry. Ford has the largest share of the UK car market − over 26 per cent in 1988 − and it produces about 335,000 cars annually in Britain. Furthermore, over 65 per cent by value of the externally purchased materials and components in UK-built cars are supplied from domestic sources (HMSO 1987). In contrast to General Motors and Peugeot-Talbot, Ford's British operations amount to significantly more than merely final assembly. Together with Rover, the company has played a critical role in bolstering the components industry. This, however, could be threatened if the company continues with its policy, as suggested by its decision to stop producing the Sierra model in Britain, to reduce the output of especially better quality cars in Britain. The justification for local components supply based upon maintaining large-scale local car output could then disappear.

In addition to facing the consequences of the European integration of production and sourcing by the car makers, British components suppliers, particularly the smaller ones, have suffered from the assemblers' move towards single sourcing from large, 'preferred status' firms. There seems to be virtually no evidence of British car makers moving towards the Japanese or the West Midlands system of the 1950s and 1960s, characterized by the supply of components from a myriad of locally based small firms and subcontractors. Instead, the assemblers have dramatically reduced their supplier numbers by awarding larger and longer-term contracts to a selection of the biggest components makers.

There appear to be several reasons for this shift towards single-sourcing. With increasing global competition in the car industry, the assemblers have sought to control the price of components at the same time as insisting for better quality, innovative capability and delivery from suppliers (Way 1989). These are conditions which have worked in favour of the large component manufacturers who have the resources to develop scale economies, devote large budgets to research and development and quality control, and utilize their organizational strength to improve on delivery. It also appears that as car makers move towards fully automated assembly, they are increasingly sourcing components in a modular form from large component manufacturers, who are given the responsibility for delivering entire assemblies of parts (Way 1989). The move towards lasting partnerships and strategic alliances between car and components makers who qualify for single supplier status has added further pressure to smaller suppliers already beleaguered by other problems such as those outlined earlier. Increasingly, the choice they face is that between collapse and becoming underpaid subcontractors for the suppliers of component systems.

This new development, however, is not just a preference for large firms, but for multinationals with a global presence, that is, companies with the capacity to supply to assemblers anywhere in the world. It is a development which has risked penalizing also the large British components, since only a few, such as GKN, Lucas and Pilkington, are global corporations. In fact, in the late 1980s, Ford, General Motors and Peugeot-Talbot increasingly have awarded major contracts to their traditional non-British global suppliers, who have established a presence in Britain through new investment or the takeover of domestic companies (Tomkins 1989). Significant examples include the US-owned Arvin Industries which dominates the global exhaust industry, and shock absorber giant Monroe Auto Equipment, Valeo from France specializing in heating equipment, and Bosch, the German multinational. In other words, the new components' purchasing strategies of the UK assemblers are resulting in the further concentration of the British components industry in the hands of global actors.

Reduced car output in Britain, tied-imports by Ford, General Motors and Peugeot-Talbot, the decline of Rover, poor levels of local content, and new supplier relations, are all developments within the British assembly industry which have crippled a very large section of the once numerous and independent components sector. In this context of globalized car production and components supply, the arrival of the Japanese car manufacturers – who have selected Britain as an export base for a potentially huge, post-1992, single European car market – has been seen as a major opportunity for revitalizing the components industry. In 1988, Nissan assembled 56,000 cars in its Sunderland factory, and is committed to building 200,000 cars a year by 1992–3. Toyota plans to build 100,000 cars a year by 1995, rising to 200,000 a year by 1997–8, at Burnaston, near Derby. Honda is to build 100,000 cars a year from 1994 at its site in Swindon in the South, which like Nissan's in the North-East, will also include an engine plant. By the second half of the 1990s, Japanese car makers will account for about a third of the prospected 2 million cars made in Britain (Done 1989). Total car production, therefore, will be back to the levels reached in the halcyon years before the 1970s, and this should give the components industry enough scale opportunities for increasing manufacturing capacity in the UK.

This optimism, however, is not fully justified. The speculated scale opportunities may not materialize, since if the Japanese assemblers significantly reduce the market share of particularly Rover, General Motors and Peugeot-Talbot, this could lead to the reduction of car output in Britain by the latter companies. In other words car production, and therefore also the supply of parts, might simply change hands, rather than double the present level. If however, the bulk of Japanese car output is for export to Europe, and achieving this will be no easy task, then, of course, there will be no deleterious impact on the output levels of other UK car producers, since their domestic market shares will remain unaffected.

In terms of local content, all three Japanese companies have agreed to source the equivalent of 80 per cent of the ex-works price of a car locally. But as this indicator includes all costs, including those of labour, marketing and so on, the real boost for British components suppliers, calculated from the percentage of externally purchased components, is likely to be significantly lower. There is little doubt, at least in the case of Nissan, who plan to establish a sheet metal stamping operation, body subassembly and a full engine plant by 1992, that the stimulus to components suppliers will be greater than that of General Motors and Peugeot-Talbot, who achieve little more than final assembly in Britain. On the other hand, it has to be emphasized that, contrary to popular opinion, the term 'local' has been agreed by the British government to mean purchases within the EC, and not Britain. This generous definition of local content has effectively ruled out any incentive or pressure to bring business to British suppliers.

Nissan, however, has promised that the bulk of its purchases, for cost and quality reasons related to just-in-time delivery, will be made in Britain (HMSO 1987). This, however, raises the question of who will be the major beneficiaries of purchases in Britain. The early experiences of Nissan tend to show that the behaviour of the Japanese multinationals may not be really that different from the new sourcing strategies being developed by the other multinationals. It appears that smaller and local suppliers in the vicinity of the Sunderland plant are not numerous, and more importantly, tend to supply only low-tech and often non-specialist parts such as plastic mouldings, trimmings, paint, seat covers, and nuts and bolts. The bigger and the more specialist contracts, predictably, have gone to the larger national giants such as TI, Lucas and GKN.

More worrying, however, for British components makers is that the vast bulk of trade with Nissan, as well as Toyota and Honda, will be snapped up by the giant companies with so-called international presence. Bosch, Devalit Plastik and Eisenwerk Bruhl from Germany, Magneti Marelli from Italy, through its takeover of Lucas's electrical operations, and several other US and French giants (Arvin, Monroe, Montupet, Faure, Valeo and Plastic Omnium) have or are about to invest in Britain in order to snap up work also from the Japanese car makers. Furthermore, there is the strong possibility of inward investment from Japanese components makers, which could lead to an onslaught on indigenous manufacturers, as it appears to have done in the US after the recent arrival of more than 300 Japanese companies which followed the assemblers (Tomkins 1989). Through takeovers, joint ventures and greenfield investments, this process has begun in Britain too, as confirmed by the presence of Ikeda (car seats), Calsonic (radiators and exhausts), Yuasa (batteries) and Nippon-Seiki (dashboard instruments). Some of the companies (e.g. Calsonic, Hashimoto and Yamato) are subsidiaries of Nissan, which represents a move towards forward vertical integration rather than the offer of new business to independent companies. This method of raising local content begs the question of whether these sources of supply are, in turn, importing the majority of their assembled parts from Japan.

A return to the old system in Britain based upon a multitude of indigenous companies supplying assemblers sourcing the entire car locally is inconceivable. Instead, the absence of a national giant (Rover) and the delivery of the car industry into the hands of the multinationals, for the variety of reasons outlined in this section, has led to the decline and concentration of the car components industry in fewer and foreign hands. The assemblers are, of course, also producers rather than simply purchasers of components. But, here too, as the next section illustrates with the example of petrol engine production, a similar restructuring has been at work.

IN-HOUSE COMPONENTS MANUFACTURE: PETROL ENGINES

The manufacture of car engines is exclusively an in-house operation and, where scale economies are forthcoming, this usually takes place in close association with assembly. Of the major assemblers only Ford and Rover have sufficient volume manufacture in the UK to justify local manufacture, although Nissan has stated its intention to establish a full engine plant at Sunderland by 1992 (HMSO 1987). Until 1984, Talbot also manufactured a small volume of engines for export at Coventry, although this business has now ceased following the demise of the Iranian car kit contract.

The gradual run-down of car engine manufacture in the UK closely parallels the contraction of the assembly industry. In 1982, just over one million units were produced compared to just over two million in 1972. In contrast to commercial vehicle engines, the most severe contraction in car engine output occurred during the early 1970s immediately following EC entry, a period characterized by a severe decline in exports. A further severe rationalization occurred at the end of the 1970s which marked the start of a major upsurge in engine imports. Although there are no separately published figures for car engines, it would seem that UK output has continued to decline during the 1980s and now stands somewhere about the 750,000 mark. However, the expansion of Ford's engine plant at Bridgend has probably slowed down the rate of contraction and served to compensate for the rationalization of engine manufacture at Dagenham and at Coventry where a Rover plant was closed in 1982. Thus a markedly favourable balance of trade during the early 1970s was gradually eroded by the mid-1970s, and after having stabilized during the late 1970s and early 1980s, was turned into a huge deficit from 1984 onwards. By 1987, the latest year for which figures are available, over 70 per cent of the domestic market was supplied through imports and the trade deficit in petrol engines amounted to over £260 million.

It is apparent from the origins of these imports that a very high proportion are of a tied nature, i.e. brought in by UK assemblers from their own production plants overseas. A major increase in engines from Japan in 1986 was to be expected following the start of Nissan's assembly operation at Sunderland. However, there was a rise of similar magnitude in the value of engines of German origin following Ford's decision to source the Sierra engine from Cologne, and also a big increase in the value of engines imported from Spain, which again suggests Ford's involvement (Fiesta engines from Valencia). Similarly, the major increase in the value of petrol engine imports from Australia in 1982 and Austria in 1987 points to their origin as being General Motors new engine plants in Melbourne and Vienna respectively. By comparison, imports from France (Peugeot-Talbot), although showing a tendency to increase, have remained at a very modest level indeed.

In contrast, exports of petrol engines, having increased during the early 1980s tailed off again after 1984. It also seems that the demise of the Iranian car kit business made only a minimal contribution to this fall. More significant has been the fall in the value of exports to Spain after 1984 and to West Germany in 1987, both of which suggest that Ford may be placing an increased emphasis upon local sourcing in Europe, which calls into question Bridgend's long-term role as a production base for Europe (although the drop in exports to West Germany may prove to be a temporary phenomenon related to currency fluctuations). Apart from Iran, other small export markets lost to the UK include South Africa and Eire. In the latter case, the lifting of import restrictions on cars in 1984 resulted in the cessation of local assembly by Ford and hence a marked decline in engine exports from the UK.

In summary, the engine market, like the original equipment industry, displays most clearly the problems of fragmentation of the UK car market and the effects of European-wide integration of production facilities by the major assemblers, leading to declining local manufacture and exports and increased import penetration of in-house components. There is no doubt, however, that without the major investment by Ford at Bridgend, the situation would have been very much worse. In 1985, Bridgend appears to have been the sole source of UK petrol engine exports, with over two-thirds of its 390,000 units exported to Europe (HMSO 1987). In view of this, Ford's stated intention to increase local sourcing in Europe, through a 'kanban'-type supply system must be cause for concern, particularly as Valencia and Cologne produce the same types of engine as those made at Bridgend (Escort, Orion and Fiesta). Nor do the prospects for Nissan's engine plant at Sunderland look particularly rosy unless the company can achieve a significant increase in its European market share. A production target of 200,000 units per annum will have to be approached if the plant is to achieve viability, and in view of French and Italian resistance to Nissan's European exports, this will not be easy. Thus the prospects for car engine components manufacturers, particularly those reliant on local assembly, look anything but bright, and as we shall see in the following section, this sector has already been decimated by the developments outlined above.

ENGINE COMPONENTS

Compared to other EC markets, a relatively high proportion of engine components are outsourced in the UK. For example, in the case of engine pistons only 15 per cent of the UK assemblers' requirements are supplied in-house, compared to 60 per cent in Spain, 55 per cent in France and 25 per cent in West Germany and Italy (Monopolies and Mergers Commission 1984). A recent trend towards increased out-sourcing to take advantage of technological developments by specialist component manufacturers has therefore had least scope in the UK, where outsourcing is already at a high level. A second distinguishing characteristic of most UK engine component markets is the high degree of dominance achieved by individual specialist manufacturers; AE in pistons and rings, AE and GKN in bearings, and TRW in valves. In fact, the level of market concentration has recently increased still further through T&N's acquisition of both AE in 1986 and GKN Vandervell in 1988, so that the original equipment markets for engine pistons and bearings in the UK are now effectively in the hands of one company. Elsewhere in Europe this situation does not appertain and the assemblers still have a choice with respect to which suppliers they use.

An increasing reluctance to depend upon one source of supply has thus motivated UK engine assemblers to turn towards alternative suppliers in Europe, thereby dragging in imports. The Monopolies and Mergers Commission, in turning down GKN's bid for AE in 1983, were concerned about the effects of the merger on the UK's balance of trade in engine bearings, having noticed the deterioration in pistons, a market effectively monopolized by AE. It is to be hoped that the bringing together of the GKN Vandervell and AE Glacier Bearing business under the T&N banner does not confirm the Monopolies and Mergers Commission's worst fears.

A consistent data series for engine component sales in the UK is only available from 1981 but nevertheless shows that in spite of an 11 per cent real increase the value of the home market, the home and overseas sales of UK manufacturers fell by almost one-third in real terms by 1987 (Table 8.5). During the same period a substantial overseas trade surplus of £78 million was turned into a deficit of £39 million as a result of both rising imports and the falling real value of exports.

The relative importance of the aftermarket for engine components varies substantially from product to product, but in 1981 would seem

Table 8.5 Sales and overseas trade performance of UK engine component firms, 1979–87 (1980 prices)

	Home and overseas sales of UK firms	Of which exports		Sales in UK market	Of which imports	
	(£m)	*(£m)*	*(%)*	*(£m)*	*(£m)*	*(%)*
1981	249	181	73	177	109	62
1983	196	129	66	172	105	61
1985	203	138	68	182	117	64
1987	169	117	69	197	145	74
Percentage change 1981–7	− 32	− 35		+ 11	+ 33	

Source: *Business Monitor*, PQ 3530, Motor Vehicle Parts

to have accounted for just over half of all UK sales (EIU 1983). The aftermarket is least important for pistons, rings and bearings which are only normally replaced as part of the engine reconditioning process, and most important for fast-moving items such as oil and air filters and fuel pumps. No published data exist to indicate whether replacement sales have kept up better than original equipment sales, although given the decline in demand for the latter, one suspects this to be the case. Certainly, a high and probably increasing proportion of UK piston ring and bearing exports are destined for the aftermarket and this is also true of bearing imports. In contrast, piston and ring imports in 1982 were overwhelmingly intended for the original equipment market, providing confirmation that UK assemblers have turned to alternative overseas suppliers as a result of AE's dominance of this market (Monopolies and Mergers Commission 1984).

Engine component imports from West Germany have, in fact, increased substantially since 1979, indicating that AE's main European competitors, Mahle and Karl Schmidt are probably the main source. In 1979, the trade deficit with West Germany in engine components was just over £40 million; by 1987 it had risen to over £100 million, and but for this the UK's aggregate balance of trade would have been substantially positive. However, another contributory factor to the UK's deteriorating trade performance was the contraction of a number of important export markets, particularly Spain, Italy and Mexico. Although not substantially increasing, exports to the US, the UK's largest single market, held up reasonably well as did those to France and West Germany. The reasons for the decline in these export markets are not clear, although both Ford and GM have in-house piston capacity in Spain and Mexico, and AE itself has a major facility in Italy (AE Borgo) which has undergone considerable expansion in recent years, primarily through the acquisition of Eaton's Italian subsidiary, Nova.

The predominant response of the major original equipment manufacturers, AE and GKN to the contraction of demand at home and the loss of overseas export markets, has been to cut back UK capacity. GKN for example, having acquired Sheepbridge's piston and ring interests in 1979, had completely withdrawn from the market by 1985 through wholesale closures involving the loss of over 400 jobs at Slough, King's Lynn and Northampton. GKN has also rationalized its UK bearings interests following a catastrophic decline in exports from 47 per cent of turnover in 1980 to only 5 per cent in 1982 (GKN Vandervell, Annual Reports). This was immediately followed by the closure of Vandervell's Tremorfa factory in Wales. Although it is difficult to say to what extent this decision was related to export replacement, GKN Vandervell does have an overseas production facility at Brunico in Italy. AE's response to falling UK sales has been equally energetic, particularly in the Cylinder Components Division where employment was cut back by over 5,000 between 1979 and 1983, involving major rationalization of Wellworthy's piston manufacturing operations at Lymington and Plymouth. AE's 1982 Annual Report indicates that these cut-backs also followed a decline in original equipment export sales, but does not indicate in which overseas markets this fall occurred. Rationalization has been less severe in the Bearings Division where sales have held up reasonably well. Nevertheless, even here, UK output declined by 14 per cent between 1980 and 1982 and there were over 1,000 job losses in the Division as a whole between 1979 and 1983 (Monopolies and Mergers Commission 1984).

In view of the continuing build-up of overseas production facilities by both companies it is difficult to accept that UK exports have not been to some degree affected. It is also difficult to accept that the original motive for overseas expansion was the contraction of the UK assembly industry when both firms had extensive interests in Europe long before the onset of decline. For example, AE acquired piston interests in France and Italy as early as 1960, whilst GKN acquired bearing interests in Italy in 1967 through the takeover of Vandervell Products. In fact, AE continued to build up its bearing interests in Europe throughout the 1970s, principally through the acquisition of Deva Werke of West Germany in 1975 and Société Industrielle des Coussinets of France in 1979. More recently, attention has switched to North America with the construction of new piston facilities in Alabama and South Bend, Indiana in 1986. GKN too has moved into transatlantic engine parts manufacture through a joint venture with Sintermex of Mexico in 1985. As this venture is primarily intended to supply the United States market, it is to be hoped that this will not be at the expense of UK exports, given that the US remains the leading market for engine parts (Table 8.6).

SHOCK ABSORBERS

From an area of specialist engineering in which the assemblers themselves have significant in-house capability in the UK, we now turn to a relatively mature product, the requirement for which is usually outsourced to demonstrate how the same processes of international concentration and quasi-vertical integration are at work. The European

Table 8.6 Overseas trade balance in engine components by source and destination countries (1980 prices)

	1979			1987		
	Imports (£m)(a)	Exports (£m)(b)	Ratio (a)/(b)	Imports (£m)(a)	Exports (£m)(b)	Ratio (a)/(b)
West Germany	37.6	6.5	5.8	58.3	10.2	5.7
Italy	10.9	3.5	3.1	14.1	3.0	4.7
France	7.5	5.3	1.4	10.0	6.4	1.6
Belgium	4.4	4.3	1.0	8.5	4.0	2.1
Netherlands	2.2	5.0	0.4	2.2	3.7	0.6
Spain	0.0	6.8	NA[a]	2.4	1.5	1.6
EC total	64.5	31.4	2.1	96.9	33.0	2.9
Sweden	2.3	5.1	2.2	4.0	5.3	1.3
Iran	0.0	7.1	NA	0.0	2.5	NA
US	23.2	22.3	1.0	21.9	18.8	1.2
Mexico	0.0	13.0	NA	0.0	1.5	NA
Japan	5.3	0.0	NA	7.3	0.0	NA
Total	105.0	175.0	0.6	145.0	117.0	1.2

Source: Overseas Trade Statistics of the UK (HMSO)

[a]NA, Not applicable

shock absorber market provides an excellent representative case study of how the approach of 1992 has stimulated a rush of cross-border takeovers, leading to the demise of smaller national suppliers and the emergence of a small dominant group of internationally integrated producers. The recent acquisition (May 1989) of Armstrong Equipment's shock absorber division by Tenneco of the United States may thus be viewed as part of a rapidly accelerating process of seller concentration with the EC, which has established four US and two West German companies as the dominant independent suppliers.

Apart from Tenneco three other US corporations have emerged as major suppliers to the car industry: ITT through its controlling interest in Alfred Teves of West Germany and Koni BV of the Netherlands; Allied Signal through its control of DBA; and Arvin Industries, a relative latecomer to Europe, but a major supplier to Ford and General Motors in the United States. Arvin's shock absorber interests date only from its acquisition of the Maremont Corporation in 1986 which brought in Gabriel, a major West German manufacturer, with facilities also in Belgium. In 1989 these interests were extended by the acquisition of AP Amortiguadores in Spain from TI of the UK, who like Armstrong also found survival in this sector increasingly difficult. Tenneco, through the takeover of Armstrong also acquired interests in Spain (Armstrong Amortiguadores) to add to existing manufacturing interests in West Germany, Belgium and France. Finally, Allied Signal's acquisition of Bendix-DBA in 1982 brought in manufacturing facilities in Italy, the Netherlands and West Germany.

Only two West German firms have proved large enough to withstand the US onslaught on the European shock absorber market: Fichtel and Sachs, recently acquired by Mannesmann, and Boge AG, the only significant independent European producer. Apart from the UK market which they have preferred to service through exports, both of these companies have manufacturing interests throughout Europe and in the United States and thus can be regarded as major players on the world scene.

Several of the major European car manufacturers also have significant in-house shock absorber manufacturing capability. In the UK car industry, for example, the market for original equipment has been mainly limited to Ford and Rover amongst the mass producers, as GM, Talbot and Nissan all have in-house capacity elsewhere in Europe. This is perhaps the major reason why scale production economies have been difficult to achieve in the UK and why the two major indigenous suppliers of original equipment, Armstrong and Woodhead have failed to survive in this market. Armstrong with 80–85 per cent of the car market sold off its shock absorber interests to Tenneco in May 1989, whilst Jonas Woodhead, with a similar level of dominance of the commercial vehicle market, disposed of its facilities in a management buy-out in October 1985. The latter is thus the only remaining indigenous UK manufacturing operation in this market, although much more heavily reliant on the aftermarket.

The inability of the UK's two leading producers of shock absorbers to survive in this highly international market, must be attributed primarily to the erosion of their domestic market position. Thus the real value of home and overseas sales of UK companies (which can reasonably be equated with the combined sales of Armstrong and Woodhead) fell by 36 per cent between 1979 and 1984, and has continued to fall at a slightly reduced rate up to the present time (see Table 8.7), so that by 1988 sales were 47 per cent down in real terms on 1979 levels. Most of this can be attributed to a fall in demand for external sales within the UK as a result of rising imports of vehicles (the real value of UK market sales in 1988 was still 21 per cent down on the 1979 value, although having recovered somewhat since 1982) and the remainder to rising imports of shock absorbers. In 1979 imports took only 10 per cent of the UK shock absorber market, whereas by 1988 they were responsible for over 46 per cent. Although some important export markets, notably Iran, were lost during this period, exports as a proportion of total sales were maintained at around 10 per cent, which, however, also represents a fall in their real value.

Table 8.7 Sales and overseas trade performance in shock absorbers, 1979–88 (1980 prices)

	Home and overseas sales of UK firms (£m)	Of which exports		Sales in UK market (£m)	Of which imports	
		(£m)	(%)		(£m)	(%)
1979	87.9	8.3	9.4	87.9	8.3	9.4
1982	56.3	7.4	13.1	57.7	8.8	15.3
1984	56.6	7.8	13.8	60.0	11.2	18.7
1986	46.4	4.5	9.7	56.4	14.5	25.7
1988	46.8	9.8	20.9	69.4	32.4	46.7
Percentage change						
1979–88	− 46.8	+ 17.9		− 21.0	+ 290.4	

Source: Business Monitor, PQ 3530, Motor Vehicle Parts

As with most other component markets, the primary source of shock absorber imports is West Germany, followed by Belgium and the Netherlands. The West German share of imports rose from 42 per cent in 1979 to 56 per cent in 1987, whilst imports from the Low Countries also increased substantially in real terms. Although Japan and Spain (Kayaba) also became important sources of imports, in real value terms, their contribution still remains small (see Table 8.8). By inference, therefore, the primary reason for rising import penetration would seem to be the assemblers' strategy of using alternative suppliers within the Community, probably Fichtel and Sachs, Boge, and Gabriel in West Germany, and Monroe and Koni in Belgium and the Netherlands respectively. It is not clear whether the motives for second sourcing in Europe have to do with cost factors or, as in the case of engine components, the assemblers' determination to break Armstrong's dominance of the original equipment market. Nor have any data been published since 1981 to indicate whether the rising tide of imports is primarily intended for the original or replacement equipment market, although between 1978 and 1981 imports of production parts rose from 37 per cent of total shock absorber imports to 58 per cent. This indicates that it is therefore the original equipment market which is primarily responsible for the deteriorating balance of trade in this sector. Further, whilst exports of replacement parts during this period comfortably exceeded imports, imports of production parts were almost double the value of production part exports by 1981.

Table 8.8 Overseas trade balance in shock absorbers by source and destination countries (1980 prices)

	1979			1987		
	Imports (£m)(a)	Exports (£m)(b)	Ratio (a)/(b)	Imports (£m)(a)	Exports (£m)(b)	Ratio (a)/(b)
West Germany	3.5	0.4	8.0	11.5	1.1	10.5
Belgium	2.2	0.4	5.0	4.8	0.1	48.0
Netherlands	1.4	0.3	4.7	2.3	0.2	11.5
France	0.3	0.3	1.0	0.1	0.3	0.3
Spain	0.1	0.1	1.0	0.5	0.1	5.0
Eire	0.0	0.6	NA[a]	0.0	0.1	NA
EC total	7.5	2.1	3.6	19.4	2.7	7.2
US	0.3	0.1	3.0	0.3	0.7	0.4
Canada	0.0	0.8	NA	0.0	0.1	NA
Japan	0.1	0.0	NA	0.1	0.0	NA
Iran	0.0	0.4	NA	0.0	0.0	NA
Total	8.3	8.3	1.0	20.6	5.4	3.8

Source: Overseas Trade Statistics of the UK (HMSO)

[a]NA, Not applicable

The loss of a number of important overseas export markets, particularly Iran, Canada and Eire, also contributed to a period of sustained loss-making at both Armstrong and Woodhead after 1981. In real terms the value of UK shock absorber exports fell by almost 40 per cent between 1979 and 1987, with only three export markets holding up reasonably well: West Germany, the US and Spain. It must be stressed, however, that in spite of this, imports of shock absorbers from West Germany still outstripped exports to West Germany by a factor of ten throughout this period and only in the case of the US was there a surplus on the trade balance in 1987. What data there are, suggest that overseas original equipment markets have been particularly hard to penetrate without local production, with at least two-thirds of UK exports destined for the replacement market in 1981. Both companies have acquired or set up overseas production facilities: Armstrong in Canada, Spain and France, and Woodhead in France. It seems, therefore, that lost export markets in Canada and France may have been the result of export replacement by local production, although exports to France, where Armstrong acquired Newton in 1979 and Woodhead acquired Amortex in 1980, were never of significant proportions.

The response of Armstrong and Woodhead to declining market opportunities in the UK has been remarkably similar. Both have sought to decrease their reliance on shock absorbers through diversification into more secure product markets both inside and outside the motor industry. Thus Armstrong has sought to build up its fastenings division in which it has a dominant position in the UK market, whilst Woodhead has increasingly concentrated upon springs and suspension systems for commercial vehicle makers in which it has a similar degree of dominance. Second, both have rationalized unprofitable motor component interests at home and overseas through plant closures and divestments to foreign competitors. For example, before selling off its shock absorber business to Tenneco in 1989, Armstrong had already sold its exhaust interests to 'an unnamed European buyer' and its radiator business to T&N (Coventry Motor Fittings). Overseas interests have also been savagely rationalized with the sale of Newton DFA, its French shock absorber subsidiary in 1985, a move paralleled by Woodhead in 1988 through the sale of Amortex CRIM. Armstrong also closed down its Australian automotive business in 1983, followed by its French and German trading subsidiaries in 1984.

In the UK both companies complain of the downward pressure on prices exerted by their major customers after 1981, with the result that cost increases in respect of purchased materials and services cannot be recovered. In 1983, for example, Woodhead was forced to abandon the production of a high-volume shock absorber for a car manufacturer because there was no profit at the quoted price. Both also suffered from the relative strength of the pound during the early 1980s as well as the increasingly complex product specifications of their customers. The former undermined the competitiveness of UK exports, whilst the latter necessitated major capital investment at a time of recurrent loss-making. It is not surprising, therefore, that they were forced to adopt draconian rationalization measures during the period from 1981 to 1985. Woodhead, for example, cut employment by almost a half during this period whilst consolidating shock absorber manufacture on one site at Ossett through the closure of the Sheffield pressings plant. Armstrong, too, cut its labour force by 40 per cent between 1979 and 1984 through the closure of Beverley and the concentration of shock absorber manufacture in the York plant in 1982. It is thus rather ironic that shortage of manufacturing capacity should lead to a need for expensive outsourcing in 1988. The resultant losses appear to have been a deciding factor in the sale of the division to Tenneco.

In summary, the sector illustrates the way in which two indigenous medium-sized original equipment manufacturers have been squeezed out of a mass-production component market by cost reduction strategies employed by multinational assemblers. Their combined monopoly or near monopoly of the UK original equipment market proved to be of little significance from 1973 onwards when the assemblers were able to import more cheaply from in-house or alternative independent sources within the EC. Partly as a reaction to these developments, both Armstrong and Woodhead attempted to internationalize their interests after 1979, but the strategy was ineffective against competitors who were much larger and more highly internationalized than themselves. The dismantling of their overseas operations was thus merely a prelude to their ultimate withdrawal from the industry. It remains to be seen whether just-in-time delivery will ensure the survival of shock absorber manufacture in the UK, given the overcapacity existing in Europe and given also the relatively small scale of operations at York and Ossett.

BRAKE AND CLUTCH LININGS

The original equipment market for brake and clutch linings provides a major contrast to the engine component and shock absorber markets in exhibiting all the features of a mature international oligopoly. It is also distinctive in that two UK-based multinational corporations, T&N and BBA, have established themselves, along with Valeo of France and Bendix of the United States, as dominant suppliers to the clutch and brake manufacturers worldwide. In spite of this, the UK industry does not seem to have greatly benefited, with declining sales and employment and a marked tendency for exports to be replaced by overseas production facilities. Nevertheless, as a result of the dominant position occupied by T&N and BBA in the UK and, indeed, within the EC as a whole, this is one sector in which imports have shown very little tendency to rise so that we must look elsewhere for explanations for decline. In fact, these are to be found in international sourcing strategies for brakes and clutches employed by the motor vehicle manufacturers which have directly reduced the demand for linings in the UK as well as in the inability of the linings manufacturers to achieve satisfactory profit margins in the UK in the face of resistance to price increases from the assemblers.

A duopolistic supply situation has existed in the UK since 1985, when Mintex, the linings subsidiary of BBA and the second largest producer of linings, acquired Don International, the third largest producer, and thereby achieved a market share equivalent to that of the market leader, Ferodo (T&N). Apart from the two majors, the only remaining significant producer of linings in the UK is Lucas Girling, which has some in-house production to service its brake manufacturing activities. Two other important suppliers, AP and H.K. Porter have recently been absorbed by Mintex-Don as part of a strategy of vertical integration into the clutch market (AP) and horizontal integration into the higher-value-added commercial vehicle clutch facings market (H.K. Porter). Both these acquisitions for the first time threaten Ferodo's almost complete dominance of the original equipment clutch linings, because until 1986, Mintex-Don was much more heavily involved in brake linings and in the aftermarket.

The dominance of BBA and T&N in this sector stems mainly from their vertically integrated asbestos-processing activities, which have given them substantial cost advantages in raw material supply. However, the switch from asbestos to glass and carbon-fibre-based linings during the 1980s has to some extent eroded these advantages and resulted in rising input costs at a time when downward pressure on prices has been exerted by their major customers. The switch away from asbestos may also in part explain the collapse of unmounted asbestos lining sales in the UK shown in Table 8.9. Nevertheless, it should be stressed that linings composed wholly or mainly of asbestos still account for the lion's share of the industry's output. For example, in 1984 only 8 per cent of Mintex's sales were non-asbestos based. However, the absence of separate sales data on non-asbestos linings makes it impossible to judge the degree to which product substitution has contributed to a 50 per cent drop in sales of unmounted asbestos linings between 1979 and 1987, although it is likely that the severity of the decline in this market does reflect this. However, between 1979 and 1987, sales of clutches and brakes in the UK fell in real terms by 49 per cent and 34 per cent respectively, which suggests that this was the main factor in the decline of linings sales. The absence of separately published trade figures for brakes and clutches until 1988 makes it difficult to assess whether import penetration, insignificant in the linings market itself, was a major factor in the collapse of demand from its major customers. In 1988, imports of clutches and brakes were responsible for 37 per cent and 28 per cent of sales in the home market respectively.

Table 8.9 Sales and overseas trade performance of UK brake and clutch lining manufacturers,[a] 1979–87 (1980 prices)

	Home and overseas sales of UK firms (£m)	Of which exports		Sales in UK market (£m)	Of which imports	
		(£m)	(%)		(£m)	(%)
1979	114.0	16.3	14.3	100.8	3.1	3.1
1981	76.5	10.9	14.2	68.7	3.1	4.5
1983	70.9	9.5	13.4	64.2	2.8	4.4
1985	68.7	9.9	14.4	61.7	2.9	4.7
1987	56.7	10.2	18.0	50.2	3.7	7.4
Percentage change 1979–87	−50.3	−37.4		−50.2	+19.4	

Source: *Business Monitor*, PQ 2440, Asbestos Products

[a]Figures relate to unmounted linings wholly or mainly of asbestos

In spite of the contraction of market opportunities in the UK, neither T&N nor BBA have shown any tendency to decrease their reliance on automotive parts. Indeed, T&N's automotive division increased its share of company sales from 27 per cent in 1979 to 45 per cent in 1985 and the high level of involvement of BBA in the automotive market has also been maintained throughout the 1980s with vehicle components accounting for around 75 per cent of total sales. Both the major firms have in fact pursued an expansionary strategy involving both diversification and vertical integration within the automotive sector. Given the overcapacity existing within the industry this strategy has been pursued almost exclusively by means of acquisition. Also, given the relatively depressed state of the UK market, expansion through takeovers has predominantly involved foreign direct investment.

In view of the recession in the UK car and commercial vehicle linings markets, the obvious strategy would have been to seek overseas export markets. However, in the case of both unmounted linings and brake pads, the evidence suggests that this strategy was largely ignored by both companies. Table 8.9 shows that exports of unmounted linings declined in real terms by 37 per cent between 1979 and 1987 and never accounted for more than 18 per cent of total sales. Similarly, exports of disc brake pad assemblies declined from £21.5 million in 1979 to £15.9 million in 1987, a fall of almost 60 per cent in real terms.

Table 8.10 Overseas trade balance in unmounted brake and clutch lining[a] by source and destination countries (1980 prices)

	1979			1987		
	Imports (£m)(a)	Exports (£m)(b)	Ratio (a)/(b)	Imports (£m)(a)	Exports (£m)(b)	Ratio (a)/(b)
West Germany	1.1	3.0	0.4	1.7	3.2	0.5
Italy	0.2	0.8	0.3	0.2	0.7	0.3
France	0.4	1.2	0.4	0.1	0.6	0.1
Belgium	0.1	0.5	0.2	0.1	0.3	0.4
Netherlands	0.1	0.7	0.1	0.0	0.8	NA
Denmark	0.1	0.1	0.6	0.7	0.1	4.5
Spain	0.0	0.0	NA[b]	0.1	0.1	1.3
EC total	2.0	7.1	0.3	3.0	6.7	0.5
Sweden	0.1	0.7	0.1	0.0	0.2	NA
US	0.6	1.0	0.6	0.1	0.1	0.8
Japan)	0.1	0.1	1.4	0.4	0.0	NA
Asia-ex. Japan)	0.2	1.5	0.02	0.0	1.3	NA
Nigeria	0.0	1.4	NA	0.0	0.1	NA
Total	3.1	16.3	0.2	3.7	10.2	0.4

Source: Overseas Trade Statistics of UK (HMSO)

[a] See note [a], Table 8.9

[b] NA, Not applicable

The reasons for this failure to expand export markets are obviously connected with the existence of overseas production capacity which BBA and T&N have built up, particularly in Europe and North America, much of it in the period since 1979. Table 8.10 shows that in that year the major linings export markets in order of importance were: West Germany, Nigeria, France, the US, Italy and Sweden; by 1987 exports to two of these markets, the US and Nigeria, had become negligible and to another, Sweden, were considerably reduced. In the meantime, Ferodo had expanded output considerably at its US subsidiary Nuturn and acquired a majority interest in Turner's Engineering Products of Ibadan where production began in 1979. Although not large in absolute terms, exports to South Africa also fell away significantly in 1987 at a time when BBA's Textar subsidiary was following a deliberate import replacement programme by importing new equipment and technology. It is not without interest also that Don International has a major manufacturing subsidiary in Sweden and Ferodo in Italy, both of which declined in significance as export markets. On the other hand, exports of linings to West Germany, where Textar has a large share of the market, were maintained at a similar level.

Both companies have thus clearly preferred to extend their overseas production facilities which were already extensive at the beginning of the 1980s. In 1978, for example, Ferodo had manufacturing affiliates in Italy, Spain, Zimbabwe, India and the United States: by 1988 further linings interests had been acquired in West Germany (Beral Bromsbelag), South Korea, Nigeria, France (Abex) and Spain (Garnecto). The acquisition of Abex's production facilities in France and Spain in 1988 represents a considerable increase in T&N's European market share, as each company has around 25 per cent of its domestic market. T&N has also greatly extended its interests in the United States through the expansion of Nuturn and the acquisition of Worldbestos. A rapid expansion of Mintex's European interests occurred in 1985 through the acquisition of Don International with manufacturing capacity in Belgium and Sweden which complemented existing facilities in West Germany and Spain. In the same year, Mintex also acquired a majority holding in a further Spanish linings manufacturer (Frenos y Embragues) and in the French arm of Beral Bromsbelag from Ferodo.

One aspect of internationalization which remains unclear concerns the location of manufacture of non-asbestos-based linings for which the market is currently expanding rapidly. There is evidence, for example, that tighter legislative controls on asbestos processing in some EC countries has encouraged at least one manufacturer to concentrate asbestos linings manufacture in the UK and expand non-asbestos linings manufacture in Europe. The total specialization of the H.K. Porter plant at Newcastle (recently acquired by BBA) in asbestos clutch facings was highlighted in a shop stewards' report (AUEW 1985) as a major factor in declining orders at the plant. Meanwhile production of non-asbestos linings has been concentrated in Porter's other plant in the Netherlands. If the major manufacturers are also encouraged to adopt this strategy, the long-term consequences for the future of the industry in the UK could be extremely serious.

As members of the 'big five' within the motor components industry (the others being GKN, Lucas and TI), both companies have sought to extend their control of specific product markets, particularly by means of forward integration. BBA, in particular has actively pursued this strategy through acquiring Britain's leading clutch manufacturer, AP, together with the brake and clutch division in the UK of the Repco Corporation of Australia in 1986. More recently, BBA has moved into the brake aftermarket through the acquisition in 1988 of CBS Automotive of Telford, a manufacturer of replacement brake shoe assemblies. The other sector of the motor vehicle industry in which BBA has sought to build up a substantial market share is that of plastic body parts through the takeover of Holden Hydroman in the UK and Guthrie Corporation in the US. T&N has been more concerned to move into higher-value-added specialized engineering areas of the motor industry, not only engine components but also radiators and fluid couplings. Some low-value-added products, particularly filters, have been divested as part of this strategy.

Given the high degree of concentration in the linings sector, opportunities for horizontal integration have been limited to a number of small to medium-sized specialists operating in the higher quality commercial vehicle linings market. It is noticeable that many of these firms have either not survived as independent manufacturers or have withdrawn from these niche markets as the majors have gradually extended their interests into non-asbestos-based materials. The example of H.K. Porter has already been mentioned; others include Brake Linings acquired by Ferodo in 1977 and Morgan Crossley acquired by Armstrong in 1978 and now closed.

CONCLUSION

Our analysis of recent developments in the British car components original equipment market has tended to suggest that the industry, in its entirety as well as different product markets, does not face a particularly bright future. The 'globalization' of the car assembly industry and the related subjugation of the components industry to international oligopolies are perhaps the two most decisive forces shaping its future.

The assembly industry does not possess a national champion capable of keeping out foreign car and car components imports, and providing adequate scale opportunities to justify large-scale local manufacture of components. Instead, the car market is severely fragmented, and that part of it which is served by companies with manufacturing capacity in Britain does not provide an adequate level of demand for the components industry. The latter is not so much the inevitable consequence of falling competitiveness within UK manufacturers, such as Rover, but rather the outcome of the deliberate choice of the multinationals in Britain (Ford, General Motors, Peugeot-Talbot) to integrate their car production and components purchasing facilities across Europe. This has significantly reduced the demand for British-made original equipment, owing to an increase in tied-imports of cars and components, a decrease in the local content of British-made cars and a decrease in local in-house components manufacture. For these companies, Britain is simply one part of a global production system.

It is in this context that the revival of car manufacture in Britain – to a limited extent by General Motors and Peugeot-Talbot, but mainly by the Japanese – ought to be interpreted. Nissan, Toyota and Honda are also global corporations which will insert their UK operations into a wider international division of labour. It is very likely that the local content of the Japanese factories in Britain will be higher than certainly that of Vauxhall and Peugeot-Talbot cars, since unlike the latter, the Japanese have much less European capacity which can be traded off against UK operations. On the other hand, their insistence in defining 80 per cent local content as purchases within the entire EC, demonstrates that there is no guarantee that British component manufacturers will be major beneficiaries.

The potential benefits of increased car output in Britain also have to be considered in the light of the question of who, in the car components industry is most likely to benefit. Here, the differences between the Japanese and the other UK-based multinationals become negligible. Both groups are converging towards single-sourcing of clusters of components from their traditional or other global companies. Whether this leads to the siting of supply outlets near to the assembly factories, rather than imports, is of little relevance to existing non-global components manufacturers in Britain without an 'international presence', since they will automatically not qualify for major contracts. Those who will, will be the Japanese and other inward investors.

This brings us to the implications of the second major development affecting components manufacture, namely the emergence of an international oligopoly of component suppliers. In part this has been brought about by the assemblers themselves who have encouraged their major international suppliers to develop a significant presence in each of their global markets. Within the EC, this process, accelerated by the approach of 1992, has increasingly involved the replacement of traditional national suppliers by members of the oligopoly whether they be European, American or Japanese. The process of international concentration has been particularly marked in certain mass-production commodity markets where scale economies have given significant advantages to the larger suppliers. The shock absorber and brake and clutch linings sector are clear examples of this; in the one case, British companies have been squeezed out of the market, in the other, they are extending their dominant positions in Europe and North America. It should be stressed, however, that the former case is much more representative of the UK car component sector as a whole, in which a wide range of original equipment commodity markets is now entirely in the hands of foreign producers, including alternators, lighting equipment, exhausts and silencers, and oil and air filters. Each of these markets has been abandoned by major British producers who have increasingly found themselves unable to compete effectively with the scale of production either of the assesmblers themselves or of their major international suppliers.

As is illustrated by the market for engine components, the assemblers have also attempted to control the nature of oligopolistic supply when threatened by a dominant national producer. We have seen how the failure of GKN to provide a viable alternative to AE led to a switching of piston and ring contracts into Europe, thus adversely affecting the UK's balance of trade in engine components. To some extent also, Armstrong's dominance of the UK shock absorber market for cars may have been instrumental in pulling in original equipment imports. The lesson to be drawn is surely that in the long run a *laissez faire* attitude to monopoly and mergers in the UK has allowed positions of dominance to be achieved which the car makers have been determined to break. In other EC markets a number of suppliers have usually been available so that switching to overseas alternatives has not been necessary. In the UK, too, the example of the brake and clutch linings sector shows how the existence of an alternative national supplier has resulted in a relatively low degree of import penetration.

What does all this imply for the future of car component manufacture in the UK? We have identified two main trends in the industry: a growing level of import penetration accompanied by an increasing degree of foreign ownership. Thus the vital question is whether the currently high level of foreign direct investment, associated with the commencement of Japanese assembly, will eventually lead to a diminution in import penetration. We feel that this is unlikely for a number of reasons. First, because the bulk of the incoming investment, whether new or involving takeovers, is in mass-production, relatively low-technology commodity markets where product scale economies are of increasing significance. The permanence of this investment thus clearly depends on the ability of the Japanese to increase absolutely the number of cars manufactured in the UK rather than to take market share from existing producers. Second, acquisition, which is by far the most significant method of foreign entry into the UK market, is more often motivated by a desire to secure distribution channels rather than to pick up extra UK capacity. A renewed downturn in the industry could thus easily lead to rationalization of incidentally acquired UK assets, especially given the lower costs of manufacturing on the Continent. Third, the requirement for 80 per cent local content in the case of the Japanese car transplants will not necessarily lead to import replacement, if Japanese component manufacturers are allowed to bring in a high proportion of their own requirements from Japan.

Finally, the process of growing internationalization and concentration in the car components industry, as identified in this chapter, strongly militates against a currently fashionable view which argues that many industries today are experiencing vertical disintegration, and, as a corollary, local linkage formation. Restructuring in this industry has, in fact, gone in exactly the opposite direction from a situation prior to the mid-1970s, of local supply networks. Today, it is an internationally integrated and concentrated industry within which local supply amounts to either the purchase of peripheral equipment from small independent suppliers or lasting and more lucrative contracts with the branches of closely affiliated multinational organizations.

9 Restructuring the Swedish manufacturing industry – the case of the motor vehicle industry

Anders Malmberg

This chapter is about the Swedish motor vehicle industry. The first part of the chapter deals with some general trends of restructuring and regional change within Swedish manufacturing as a whole. It includes a short presentation of a structural approach to industrial location analysis that is adopted in the subsequent sections. After that, a brief description of the Swedish motor vehicle industry is given, followed by a section dealing in more detail with the history and present structure of the production of cars within the Volvo company.

RELOCATION AND RESTRUCTURING – SOME GENERAL TRENDS

As in most capitalist industrialized countries, the manufacturing industry in Sweden has been in the process of decentralization since the end of the 1960s. The process can be described as a shift from large cities and industrial core regions to small towns and peripheral regions (Fig. 9.1). Compared to other countries, however, the spatial redistribution has been of moderate extent (Lundmark and Malmberg 1988).

Only occasionally has manufacturing employment increased in the periphery, and decreased in the centre regions at the same time. More often, the redistribution of employment is the result of a faster growth (up to 1976) or slower decline (after 1976) in the periphery. In the early 1970s, peripheral communes in northern Sweden experienced the fastest growth, whereas after 1976 peripheral communes in the south have had a more positive development.

A survey of manufacturing employment changes at the county level (Sweden is divided into twenty-four regions) shows, perhaps more surprisingly, that the redistribution from metropolitan regions (i.e. Stockholm, Gothenburg and Malmö) and other industrial core regions has been going on at least since 1940 (Malmberg 1987). One conclusion to be drawn from this is that regional policy measures, such as capital subsidies to manufacturing plants locating in assisted ('peripheral') areas, can hardly be regarded as the chief explanation for decentralization, since such policies were not initiated until the mid-1960s, some twenty-five years after the process of decentralization began.

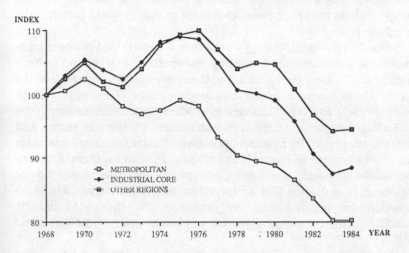

Figure 9.1 Employment changes in Swedish manufacturing industry in different types of municipalities (communes), 1968–84
Source: Industrial statistics

Neither does traditional shift-share analysis – questioning to what extent the inherited industrial structure is the root cause of regionally divergent industrial development – explain the redistribution of manufacturing employment between regions. The decline of manufacturing in metropolitan regions occurred despite their favourable industrial structure, and the growth in peripheral regions took place despite their unfavourable industrial structure (Håkansson and Danielsson 1985; Lundmark and Malmberg 1988).

As a more fruitful explanatory framework, I would suggest the adoption of a structural approach to changes in industrial location and similar to that developed in the writings of Massey (1979, 1984), Walker and Storper (1981), Hudson (1988), Maskell (1982, 1988) and others. I will here comment briefly on four major elements in such an approach.

First, firms may be assumed to search for optimal locations, but the decisions about location are necessarily connected to investment decisions, and are therefore always part of the overall strategy of the firm. The optimal location cannot, therefore, be defined separately from the characteristics of the product, the production organization and the functioning market. If a given location, in the course of time, turns out to be suboptimal, production may be moved to another location. More often, though, the firm tries to adjust production to prevailing conditions at the existing location, or through various measures tries to change conditions there so that they will better fit the needs of production.

Second, the overall strategy of the firm is constrained by the macroeconomic structures (the prevailing institutional, market and technological conditions, etc.) that form the economic environment of the firm. These macroeconomic structures change constantly, due to technological and other changes in production and circulation.

Third, the physical and social structures of specific places and regions are shaped by historical processes. Different elements in these structures become resources if and when a demand for them is created by some economic activity. Correspondingly, they cease to be resources if and when that demand disappears. The way in which the spatially varying resources are exploited give rise to historically specific forms of spatial divisions of labour (Massey 1979; Lipietz 1980).

Finally, the relation between industrial location and the spatial structure of resources is reciprocal. When industry is located in an area, the physical and social structure of that area changes. This may increase the attractiveness of the area to other firms – the idea of the concepts of external economies of scale or agglomeration economies – but the structures which are formed around existing firms may also hamper subsequent industrial growth.

One immediate consequence of adopting a structural approach of this kind is that the focus of research shifts. Instead of conceiving of the decentralization issue as a question of relocation, it becomes a question of restructuring.

A number of significant restructuring processes can be identified, most of them associated with a growing internationalization of the economy. Foreign trade has increased, as has foreign ownership within Swedish industry. Today, about 15 per cent of total Swedish manufacturing employment is within companies owned (by more than 50 per cent) by foreign capital. At the same time Swedish investments abroad increase, and this flow of capital is mainly directed towards countries within the European Community.

One important outcome of the restructuring process is that of sectoral transformation – the rise of certain industries and the virtual collapse of others. This has to a large extent influenced the internationalization process, as well as the spatial redistribution described above. In Sweden the iron and steel, shipbuilding, textile and clothing and wood industries accounted for the major part of manufacturing employment decline during the years 1968–84, and this partly explains the employment decline in the old industrial core regions outside the major metropolitan areas.

In the same period parts of the engineering industry, most notably the electric and motor vehicle industries, showed considerable growth. Empirical findings support the idea that employment growth within these industries in the periphery to a large extent is associated with standardized and routinized production, utilizing the relatively cheap labour and land in peripheral regions (Lundmark and Malmberg 1988).

THE MOTOR VEHICLE INDUSTRY

The growth in the Swedish motor vehicle industry (ISIC 3843) is remarkable, since employment continued to increase all the way through the deep recession 1976–82. During the period 1968–84, when almost 12 per cent of overall manufacturing employment disappeared (103,000 jobs), employment in the motor vehicle industry almost doubled, as 33,000 additional jobs were created.

There are a number of explanations for this. One is that the Swedish automobile industry in the 1970s shifted from a previous concentration on production of ordinary cars for average income households, to more luxurious cars for people with higher incomes. This turned out to be a successful strategic choice, since this segment of the market proved to be less affected by market decline following the oil crises (Bäckström 1988). In the home market, though, both Volvo and Saab predominantly sell the cheaper models, and the cars are still regarded as ordinary.

The success of the Swedish motor vehicle industry in foreign markets during the 1980s has also been strongly reinforced by several devaluations of the Swedish currency between 1980 and 1982. A more long-term explanation lies in the Swedish 'wage policy of solidarity', stemming from the early 1960s. The original aim of this policy was 'equal pay for equal work', but it turned out to be a major force speeding up the restructuring process, since all firms were required to pay similar wages, regardless of their profitability. By international standards, wage levels in industries such as textile and clothing became high, while on the other hand wage levels in engineering, and particularly in the motor vehicle industry, became relatively low.

In 1986, the latest year for which statistics are available, the motor vehicle industry accounted for around 10 per cent of the Swedish manufacturing industry, in terms of employment as well as value added. The value of exports reached 40 billion SEK, which is 15 per cent of total Swedish exports. The same year 421,000 Swedish cars were produced. Of these, just below 20 per cent were sold in Sweden, while the rest were exported, primarily to North America (42 per cent) and Europe (35 per cent). Although this industry is of enormous importance in the national context, Sweden accounts for only 1 per cent of global car production.

The picture is different when production of trucks is considered. One out of every six medium-size or heavy trucks produced in the Western world is either from Volvo or Saab. More than 90 per cent of Swedish truck production is exported, two-thirds of the export being directed towards Europe (*Svensk industri och industripolitik* 1988).

The Swedish motor vehicle industry is almost totally dominated by two companies – Volvo and Saab. Before looking more closely at the bigger of these companies, Volvo, a few general characteristics of the industry will be outlined.

First, ever since the fast expansion started in the early 1960s, the motor vehicle industry in Sweden has shown many characteristics typical of a propulsive industry, being in a Perrouxian sense a central focus of a growth pole (Perroux 1955), as the effects of growth within the sector are widespread. Apart from its manifold linkages to other parts of the manufacturing system (steel, engineering products, rubber, plastics, textiles, etc.), the growth of the sector also promotes investment in transport infrastructure and thereby affects growth in the building and construction sector, as well as the general conditions for transport of goods and people.

Second, mass production is a characteristic feature of the motor vehicle industry. This means that large-scale technology dominates, and that various forms of production rationalization, in order to cut costs, are the main means of competition. This, in turn, reflects the fact that even though a modern car is technically complicated, it mainly consists of technologically mature products. Single components or functions may be newly developed and of a 'high-tech' character, but the general concept of how to build a car is well established, and spread all over the world. Also production technology is mature and shows great similarities from one company to another. Only in the case of a very small segment of exclusive products (i.e.

luxury cars) can large-scale production be set aside (Karlsson 1985). In general, I would argue, the dominance of mass production still prevails, in spite of the propositions being made recently concerning the shift from Fordist to some form of post-Fordist production organization (see for example Schoenberger 1987).

Third, the motor vehicle industry is organizationally and geographically concentrated, in the sense that a limited number of companies and a limited number of regions dominate world production. This is reflected in the regional pattern of growth within the Swedish motor vehicle industry, as it differs significantly from that of the manufacturing industry as a whole. The peripheral regions have experienced the fastest growth in relative terms, but the rate of growth was also considerable in the metropolitan and industrial core regions (see Fig. 9.2). As a matter of fact, in absolute terms the majority of new jobs within the motor vehicle industry were located in the latter regions. This concentrated pattern is reinforced by the fact that the large automobile companies are primarily characterized by assembly work, and that they tend to gather a net of subcontractors quite close to the assembly plants, which are often considered to be the core of the industry.

The geographical concentration does not, however, mean that the locational pattern has been a static one. On the contrary, on a world

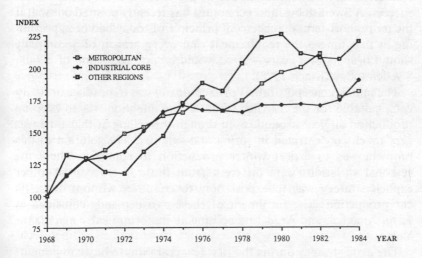

Figure 9.2 Employment changes in the Swedish motor vehicle industry in different kinds of municipalities (communes), 1968–84
Source: Industrial statistics

scale the history of the motor vehicle industry shows a number of geographical shifts, where the 'core region' of the industry has been relocated. After the breakthrough in the north-eastern part of the US in the beginning of the century, Europe became the fastest growing area from the 1930s, and from the late 1960s Japan and a couple of non-OECD countries have rapidly increased their share of global automobile production, and actually seem to be taking over the leading position.

THE VOLVO PRODUCTION OF CARS – STRATEGY AND STRUCTURE

The history of the Volvo company goes back to 1926, when it was founded as a subsidiary of SKF, the producer of ball bearings. Production of private cars today dominates sales as well as profitability, but that has not always been the case. Even though it was the vision of a Swedish production of cars that guided the founders of Volvo, for the first thirty years it was the production of trucks and buses that kept Volvo in business. (For a more detailed account of the history of Volvo, see Hermele 1982; Ellegård 1983; or Kinch 1988.)

It was not until the mid-1930s, after ten years of experimentation with different models, that the marketing of cars started to show some success. A Swedish business economist has recently pointed out that if the more short-term management principle of today had been prevailing at that time – the requirement that every branch of a company should bear its own costs – there would be no production of cars in Sweden today (Kinch 1988).

The initial 'concept' of the Volvo company was to produce ordinary cars, suitable for the Swedish climate. The intention was to keep up production all year around, even though the selling at that time was very much concentrated in spring and summer. The solution to this problem was to export winter production to countries where the seasonal variations were different from those in Sweden. Another explicit strategy was to export only to countries without domestic car production. The fulfilment of these two demands coincided in Latin America, and Argentina became an important early market for Volvo.

The main strategy during the first few years was to buy components from independent, competing firms (Ellegård 1983). Volvo, located in Gothenburg, intended to remain an assembler of bought components – this was one of the general ideas behind the slogan 'the Volvo way of producing a car'.

This strategy was, however, partly abandoned in 1930 when Volvo bought the supplier of engines, Pentaverken, which was based in Skövde, some 150 km north-east of Gothenburg. From then on, the strategy was to take over subcontracting firms that had difficulty in changing because they could not afford the investment programmes considered necessary. In 1935, Volvo was separated from SKF and became an independent company.

From 1950, passenger cars became the company's leading product. The period 1950–70 can be characterized as the major phase of growth of the Volvo company (Ellegård 1983). That period meant a fast growth in productivity as well as production and employment. The strategy from the 1920s, not to export cars to countries with domestic car production, was abandoned and from 1956 exports to the US started to grow. From then on, a number of new strategies were adopted. In 1958, Volvo established its first branch plant, production of brake drums in Floby, 100 km north-east of Gothenburg. In 1963, the assembling of cars outside Sweden started, as the previous marketing company in Canada took up production (in Halifax). During this period, assembly plants were also located in Ghent, Belgium, and – in the regime of another company – in Malaysia.

Also of great importance was the organizational restructuring during the 1960s, when the car production subsidiaries were merged with the mother company, in order to strengthen coordination and control over production.

The period since 1970 is characterized by growing investments outside the production of cars. There had been a moderate attempt at diversification in the 1940s (Svenska Flygmotor in Trollhättan, 70 km north of Gothenburg, producing engines for aeroplanes) and in the 1960s (Bolinder-Munktell in Eskilstuna, 90 km west of Stockholm, today producing tractors under the name of Volvo BM), but the 1970s has seen the entry of Volvo into new and different sectors, most notably the food industry and trade (predominantly with oil and fruits).

Another characteristic of the period since 1970 has been the setting up of a number of new plants in Sweden (Bengtsfors, Lindesberg, Kalmar, Vara, Tanumshede, Färjelanda) – all except Lindesberg (mid-Sweden) and Kalmar (south-east Sweden) located within 2 hours' drive (i.e. 150 km) of Gothenburg, and all of them in rather small, previously not heavily industrialized towns. Intensified cooperation, in various forms, with car producers outside Sweden (DAF in the Netherlands, Peugeot and Renault in France, British Leyland in the UK, General Motors in the US) was a third significant feature of this period.

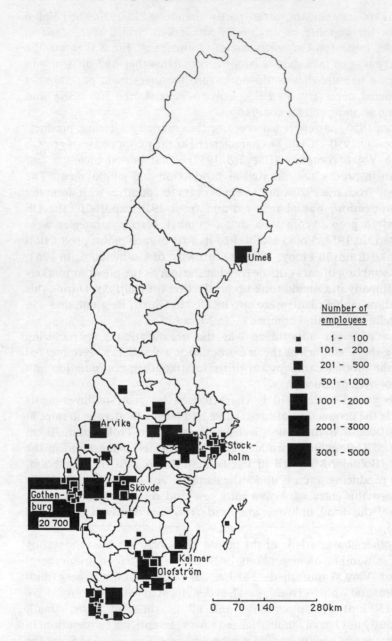

Number of
employees

■   1 – 100
■   101 – 200
■   201 – 500
■   501 – 1000
■   1001 – 2000
■   2001 – 3000
■   3001 – 5000

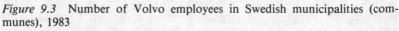

Figure 9.3 Number of Volvo employees in Swedish municipalities (communes), 1983
Source: Company Register, National Bureau of Statistics

In the following, two themes related to the present and future structure of the Volvo production of cars will be commented upon – that of production organization, linkage systems and location, and that of the relation between capitalist manufacturing industry and the state in a social democratic welfare nation like Sweden.

PRODUCTION ORGANIZATION, LINKAGES AND LOCATION

Volvo's annual production of more than 400,000 cars (half of which is in Sweden), almost 50,000 trucks and 4,000 buses and coaches makes up, evidently, an extensive and complex production system. Figure 9.3 shows the regional distribution of the company's 50,000 employees in Sweden (if Volvo activities abroad are included, employment reaches almost 75,000). From a quick glance at the map, we can conclude that production is spread all over southern Sweden. Although there are small clusters of production units around Stockholm and Malmö, as well as in the South-east of Sweden, the most noticeable feature is the concentration around the Gothenburg area. Especially plants involved in automobile production tend to be clustered in this region.

At Torslandaverken in Gothenburg, the main car assembly plant of Volvo, 100 trucks daily unload 5,000 pallets with materials and components. Much of this comes from plants owned by Volvo, but a considerable proportion is delivered by independent subcontractors. Estimates made by the State Board of Industry (SIND 1980) indicated that, by the end of the 1970s, 65 per cent of the value of a car was produced outside the Volvo company. According to estimates by the Volvo company, 10,000–12,000 people are employed by subcontracting firms in Sweden (that is, subcontractors, producing components for cars), which can be related to the around 25,000 employees engaged in car production within the company (1986).

This ratio between internalized and externalized production (2:1, in terms of employment) makes Volvo comparable with the large American automobile companies (Ford, GM), but it differs sharply from that of Toyota and other leading Japanese companies. To a much larger extent they produce cars in accordance with the original strategy of Volvo back in the 1920s; the ratio between the number of employees within the Japanese automobile companies and that of their subcontractors has been estimated to be 1:4 (SIND 1980).

The Volvo car production system makes a large number of towns and municipalities, often small in size, heavily dependent on the success of Volvo in the market. Apart from the latent risks of this dependency, which during the 1980s has not caused any serious problems anywhere since production has grown steadily, the system is undergoing substantial changes. Two interrelated processes of strategy re-orientation can be identified, both of them having obvious spatial implications.

One is the more explicit orientation towards what is often referred to as just-in-time organization of production. Even though the concept of JIT has become widespread since the mid-1980s, it must be recognized that logistic strategies of a similar kind were adopted much earlier, not least in the motor vehicle industry. During the 1980s, however, Volvo has tightened the time schedule of its subcontractors as the demand for quick and safe delivery of components has increased. For many products, a couple of days may pass from the time that the order is transmitted until the component enters the assembly line, but efforts are continuously made to reduce this time.

Some of the subcontractors today have a permanent on-line connection to Torslandaverken. One example is the firm Sunwind, a producer of floors for the luggage boots of Volvo cars, located at Säve some 15 km north of Torslandaverken. Sunwind continuously receives computerized information about what cars are entering the assembly line at Torslandaverken (model, colour, etc.). Within a couple of hours the floor is delivered, in time for when a certain car reaches the floor-fitting station. This kind of 'sequence-delivery', it is planned, will be practised by ten subcontractors within a couple of years.

Another change, which is likely to affect Swedish subcontractors, is Volvo's intention to diminish its dependency on small firms delivering single components, in favour of those producing more complex systems of components. As more complex systems to a large extent are imported, mostly from West Germany, this re-orientation may have negative consequences in many places around Sweden.

Some obvious effects of the changing logistic strategies and spatial structure of linkages may be identified. One is that the spatial concentration is likely to increase. The Swedish motor vehicle industry has always been located predominantly in southern Sweden, and in the case of Volvo the west coast has been the core region. This pattern is being reinforced as a dominating share of investment is made within, or close to the Gothenburg region.

A second effect is that rapid transport is regarded as a necessary condition for the successful production of cars. Rail transport is considered to be too slow and non-adaptive. Instead trucks have become the preferred mean of transport, leading to specific demands on the state in matters of infrastructure (see below) and a permanent conflict between the motor vehicle industry and the environmentalist organizations in Sweden.

Third, as JIT production is vulnerable to disturbances of any kind, the importance of labour relations has been highlighted in the last few years. For example, when the white-collar workers in the Swedish manufacturing industry went on strike in January 1988, it took only a few hours before all production at Torslandaverken stopped as no components entered the assembly line, and the very same day 6,000 blue-collar workers were dismissed temporarily. The effects spread rapidly to the subcontractors as they did not have the inventory facilities necessary to keep up production when delivery to Torslanda-verken had to stop.

For a number of years, Volvo has had to face problems of high labour turnover and high rates of absenteeism, especially at Torslandaverken. Efforts to cope with these problems include different types of re-organization of production processes as well as experiments with flexibility in work-time schedules. The Volvo plant in Kalmar, established in 1974, became world famous as the first modern automobile assembly plant without an assembly line. Instead production was organized around groups of workers (15–20 persons) being responsible for the assembly of larger sections of the cars. Experiences from this experiment were fairly positive, from the point of view of the company as well as the workers (Agurén *et al.* 1984). At some of the Volvo plants, for example those in Skövde (motors) and Kungälv (wheels), the employees may choose between a large number of different time-schedules, some of them including work only during the weekends (with full pay).

The re-organization of the production process also, of course, includes introduction of new technology, often with the explicit purpose of creating jobs that will allow more women to work on the assembly line (Ahlinder 1988).

The problem of recruiting labour, and keeping it within the company, has sharpened during the last few years as labour shortage has come to be a general characteristic of the Swedish labour market. Current predictions (Olsson and Broomé 1988) indicate that labour shortage can be expected to prevail for the next 10–15 years, primarily due to demographic reasons.

VOLVO AND THE STATE

In a speech in the early 1980s, the managing director of the Volvo company, Pehr G. Gyllenhammar, stated that:

I personally believe that the automobile industry marks the limit of the sustainability of industrial society. If you, as a country or a nation, state as a fact that you are not competitive within this industry, then you have also abdicated from industrial society.

(Gyllenhammar 1981, author's translation)

True or not, to a large extent this seems to be the view of governments throughout the Western world as enormous efforts are made to promote growth, or at least to prevent decline, in the automobile industry (Hedlund and Steen 1985). In Sweden, the relations between the automobile industry and the state are close. These relationships are expressed in many ways, as a few examples will illustrate.

When the shipyard in Uddevalla, 100 km north of Gothenburg, was closed in 1986, Volvo offered to locate an assembly plant in the town, as a replacement. In return, a number of favours were requested. Direct and indirect capital support was given, in total two or three times as large as the overall annual capital subsidies given to firms locating in the assisted areas. This generosity was later repeated when Saab, as a 'matter of justice', received similar support in order to locate an assembly plant on the premises of the former shipyard in Malmö. Volvo also claimed that the highway between Gothenburg and Uddevalla needed large investments, in order to satisfy the need for quick and safe transport by truck between Torslandaverken and the plant in Uddevalla. The 'missing link' of the motorway between Gothenburg and Uddevalla is today being built, despite strong protests from environmentalists all over Sweden. The west coast is the region in Sweden where the sea is most overfed with nitrogen and forests are most seriously affected by acid rain.

Also in a more general sense, the Volvo company is the main lobby in Sweden when transport and communication infrastructure is discussed. The so-called Scandinavian Link project (the vision of a motorway from Oslo, along the Swedish west coast through to Denmark – via a bridge connecting Malmö and Copenhagen – and onwards to Europe) was launched in Sweden by the managing director of Volvo a few years ago. The idea would presumably have been dropped quickly, for environmental reasons, were it not for the pressure from Volvo.

Another issue concerns import regulations. In 1988, several contacts were made between the Swedish and Japanese governments in order to reach an agreement limiting Japanese car sales in Sweden. This has been heavily criticized as being a result of Volvo and Saab putting pressure on the Swedish government, to the detriment of Swedish car buyers.

CONCLUSION – POST-FORDISM EMERGING?

The changes within the motor vehicle industry have many characteristics in common with the restructuring of the Swedish manufacturing industry in general, but also a number of features that make this industry distinct. The tendency towards internationalization (in sales as well as production), the location of branch plants in small towns, and a strong awareness of the importance of capital–labour relations is similar. So are the close and manifold relations between the large companies and the state.

At the same time, it is obvious that some trends and structures identified in the analysis of overall manufacturing restructuring – spatial decentralization of standardized and routinized production and spatial concentration of management, R&D and sales departments (Lundmark and Malmberg 1988) – become less significant in the case of the motor vehicle industry, as much of the relatively routinized and low-paid work is still carried out in the metropolitan regions.

A plausible explanation of this difference may be found in the logistic strategies being adopted in the Swedish automobile industry. While the impact of distance and transport costs has gradually come to be regarded as almost insignificant as a locational determinant for many industries, it seems to be of great importance within the motor vehicle industry. Modern logistic strategies may therefore bring back the issue of transport costs to the heart of industrial location analysis (Estall 1985). This time, however, it is not transport costs in the traditional Weberian sense (tons per kilometre) that matters, but efforts to reduce time and increase stability in deliveries from branch plants and subcontractors producing components for subsequent assembling.

These kinds of logistic changes are, together with some other trends of production re-organization, such as vertical disintegration of firms, adoption of more flexible production techniques, etc., nowadays often discussed in terms of an emerging post-Fordist mode of capitalist production (see, for example, Harvey 1987; Schoenberger 1987, 1988; Holmes 1988). The shift to flexible specialization, flexible accumulation – or whatever the supposedly emerging form of production is termed – is argued to have profound effects on the location of industrial activities, since it means the revival of the agglomeration economies that have been more or less out of the discussion during the 1970s and early 1980s.

Whether this change is likely to characterize most manufacturing industries in the future, as is suggested by some writers (e.g. Piore and

Sabel 1984; Scott 1988a; Storper and Scott 1989), remains, though, to be seen. Gertler (1988: 430) claims that:

> Much of the 'Geography of Post-Fordism' literature has been explicitly inspired by very real and impressive changes underway in the automotive sector in Japan, North America, and U.K. and Western Europe. And yet, one should be as wary of generalizing from the automotive sector now as one should have been at the zenith of Fordism. Just as many sectors never reached the level of technical prowess, capital-intensity and rigidity which was evident in automobile production under Fordism, so too will few of them follow the auto industry's footsteps with the assembly of large complexes of flexibly automated capital.

From a Swedish point of view, this suggestion has much in its favour. Important changes are occurring in the way that, for example, the Volvo company is re-organizing the production of cars. But, just as mass production in the Fordist sense never became generally dominating in Swedish industry, it would not be sensible to expect a massive shift to post-Fordism in the coming years.

10 Subcontracting in the motor industry: a case study in Coventry

Mike Rawlinson

The motor vehicle sector has been important in the Coventry local economy since the early 1900s, securing employment not only in the manufacturers, but also in an extensive network of component suppliers and subcontracting firms. Throughout the development of the Coventry manufacturing economy many firms have been inextricably linked into the fortunes of the large motor vehicle manufacturers. Friedman (1977) characterized the Coventry local economy as a dual economy, with a core of a small number of large dominant firms mostly in the motor industry and a larger number of peripheral, functionally subordinate and dependent small firms. The dominance of these large motor vehicle firms both prior to and after the recent recession has been documented by Healey and Clark (1984) and Thoms and Donnelly (1985). Even after this sector had lost over 33,000 jobs between 1974 and 1982, motor vehicle manufacture still employed 32,800 or over 37 per cent of all manufacturing workers in the local economy by 1982 (COVRIED).

Watanabe (1987) considers that the structure of the motor vehicle industry is made up of three distinctive sectors, all of which are represented in the Coventry local economy. First, there are the vehicle assemblers, such as Jaguar, Peugeot-Talbot and Massey Ferguson, who produce the chassis and some key components. Second, there are the component manufacturers, who develop functional components in collaboration with the assemblers, for example Automotive Products who produce clutch and braking systems. Third, there are the subcontracting firms who produce or process parts and simpler components according to specifications given by the assemblers or component manufacturers. This third group of firms may also work for component suppliers as well as the assemblers.

The difference between component suppliers and subcontractors is that component suppliers have the technological capacity to develop their own products. However, within the studies of subcontracting in the motor vehicle industry (Holmes 1986; Morris 1988) the component suppliers have been considered as forming part of the same functional group in the economy as the generally much smaller and independently owned subcontractors. However, the subcontractors tend to concentrate on relatively smaller batch production, manufacturing components entirely to specifications which are set down by their customers. Subcontracting has received revived interest over the 1980s, in particular it is seen as an integral strategy of manufacturing firms aiming for flexibility in the production process (Atkinson 1984; Imrie 1986; Morris 1988). However, these third-level firms have received little attention, and their importance within the motor industry and to a local space economy is little understood. This chapter focuses on the use of subcontracting in the motor vehicle industry in the Coventry local economy.

LINKAGES, SUBCONTRACTING AND THE MOTOR INDUSTRY

The study of inter-firm relationships in industrial geography has traditionally been founded within linkage studies (see Marshall 1987). The generally accepted definition of an industrial linkage is that which occurs when one manufacturing firm produces inputs of goods or services from, or sells output to, another manufacturing firm (Keeble 1976). Linkages can be either forwards or backwards. A forward linkage from a motor vehicle manufacturer is traditionally the sale of output to a dealer network, either legally dependent or independent. A backward linkage has traditionally been associated with the purchase of raw materials and components from stockholders or other manufacturing companies. A backward linkage represents vertical disintegration within the production process.

Motor vehicle manufacturers in the Coventry and UK economies realized by the turn of the century that they could gain from scale economies achieved at component supplying firms (Thoms and Donnelly 1985). They could avoid paying directly for the expensive development costs, and for a diverse range of manufacturing technologies. They could instead concentrate their investment on the production of drive trains and (later) body shells. The production of motor vehicles is a complex operation, however, it can be understood as the assembly of different 'bundles' of technology. These bundles are: the body shell, the power train, the suspension and steering, the glass, the clutch and braking systems, the electronics, the seats and trim, the exhaust and carburetion, the cooling system and the wheels and tyres. The first two bundles are almost invariably retained in-house as they are considered strategic fuctions, however, the latter tend to be bought in on a contract basis from component suppliers and added onto the vehicles by the assemblers. The buying-in and assembly of components represents vertical disintegration in the production process, consisting of free market transactions between separate companies. The in-house production of the body shell and drive train represent vertical integration.

However, between these two forms of production, vertical integration and vertical disintegration, there lie several intermediate inter-firm linkages, that are not solely based on free market transactions. These alternative, intermediate forms of production organization are little researched and not treated explicitly by traditional economic theory. They are forms of inter-firm relationships that may involve a power relationship, for example a purchasing firm may be able to force the price of bought-in components down. This may be due to the dependency of the supplier on that customer for its livelihood. This customer dependence results in what is known as a 'monopsonistic' relationship. The use of this type of relationship to force down the price of supplier firms' products has been identified in the clothing industry by Rainne (1985). The notion of a backward linkage, based on neoclassical economics, therefore becomes somewhat problematic when considering the nature of relationships which involve power differentials (Sheard 1983; Holmes 1986; Imrie 1986). Many alternative relationships for production exist that are not strictly based on the neoclassical notion of a free market transaction. These intermediate forms are shown in Table 10.1. Of these alternative arrangements subcontracting has been widely used by motor vehicle manufacturers. This particular form of linkage within an economy has been little researched in the past, even though it has been known to exist since at least before the Second World War in the Coventry and UK economies.

Subcontracting refers to a situation where the firm offering the subcontract requests another, legally independent, firm to carry out the processing of a material, component, part or subassembly for it, according to specifications provided by the firm offering the subcontract (Watanabe 1972). There has been little empirical research on subcontracting, but of the literature that is available Holmes (1986) suggests that there are three main types: specialist, capacity and supplier subcontracting. Specialist subcontracting is where the customer relies on the specialist skills of the subcontractor and design decisions are usually left to the subcontractor. The benefit to the

Table 10.1   Alternative strategies for the manufacture of a product

Organization of production	Form of production
Buying-in and assembly of components	Vertical disintegration
Production through subsidiary or affiliate Product licensing or joint ventures Franchising Subcontracting Outworking	Intermediate forms of production organization. Not always based on free market transactions
In-house production	Vertical integration

customer firm is that it does not have to invest in new technologies for limited use. Scott (1983) reports that in the semiconductor industry in California many firms contract out specialized operations in the production of printed circuit boards which involve relatively high expenditure on capital equipment. Thus specialized subcontracting is a means of 'collectivizing work tasks so as to avoid heavy cost penalties incurred by the partial or inefficient use of capital' (Scott 1983: 359).

Capacity (or concurrent) subcontracting refers to a situation where the supplier produces the same component that the customer firm produces in-house, or normally would produce in-house. The need for this type of subcontracting may arise when the customer cannot meet all of the demand for its product using in-house production alone. Capacity subcontracting may be the result of: poor production planning, a machine breakdown, a sudden unforeseen increase in demand, or when there is a cyclical demand for the firm's product. A cyclical demand gives rise to what Berger and Piore (1980) refer to as 'stable' and 'unstable' components of demand. The stable component of demand is essentially the proportion of demand that can be predicted, and production to meet this level will be done in house. The unstable component of demand, that is anything above the minimum demand level will be 'farmed out' for other firms to produce. These two components of demand are illustrated in Fig. 10.1. The advantages of this system are that the customer can externalize the uncertainty of production planning, lay-offs, short-time and any labour relations problems to the supplier.

The third category of subcontracting is that of supplier subcontracting. This is defined by Holmes (1986), and derived from Chaillou (1977), as referring to a situation where an independent subcontractor develops, designs and makes a product and enters into an agreement

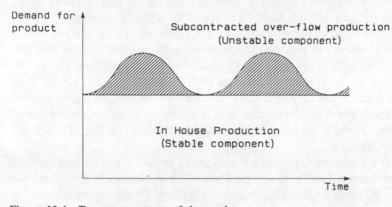

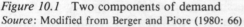

Figure 10.1 Two components of demand
Source: Modified from Berger and Piore (1980: 66)

to supply a dedicated or proprietary part to a customer firm. This is not in fact a form of subcontracting, but is actually a form of component supply associated with Watanabe's (1987) level-two firms. Watanabe's distinction between component suppliers and subcontractors is valid when the structure of the automotive industry is empirically examined. Generally the firms that develop parts are those that produce functional subassemblies or systems, such as the clutches, brakes and electronics, either separately or in conjunction with assemblers. The firms that produce these different 'bundles of technology' are generally large, multi-plant and often multinational companies, for example, GKN, Lucas Industries and the BBA Group. Many of these companies are actually larger than the vehicle assembly firms that they supply, and it is not unreasonable to expect that they have extremely different relationships with the firms that they supply than small 'jobbing shops'. Often the component suppliers design and develop a system and then attempt to sell it to as many different customers as possible, with slight modifications to fit each customer's particular models. Examples of such components are starter motors and alternators which remain standardized and completely designed by the suppliers who compete for the original equipment (OE) orders from major motor manufacturers. These firms may also produce key components such as engines (e.g. Perkins of Peterborough and Cummings of Daventry for diesel engines) and gearboxes. Basically the customer aims for as much component supplier input as is possible.

This is because the development of a component is expensive. These level-two firms supply the assemblers with components that are more akin to off-the-shelf parts. 'No off the shelf part actually exists because you always have to tailor it in some way to what you're actually looking for yourself. But the closer you can get to something that is already in production for somebody else, the cheaper it is and the quicker you can get it' (respondent at vehicle assembly firm). For example, the automatic gearbox that Jaguar buy from ZF in West Germany is about 90 per cent identical to the unit that goes into all BMW Series 6 and 7 vehicles, and the manual transmission purchased from Getrag is 90 per cent common to the unit on the 911 and 928 Porsche cars.

The component producers also make frequent use of smaller sub-contractors. They tend to operate on a considerably larger scale than the subcontractors, and have markedly different production processes, types of capital ownership and management, possess different technologies and play different functional roles within economies. Some of these component suppliers operate in oligopolistic systems, for example, there are only three suppliers of glass to the automotive industry in Western Europe. Therefore it is really a mistake to try to fathom out the intricacies of production subcontracting by including these two different types of firms under the same heading (e.g. Holmes 1986; Cooke 1988; Morris 1988; Gertler 1988). The confusion over these different categories may be due to the relative lack of empirical evidence on production subcontracting.

The component suppliers can be considered as 'main contractors'. They tend to have written contracts to supply a certain amount of components per year, month or day, that they may well have designed or partly designed themselves. Subcontracting often involves no actual written contract and tends to be more 'informal'. The accountancy procedure is often more like giving a bill for services rendered. For example, an order may involve a buyer from a customer firm giving a subcontractor a drawing of a component or part and then agreeing a price. The components are then made and sent to the customer together with an invoice.

In order to assess the nature of subcontracting and its use by firms in the motor industry a study was undertaken in the Coventry local economy; comprising the City itself plus the Districts of Warwick and Leamington Spa and Nuneaton and Bedworth. Three motor vehicle assemblers were examined: Peugeot-Talbot, Massey Ferguson and Jaguar, and a major component manufacturer Automotive Products whose main plant is in Leamington. Fifty-nine precision engineering subcontracting firms were also examined. All of these engineering firms were independent and were locally owned or controlled. They consisted of all but one of the precision engineering subcontracting firms that had survived over the post-recessionary period of 1982–7. These firms were horizontally linked, in that they were competing in the same market using metal-cutting machine tools for batch production. The firms employed 663 workers in 1982 and 787 in 1987, giving an increase of 124 workers and a mean size of about 13 employees per firm in 1987. The vehicle assembly firms consist of two low-volume 'quality' producers, Jaguar and Massey Ferguson, with outputs of about 45,000 units each in 1987, and one 'medium-volume' car producer with a 4 per cent share in the UK passenger car market, though production at Peugeot-Talbot had fallen from 120,000 cars in 1983 to only 45,000 in 1987 (*Coventry Economic Monitor*). Automotive Products is one of the largest manufacturers of clutch and braking systems in Europe and produces components for motor vehicles in large batches (100,000s) down to single units for competition use. In total the four large firms employed over 19,358 workers in 1982 and 18,502 in 1987 (*Coventry Economic Monitor* and COVRIED).

It is argued here that the changing production strategies of these firms has led to a qualitatively and quantitatively different use of subcontracting. By interviewing the owners of the precision engineering firms, senior purchasing managers within the 'customer' firms and trade union representatives, an accurate picture of the nature and extent of subcontracting prior to, and during, the 1980s could be constructed. These two time periods can be equated with the end of the 'Fordist' production regime and the start of the emerging 'neo-Fordist' period (Tolliday and Zeitlin 1986) and also the impact of 'Japanization' on the UK manufacturing economy (Oliver and Wilkinson 1988).

THE 'OLD REGIME' OF PRODUCTION SUBCONTRACTING

The characteristic use of production subcontracting by firms in the motor industry prior to the 1980s was essentially that of capacity or concurrent subcontracting. The small firms were used to supplement in-house machining capacity. 'A lot of companies used subcontracting as a buffer so for the subcontracting firms when work was plentiful they were OK, but in the recession the work stopped and this caused lay-offs in the subcontracting firms' (AEU respondent). During the recessionary period subcontracting firms were generally dependent on

2–3 major customers, and it was not uncommon to find firms working almost exclusively for one customer.

Many of the batches that were subcontracted out were 'rush jobs' that would often be required back, completed, within a day of being given out. These rush jobs mostly arose out of poor production planning by management in the customer firm, a machine breakdown, or a sudden increase in demand that could not be met with by the available in-house capacity. The element of poor production planning often prompted queries by subcontractors as to how the customer firms could ever hope of successfully implementing just-in-time production, when they frequently had difficulty in successfully planning production with large buffer stocks. The size of batches that were put out for machining could be of any size, which reflects the *ad hoc* way in which subcontracting was often used. This period also saw the 'free issue' of raw materials, tooling and checking fixtures. If castings were to be machined they would be supplied by the customer out of its own stock. The material would be machined by the subcontractor and returned for quality control inspection by the customer firm.

The in-house machine shops of large manufacturing firms are often expensive to run due to the high overheads they receive from the rest of the company, these are *inter alia*: costs from management, supervision and office functions, heating, floorspace and rates, and the subsidization of canteens. Small firms generally have much lower overheads, though labour rates are about the same, and this is reflected in running costs which are typically one-third of those of the large firm machine shop. This helps to explain why subcontracting remained a competitive option for the production of smaller batches (from 1 to 5,000 units). Generally in mechanical engineering, the smaller the batch size, the more expensive per unit the component is to produce. This is because the cost of the tooling and setting-up time is spread over less components. As a result, smaller batches tended to be subcontracted out and were done on general-purpose machine tools, and larger batches would be done in-house on automatic (mechanically or microelectronically controlled), or special-purpose machine tools. For the period prior to 1982 the batch sizes between O and Q_1 in Fig. 10.2 would be subcontracted out, whereas Q_1 upwards would be retained in-house. The value of Q depends on the nature and complexity of the component, typically a value of 5,000 components would be a reasonable estimate. Q_2 would be about 50,000 units.

The location of where a particular batch would be produced was calculated by comparing a subcontractor's quote with the cost of doing the job in the customer's own machine shop. The usual method

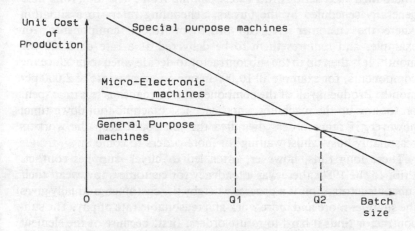

Figure 10.2 Machine tool choice and batch size
Source: Watanabe (1986: 245)

was to circulate drawings of the component to be manufactured to six prospective suppliers, who were asked to submit a price quotation. If none of the quotes were cheaper than the estimated in-house cost of production then the job would not be subcontracted out. If a quote for outsourcing was lower then the job would go to the firm which gave the lowest quote. If dual-sourcing was required then the customer would ask a second supplier to produce the components at the same price as the firm that submitted the lowest quote. The pricing of batch engineering components has always been notoriously difficult and so many owners agreed to the lower price. The use of dual-sourcing also enabled the prices of established batches to be reduced. The customer could say to a firm that the second source had agreed to do the work for less money, and that if they did not lower the price to the level of the other source then the other firm would be given all of the order. Suppliers rarely knew the customer's other sources, as they may have been in a different town or city, and so they had to accept the buyer's word and comply with the price reduction or risk losing the order for the next batch.

Long runs, or larger batch sizes, were given out on a subcontracted basis if an external cost quotation for a component was lower than in-house production. These long runs were much sought after by the small firms as they gave them an element of stability and they could better plan their production. Production planning has always been difficult for subcontractors as frequently they were not sure of when or where their next set of orders were coming from. The long runs were generally scheduled by the buyers. Scheduling refers to a situation where the customer gives an order for 10,000 components, for example, and requires them to be delivered at a rate of 2,000 per month. It is then up to the subcontractor to decide when to produce the components, for example all 10,000 in one go, or at a rate of 2,000 per month. Producing all of the components at once means less time spent on tooling-up the machines, and hence less machine-tool down-time; however, if other orders dwindled the job could keep the workers reasonably busy whilst waiting for more orders to come in.

These long runs, however, often led to buyer–supplier conflict. Prior to the 1980s there was a tendency for customers to 'sweat' their subcontractors. This is a process whereby the customer gradually gives the supplier more and more work at a reasonable rate of pay. The subcontractor finds it hard to refuse orders, first, because of the element of stability and good income that long runs offer, and second, for fear of losing work from its major customer. Once the supplier is dependent, the customer then demands price reductions for the components. The subcontractor is forced to comply, because if the work is withdrawn it may not be sure of picking up sufficient new orders quickly enough to avoid bankruptcy. This type of relationship did often result in bankruptcies in the subcontracting firms; though with policies of dual- and multi-sourcing during this period the large firms were not worried about bankruptcies in their suppliers (Friedman 1977: 122). The only time that the subcontractor had a noticeable amount of power was when doing the rush jobs. The nature of a rush job means that the customer is desperate for the work. In this circumstance the subcontractors may ask for a much higher rate of pay for the job, up to ten times the normal cost was not unusual. The customer would pay the higher rate for the work, accepting that the subcontractor is helping it out of a difficult situation and will probably have to pay its workforce overtime. The main focus of component buying prior to the 1980s was the price of components, then their quality and their delivery times. Delivery was not crucially important, except for rush jobs, because large buffer stocks were maintained in the motor firms' stores or warehouses.

THE 'NEW REGIME' OF SUBCONTRACTING

Throughout the 1980s new production subcontracting relationships have been evolving. These changes can mostly be attributed to the nature of the investment and disinvestment strategies of the motor industry over this period. They can be seen as part of a strategy of reversing the trends of huge capital losses and internal inefficiencies that became apparent in the late 1970s, by reconsidering and consolidating the 'core' activities, and a disintegration of the more 'peripheral' aspects of production. All four of the large firms have made use of capacity subcontracting for batch engineering work. However, this type of subcontracting is now rarely used, mainly because the closure of in-house machine shops in the customer firms has resulted in a situation where batch production can no longer be done in-house. This represents a shift from capacity to specialist subcontracting, as the components can no longer be produced at all in-house. Massey Ferguson closed down half a million square feet of machine-shop capacity at Banner Lane's satellite machine shop in Baginton. This was part of the rationalization to cut the over-capacity of the Coventry-based tractor operations following the drop in demand in the world tractor market in the 1980s. During this period of decreased demand subcontracted work was not recentralized, as there were insufficient tractors being made to require the components.

Shortly after the BBA takeover of Automotive Products in 1986, they closed down one of the largest collections of multi-spindle automatic machine tools[1] in Western Europe at the Leamington plant. As a direct result £13 million per year of batch machining work was subcontracted into the local economy compared with £4 million in 1982. The reason for the closure of this machine shop was that some of the machines were old and needed replacing. A long-term accountancy decision was taken, comparing the cost of renewing machines and their running and overheads costs, against the cost of buying-in components on a subcontracted basis. Virtually all of the small and medium batches are subcontracted out, with in-house machining done on purpose-built machines. These machines are designed to produce one type of component, for example a disc brake calliper, and cannot be used to produce anything else, they are not very 'flexible' machines. However, once they are tooled up to produce a component, which can take up to a week, they can turn out vast quantities at a rate quicker than any other type of machine. These machines tend to be used for current production runs, with batch sizes of 50,000 upwards (see Fig. 10.2).

Jaguar has reduced in-house machining of small batch components and castings. The reason for the reduction in machining capacity is partly strategic and partly geographical. Over the post-recessionary period Jaguar has preferred to invest in assembly and production control systems, such as engineering development, robotized welding and paint spraying, CAD and computerized management information systems. The company has also laid down an assembly track for the third engine that it now produces, the AJ6. The Jaguar sites are constrained by their location, they are either built-up around or adjacent to green-belt land. This leaves no room for expansion in the established plants. So in order to introduce a new manufacturing facility another one has to be removed to make way for it. As a direct result of the new assembly line for the AJ6 a machine shop had to be closed down to make room for it. This now means that an extra £2 million of subcontracted machining goes into the local economy. Other areas of machining have been retained or expanded, in particular the machining of engines and cylinder heads, with a flexible 'pilot build' facility. This type of work has always been performed in-house and is unlikely ever to be decentralized as it is a key activity, alongside bodyshell assembly.

Peugeot-Talbot used to use capacity subcontracting to supplement in-house machining for the production of the ckds of Peykans (Hillman Hunters) for assembly in Iran. However, with the cessation of this contract in 1987, and the closure of the foundry and engine shops at the Stoke Plant there is negligible machining work subcontracted from this plant. There is also very little work put out on a subcontracting basis from the Ryton plant. Ryton is for the most part a 'screwdriver' plant, concentrating on assembly only. All of the drive train and body panels are shipped from France. The bodies are manually spot welded and then bought-in components are added on the production track. Subcontracted machining from Peugeot-Talbot into the local economy is now of minimal proportions. The small amount of work that does go out is for non-standard fixings and studs and some tooling repair services.

Jaguar and Massey Ferguson have also externalized a large proportion of their prototype and development work, and in the process have created a dense network of local subcontractors specializing in this type of work. The customers need to have these firms located very close to them due to the nature of prototype and development work. Even with the use of CAD to design prototypes they often require slight modifications. This often means a series of trips to and from the customer several times in one day, in order to fit and re-machine the component. To cut down on development time the firms must be located within a few miles of the customer. Generally, for all of the firms, the more non-standard or smaller the batch size the closer to the customer it is made. Automotive Products also has a closely knit group of production subcontractors in and around Leamington and Coventry, in order to speed up the pace of batch production process. The customer firms have not caused firms to move into their immediate vicinity, they have concentrated on encouraging existing batch engineering firms in the local economy.

The nature of the dependency on the customers has changed. This is as a direct result of the lesson of the recession learnt by both sides. Thirty-five subcontracting firms went out of business between 1982 and 1987. Many of these are believed to have gone out of business as a result of over-dependence on too few major customers. The surviving firms had all successfully managed to increase and diversify their customer base. Of the fifty-nine surviving firms, they had all, bar four, managed to become less than around 30 per cent dependent on their major customer. The bankruptcy of subcontractors that had not previously worried the vehicle firms prior to and during the recession did concern them after the recession. They found that when they had cut back orders it caused a loss of a major portion of their supply base. When demand picked up again they found a relative shortage of subcontractors to do their work. Massey Ferguson now only allow their suppliers to do a maximum of 15 per cent of their work for them. Jaguar also encourages customer diversification in its suppliers, first to make sure that the subcontractors survive should the Jaguar orders be reduced or cut, and second, so that the subcontractors will pick up new technologies and production methods when working for other customers. This is contrary to Gertler's claim that 'from the supplier's viewpoint, there is a reduction in the number of firms to which it sells' (1988: 422). When assessing a firm to be a subcontractor Automotive Products, Massey Ferguson and Jaguar all carry out audits and capability studies on the suppliers, to make sure that they are financially viable and are capable of producing work of the quality they demand.

The users of subcontracting in the motor industry in the Coventry local economy are now more concerned with good quality at a reasonable price, rather than a good price with reasonable quality. The subcontracting relationship is seen more as a long-term 'partnership' strategy. The firms carefully pick their subcontractors and want them to survive even if orders are cut back. The large firms still possess the power in the relationship; however, rather than trying to 'screw them down on price' they allow their suppliers to earn a reasonable amount, and every effort is made to help, or encourage them to improve their production process. Customers are more interested in using their power to improve component quality rather than to force price reductions. Jaguar and Massey Ferguson have to do this through co-operation and persuasion, whereas Automotive Products, who sub-contract out substantially larger batches and longer runs, can do this by insistence, by virtue of greater economic leverage. This has led to the insistence on strict delivery and quality control programmes such as JIT and statistical process control. All of the large firms are moving towards the acceptance of 'zero defects' from their suppliers. The implementation of these quality related programmes has effectively externalized the cost and functions of quality control onto the supplier. All three of the vehicle firms that are still using production subcontracting have removed their teams of line inspectors, generally the operators or fitters check the components as they use them or put them on.

Supplier loyalty is rewarded by attempting to make sure that a company that helps with the development of a component, by doing the relatively lower paid prototype work, is rewarded with the final production run. This was not always the case prior to the 1980s when the development firms were often undercut on price by other companies when the six-quote system was used. The loyalty of the subcontracting firms can be seen first, in that they introduce the quality control and inspection procedures insisted upon by the cus-tomers, and second, they still do the inevitable rush jobs that arise. Many of the Automotive Products' subcontractors are prepared to receive a job and to work all night if it is really necessary. 'If they can't do this and do the job correctly then AP doesn't survive and they don't survive' (Automotive Products respondent).

Dual-sourcing, and duplication of production in-house and by a supplier are no longer used as production strategies. Massey Ferguson decide at the conception stage where a component is to be produced in-house or externally. If a component is to be outsourced then Massey Ferguson still use the six-quote system. Massey Ferguson pay for, and therefore own, any necessary tooling to make a component. It is now considered extravagant to make two sets of tooling. The desire to avoid paying for two sets of tooling also helps to explain why capacity subcontracting is no longer used. If there is a chance of disruption in production due to industrial relations problems in a supplying firm then Massey Ferguson will 'pull' the tooling and give the work to another firm.

CONCLUSION

The use of production subcontracting in the Coventry local economy by motor vehicle firms has undergone a qualitative change and a net quantitative increase, despite the loss of work put out by Peugeot-Talbot. The subcontracting relationship is still dominated by the larger customer firms who seek to use their power in an effort to increase the quality of bought-in components. This is mainly because all of the motor firms are moving towards a concept of 'total quality control' (Feigenbaum 1983) in their production process. The small subcontracting firms are no longer forced into bankruptcy, partly because of the abandonment of this policy by customers and partly because the suppliers that have survived since 1982 have diversified the structure of their customer base. The expansion of the subcontractor's customer base has been encouraged by the customer firms, realizing the strategic role that the subcontractors play in their own production process. The change from capacity or concurrent subcontracting to specialist subcontracting has been as a direct result of the disinvestment in machining capacity in the motor firms. Other areas of disinvestment have resulted in the subcontracting out of other 'peripheral' functions, these include: toolroom work, canteens, cleaning, security and transportation. Investment has been concentrated on assembly functions, with the introduction of automated welding, paint-spraying and transfer machines, and computerized design and management information systems. The decentralization of production outlined here challenges Marshall's statement that 'the major motor manufacturers in an attempt to achieve greater economics of scale in production, have . . . introduced greater vertical integration' (1987: 114). Finally, given the subordinate role of the subcontracting firms it might be wondered why they do this type of work. The answer is simple, 'there's a lot of money to be made in subcontracting' (subcontracting firm owner).

NOTES

1 The work done by these mechanically automated machines is on a large batch size basis, typically 5,000 to 50,000. These machines require special cams to be made to control the movement of the machine's cutting and forming tools. Once set up these machines can turn out components at a much faster rate than microelectronically controlled machine tools, and usually a semiskilled operator can 'mind' up to three machines at a time. The use of these machines lies between microelectronically controlled machine tools and special-purpose machine tools on Fig. 10.2. Special-

purpose machine tools take even longer to tool-up, but can produce at an even faster rate than multi-spindle automatic machine tools.

11 Industrial restructuring and the labour force: the case of Austin Rover in Longbridge, Birmingham

Dennis Smith

FOUR GENERATIONS AT LONGBRIDGE

This chapter is about the responses of car workers and management to the attempts made in recent years to increase flexibility in the use of labour and technology. This analysis is specific to the Austin Rover plant at Longbridge from early 1986 to early 1988.[1] It is based upon interviews with management and shopfloor workers.[2] The research was undertaken before the announcement of the takeover of Austin Rover by British Aerospace. Since organizational change occurs rapidly in the car business, this chapter only claims to be reporting as history, facts which may have since altered in some respects.

A company workforce is a historical product. Four generations may be identified at Longbridge. The earliest generation includes employees who were recruited in the period ending in 1952, the year when Austin and Morris merged to form the British Motor Corporation. A few remain still. They joined in the post-War years when a powerful shop steward organization was consolidating its position.

The next generation consists of recruits from the period between 1953 and 1967. During these years, shop stewards and foremen negotiated local shopfloor agreements. Piecework reigned. Buoyant home demand disguised inefficient and irrational management. Too many models were produced on too many sites.

The subsequent generation – 1968–77 – stems from the era of the British Leyland Motor Corporation (or BL). This was managed by Lord Stokes until 1975. Measured day-work replaced piecework during this phase. After 1975 British Leyland became a publicy owned company run by Sir Don Ryder. Formal consultative or participation arrangements within the company strengthened the higher echelons of the plant-based union bureaucracy at the expense of the shop floor.

The fourth generation begins in 1978 and includes employees

recruited during or after the regime of Michael Edwardes. For some purposes it is possible to subdivide this fourth generation, separating out recruits during the Edwardes regime (1978–82) – which saw the Longbridge shopfloor workforce fall from about 15,000 to about 11,000 – and those who joined after 1983. In the years before 1983 considerable investment in new technology took place, including the building of the New West factory to house body production for the new Metro.

At the same time a frontal attack took place upon trade union power. The chief convenor, Derek Robinson was sacked in 1979. New conditions of work were implemented, some immediately, some gradually and not, even now, fully. These included: an end to shop-floor bargaining over job times; the introduction of teamworking by flexible workers within zones controlled by supervisors; and the inauguration of 'two-trades maintenance' based upon mechanical and electrical skills.

THREE APPROACHES TO FLEXIBILITY

During the past decade three approaches to flexibility have been tried by management at Longbridge. They are summarized in Table 11.1.

Table 11.1   Three approaches to flexibility

Management strategy	Characteristic of labour force emphasized

A Involvement
  (1) Participation
  (2) New technology training; Quality circles
	Capacity for commitment

B Automation	Dispensability
C Domination	Vulnerability

The strategy of encouraging worker involvement (A in Table 11.1) has taken two forms, both of which have been indicated. In each case the object was to elicit positive cooperation from the workforce. During the Ryder years, participation (involvement strategy mark 1) was a means of coopting the trade union bureaucracy in favour of the firm's recovery strategy. More recently, another approach (involvement strategy mark 2) has been adopted, one which as far as possible by-passes the trade unions and appeals directly to the shopfloor.

During 1986 a series of management initiatives began, designed to improve communications and raise the level of employee involvement. These included: a 'Working with Pride' programme of film shows, talks and site visits; a new system of regular line (or zone) briefings of the shopfloor workforce conducted by supervisors; a re-training programme for supervisors stressing team-based work methods, quality control, and getting it right first time (with every production worker acting as his own 'inspector'); and a programme of quality (or zone) circles designed on classic lines, i.e. technical problem-solving meetings by small groups of workers under the guidance of a management 'facilitator'. Running through all these initiatives was an emphasis upon teamwork and responsible cooperation.

Another approach to flexibility is labelled the automation strategy (B in Table 11.1). Its ultimate object is to dispense with as many of the shopfloor employees as possible, replacing them with hard-working and compliant machines. The ideal factory would have no workers beyond a few skilled engineers and supervisors: maximum technological flexibility; minimum labour.

This approach was illustrated in the flexible manufacturing system (FMS) operating in part of Longbridge's South Works. Nine million pounds had been spent on the FMS facility which was being used to machine cylinder heads and cam carriers for the M16 engine used in the Rover 800 series. The director of manufacturing operations in Birmingham recently speculated to the press about the possibility of a complete 'lights out' operation, in other words a factory run by machines and robots serviced by a small, elite workforce (*Birmingham Post*, 30 September 1987).

The third approach to flexibility is to seek maximum domination by management over the workforce, weakening the defences of the latter against commands from above (C in Table 11.1). Such an approach depends upon the existence of strong feelings of vulnerability on the shop floor. It is likely to appeal to a management which is itself feeling highly vulnerable. The domination approach is likely to entail some shedding of labour, especially in its early phases as in the late 1970s and early 1980s at Longbridge. If the assertion of managerial domination is closely associated with an automation strategy, it may be possible to blame some of the job losses onto the constraints of new technology, exaggerating the effects of the latter and using it as cover.

All three strategies are designed to improve profits by increasing productivity. They are obviously related. For example, increased automation combined with labour-shedding places an additional burden on the remaining workforce. Direct workers may be expected to monitor process and product to a higher degree than before, incorporating inspection and quality control functions, implementing statistical process control techniques, adapting to new machines and so on. In other words, a management which automates is probably also going to have to dominate and involve its workforce to a greater degree than previously.

THREE STAGES OF MANAGEMENT FOR FLEXIBILITY AT LONGBRIDGE

Since the late 1970s the pursuit of flexibility has passed through three stages at Longbridge. First, the strategy of involvement in its guise as formal participation was used as a means to achieve trade union cooperation with the implementation of the strategy of automation, most obviously in the form of the robotized tracks for the new Metro. Once the recovery plan was underway, the strategy of involvement was dropped by management. A second stage was inaugurated in which the glamour, prestige and new optimism associated with the Metro project helped management in a campaign to enforce more flexible working practices through a strategy of domination; even if such practices were not directly related to the technology (cf. Willman and Winch 1985).

Under the Edwardes regime management insisted upon its right to move workers around between different jobs and parts of the factory in the course of a shift. This principle was operating widely during the period of the research. From the top downwards the managerial style was autocratic. Labour was, in effect, told to bend or it would be broken.

By the mid-1980s management at Longbridge had, then, used involvement strategy mark 1 as a means to implement an automation strategy; withdrawn involvement strategy mark 1; and used the automation strategy as a lever to enforce a domination strategy.

A third stage was underway in the years from 1986. Greater involvement was required from the workforce because as manning levels were cut to the bone the workers remaining were being required to take on new tasks such as quality control, previously the function of the dwindling band of shopfloor inspectors. They were having to be moved around more and needed to pay more attention to what they were doing and understand its significance. Pursuit of greater involvement had two aspects.

First, the domination strategy was used in an attempt to create shopfloor conditions which would increase employee commitment. Second, this same involvement strategy was cultivated by, in effect, selling specific new technology projects to the workforce and offering 'select' workers the chance to be closely involved with what was presented as the future of the company. In other words, automation was used as a bait to entice workers into a greater degree of commitment.

The second aspect is illustrated by the training programmes associated with projects such as the new PGI gearbox. As one manager, interviewed in November 1986, explained:

> We bring all the managers up from within the [PGI] area up to talk to the group of operators which has never been done before. We have the production manager who comes up and explains all about the component they are going to make . . . he talks about the facilities they are going to have to machine it, the volumes . . ., the need for quality, the introduction of statistical [process] control, the role that they have got to play. We have the industrial engineering manager up who actually talks about . . . the need for us to have work standards. We bring the quality manager up. . . . We bring up the manufacturing manager who will talk about the need for them to work together as a group. [We] tour them round the actual facility where the PGI gearbox is being installed so they understand if fully. . . . And we also let them have a ride and drive and [say] 'This is a PGI gearbox. Doesn't it feel good? And this is a Volkswagen gearbox. Isn't it crap?'

Similar programmes had been carried out for operators on the 'K' series engine and the flexible manufacturing system. They had even taken the operators to Cowley to see related aspects of production there. The manager concluded: 'Now the reaction that we had from that was extremely positive because they felt they belonged and they knew what they were doing and why they were making it.'

The other approach to involvement is, as indicated, through a particular application of the domination strategy. This can best be illustrated by the history of quality circles (or zone circles as they were known) at Longbridge. The zone circle scheme was introduced to the employees with minimum (in effect no) consultation with the trade unions. It was a 'soft' strategy imposed in a 'hard' way. The zone circle scheme began in February 1986 and lasted about a year. It never engaged the active support of more than about 200 workers. Trade union resistance brought it to a halt by the middle of 1987 (see Smith 1988). It was subsequently replaced with a programme of 'discussion groups' with built-in rights for shop stewards to attend such groups if they wished.

Between 1986 and 1988 much of the flexibility achieved by management depended upon shopfloor acquiescence in processes of intensification – in other words, being required to work harder and faster – in return for not losing their jobs. However, the picture is a complex one which differs to some extent depending on what part of the factory you look at, the age and recruitment generation of the interviewee and whether you are talking to hourly-paid operatives or first-line supervisors. Some of the detail may now be examined.

AUTHORITY AND MORALE

Interviews with seventy-three shopfloor workers (see Table 11.2) carried out in the summer of 1986 made it clear that the authority of the trade unions had decreased and that of management increased over the previous decade. Workers had considerable reservations about both parties. However, there was a high degree of confidence in the future of Longbridge. On the shop floor, changes had been noticed both in the type of worker being recruited and the attitude of first-line supervisors.

Table 11.2 Proportional distribution (%) of Longbridge shopfloor workforce by age and date of recruitment (October 1985)

Age	Recruitment				
	Before 1953	1953–67	1968–77	After 1977	Total
Up to 26 years	0 (0)[a]	0 (0)	1 (1)	11 (14)	12 (15)
27–46 years	0 (0)	6 (8)	20 (10)	14 (11)	41 (29)
Over 46 years	4 (3)	21 (15)	17 (7)	5 (4)	47 (29)
	4 (3)	27 (23)	38 (18)	30 (29)	100[b] (73)

$n = 10,289$

[a] Figures in parenthesis indicate the number of interviews carried out with shopfloor employees in each category

[b] Calculated on the basis of data supplied by the company relating to the shopfloor workforce in October 1985. All percentages are rounded up or down

Only about a fifth of the shopfloor interviewees expressed strong support for the local trade union organization or indicated that unions were necessary for the protection of employees. Over a third were hostile or negative in their comments. Some typical reactions were:

'They've not got a good name. The membership feel let down' (quality inspector, 55, car assembly buildings); and 'I pay my [union] money but I'm not interested. You've got to look after yourself' (Metro assembler, 32). A common view was that the unions had been over-mighty during the 1960s and 1970s, had been taken down a peg or two, and now were too weak to be effective. Their record over strikes was a bad one. They almost always lost and the workforce were invariably left out of pocket.

According to this view, the unions would still be missed if they were not there to take up cases relating to working conditions or individual grievances. But they were generally out of touch with the membership: 'People don't accept trade-union opinions straight off. They didn't question it before. They do now' (production marshaller, 52, car assembly buildings). There was even some slight evidence that in parts of the plant management were beginning to supplant the local union representatives as the channel for expressing grievances. For example: 'People don't go to the shop steward like they used to. They tend to talk things over with the supervisor' (guage maker, 54). This particular respondent was an active member of a zone circle.

A consensus with respect to company strategy emerged from the interviews. It was that the company was improving its model range and the level of quality. The shop floor was doing its bit. Everything depended upon how well the salesforce performed. There was anxiety about the Honda merger, about perceived managerial incompetence and infighting and about the effect on Longbridge of competition from Rover's Cowley plant. However, it was generally thought that the company was doing sufficiently well to guarantee a future for the Longbridge works, if not necessarily for individual workers.

There was very strong support for two propositions: that the main factor responsible for improved cooperation at shopfloor level in recent years was fear of redundancy (see Table 11.3, column B); and that management treated people like numbers and not as human beings. The suggestion that improved quality was a consequence of increased trust was accepted by well under a third of the employees asked. The more recent recruits rejected it more thoroughly than their predecessors: nearly seven out of ten of the post-1977 recruits dismissed the idea (column A).

However, more encouraging from the company's point of view is that when asked to consider the idea that management were genuinely interested in the well-being of the workers the size of the minority prepared to agree steadily increased — from one in five to two in five — when moving from the earlier to the more recent recruits.

Table 11.3 Responses to statements relating to management/employee relations at Longbridge

A = quality/trust; B = redundancy/cooperation; C = managerial interest in well-being; D = 'put one over'; E = numbers/human beings; F = football team; G = automation (the full versions of the statements are given below)

| | Recruitment generation[a] | | | | | | | | | | | | | | | | | | | | |
| | Up to 1967 (n=19) | | | | | | | 1968–77 (n=17) | | | | | | | After 1977 (n=26) | | | | | | |
Response	A	B	C	D	E	F	G	A	B	C	D	E	F	G	A	B	C	D	E	F	G
Agree	32[b]	63	16	63	79	42	74	35	71	29	47	71	71	77	12	65	39	81	85	62	62
Disagree	21	16	37	21	21	16	5	47	18	41	18	18	18	6	65	23	42	12	15	15	23
Don't know	26	11	42	16	0	6	21	12	6	29	35	12	6	12	15	8	19	8	0	4	8
No reply	21	11	5	0	0	37	0	6	6	0	0	0	0	0	8	4	0	0	0	19	15

[a]The two earliest recruitment generations – up to 1952 and 1952–67 – have been combined in this table
[b]Percentages have been rounded up or down

Interviewees were asked to respond to the following statements:

A 'The Company has managed to improve and maintain its reputation for high quality because it has cultivated a spirit of trust between management and workers'

B 'The major factor in improving the degree of cooperation between management and workers in recent years has been the widespread fear of redundancy'

C 'The management at Austin Rover are genuinely interested in the well-being of the workers'

D 'The management at Austin Rover would put one over on the workers if they had a chance'

E 'Nowadays management at Austin Rover treat people like numbers and not as human beings'

F 'Working in industry is like belonging to a football team. Managers and workers are playing in different positions but they are all trying to score goals for the same team'

G 'Automation is supposed to benefit everybody but the worker generally loses out when you put in new machinery'

Furthermore, employees taken on since 1977 were, compared with earlier recruits, four times as likely to disagree with the proposition that the worker generally loses out as a consequence of automation (column G): almost a quarter of these recent recruits were prepared to see the benefits of innovation, for example in terms of eliminating unpleasant and heavy work.

The longer established employees were well aware that a new type of worker had been taken on in recent years. The newcomers were worried about mortgage repayments. Some of them had had a taste of the dole queue. They were 'under pressure, worrying about the job. It makes them less sociable' (con rod operator, 53, South works). According to a 35-year-old machine shop operator in the East works, the new recruits were 'a load of zombies. They are not allowed to think'. Another man commented: 'They are not as cheerful as they used to be because of the pressure. They are more aggressive. It used to be fun here. Not now' (machine tool fitter, 58). The new workers were 'Not so happy-go-lucky.' They were 'more uptight with each other. Just get on with their jobs. The communication has gone' (51-year-old layout inspector).

Another aspect was also acknowledged: 'The new people have different attitudes. We used to be very negative, saying "This will never work" and so on. You don't get so much of that now. The younger ones will have a go' (car assembler, 32). A 25-year-old paint shop operative taken on in 1984 provided a view from the other side. He commented: 'The old blokes used to tell you not to stand for things. They don't now.'

There was a similar broad consensus about the character of first-line management. Supervisors were seen as being under intense pressure from higher up to reach their production quotas. Over the years they had become much harder although there had been some easing up since the mid-1980s. An established attitude of resentment mixed with pity was punctuated with occasional signs of respect as the following quotations show:

> At one time you could get away with a good many things but they're more strict now. You've got to abide by the rules. You need them to run the place properly. At one time you'd get a warning but now you could get the sack.
>
> (Material handler and storekeeper, 50)

> If you work they're fair enough. They have a tougher job than they used to. They get hauled over the coals if things go wrong, machine break-downs and so on.
>
> (Machine shop operator, 53)

They're scared of their jobs. And helping out on the tracks. It wouldn't have been allowed before.

(Machine tool fitter, 58)

It's hard for shopfloor workers to accept that the supervisor wants to know what they think. The company has changed unbelievably.

(Training instructor, 39)

The supervisors seem to be more pleasant lately, less worries.

(General machinist, 61)

I'm on first-name terms. They can be quite helpful.

((Maintenance fitter, 20)

Following this discussion of general conditions at Longbridge, attention will now be focused upon specific parts of the operation, looking in turn at maintenance, body and assembly and power train.

MAINTENANCE

The development of the maintenance function illustrates the complexity of relationships between the automation, domination and involvement strategies. First, the introduction of new technology increases rather than decreases the demand for trade skills. For example, in the mid-1980s approximately a third of the shopfloor workforce in the New West works consisted of maintenance teams. As Tables 11.4 and 11.5 show, maintenance workers in the New West were, on average, younger and recruited more recently than the maintenance workforce in body and assembly as a whole. If the power train maintenance workforce is also included (Table 11.6), the average age goes up even further as does the proportion of workers from earlier recruitment generations.

Second, the commitment of skilled mechanics, electricians and so on to their occupations was well above average. However, it was expressed in a spirit of separateness or independence rather than total identification with the company.

The company's response was two-fold. On the one hand, it cut down on the size of its maintenance workforce and made them work much harder. It got them out of their central pens and located them close to the track. On the other hand, it invested in training systems designed to produce a new breed of tradesmen with a wider range of skills. Instead of the complex demarcations between pipefitters, electricians and so on, the new generation of apprentices would be

Table 11.4 Maintenance workers in New West works by age and date of recruitment (%)

Age		Date of recruitment	
Up to 26 years	22[a]	Up to 1952	5
27–46 years	54	1952–67	7
Over 47 years	25	1968–77	26
		Since 1977	63
Total	100	Total	100

n = 192

[a] Calculated on the basis of data supplied by the company relating to the shopfloor workforce in October 1985. All percentages are rounded up or down

Table 11.5 Maintenance workers in body and assembly (including New West) by age and date of recruitment (%)

Age		Date of recruitment	
Up to 26 years	17[a]	Up to 1952	7
27–46 years	47	1952–67	18
Over 47 years	36	1968–77	29
		Since 1977	46
Total	100	Total	100

n = 414

[a] Calculated on the basis of data supplied by the company relating to the shopfloor workforce in October 1985. All percentages are rounded up or down

Table 11.6 Maintenance workers on Longbridge site (including body and assembly) by age and date of recruitment (%)

Age		Date of recruitment	
Up to 26 years	15[a]	Up to 1952	8
27–46 years	44	1952–67	27
Over 47 years	41	1968–77	32
		Since 1977	33
Total	100	Total	100

n = 718

[a] Calculated on the basis of data supplied by the company relating to the shopfloor workforce in October 1985. All percentages are rounded up or down

general electricians with some mechanical skills or general mechanics with some electrical skills.

The tradesmen interviewed displayed a sharp conflict between intellectual enthusiasm for the challenge of advanced technology and physical exhaustion in the face of higher workloads. A 58-year-old machine tool fitter working on the Mini said that six people had left since Christmas and not been replaced. He was having to work through the dinner break to keep up. There had been two heart attacks among his colleagues in the previous few months. One of his colleagues in the Old West, a 40-year-old pipe fitter, was adapting to the company line. He commented: 'We're getting a lot of training at the moment. We have to go to work with another trade for three months. I've been working on pneumatics, hydraulics, conveyors and pumps. The technology is changing. We've got to be efficient and competitive and get rid of demarcation.' A training instructor was even more positive, declaring 'I've never looked forward to work before. Now I love coming here'.

BODY AND ASSEMBLY

Three main production lines were operating in the body shops and assembly buildings. The Old and New West works housed body shops for the Mini (in the former) and the Metro and Rover 200 (in the latter) (Fig. 11.1). The New West is the Longbridge showplace. There are frequent groups of visitors inspecting its overhead conveyor system, driverless transport vehicles, sophisticated inspection department, automated panel store and robotic welding machines. Compared to the hi-tech New West the Old West is, in the words of one employee, like 'the black hole of Calcutta'. It is much less automated and much more human. There is even graffiti. Rover bodies pass through to one of the two car assembly buildings (or CABs). Mini and Metro bodies go into the other CAB.

As Tables 11.7–11.9 show, Mini workers were, on average, the oldest and longest established. Rover 200 workers were the youngest and most recently recruited. Metro workers held an intermediate position. Workers on all three models in the CABs, both track and off-track, emphasized the need for cooperation to make the job manageable. If operators got 'out of station' things got heated: 'we work as a team. It makes it easier' (car finisher, 24). The same went for rectifiers correcting faults on cars coming off the end of the track. However, this was not teamwork in the 'Japanese' sense of feeling strong group membership combined with sentiments of pride and

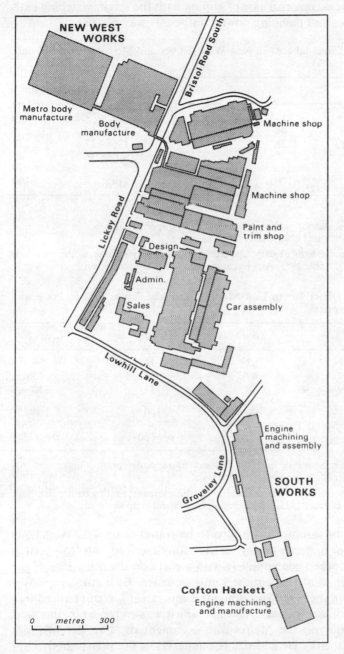

Figure 11.1 General layout of Longbridge factory

belonging. It was more a case of coping with the track, watching each other's backs and damping down conflict. It was reactive.

Table 11.7   Direct labour[a] in New West (Rover and Metro) by age and date of recruitment (%)

Age		Date of recruitment	
Up to 26 years	17[b]	Up to 1952	1
27–46 years	48	1952–67	8
Over 47 years	36	1968–77	48
		Since 1977	43
Total	100	Total	100

n = 681

[a] The term 'direct labour' indicates the exclusion of inspectors, production and material control operators and maintenance workers

[b] Calculated on the basis of data supplied by the company relating to the shopfloor workforce in October 1985. All percentages are rounded up or down

Table 11.8   Direct labour[a] on Mini, Metro and Rover 200 in body and assembly by age (%)

Age	Mini	Metro	Rover 200
Up to 26 years	2[b]	14	36
27–46 years	49	53	45
Over 47 years	48	32	18
Total	100	100	100
	n = 356	*n* = 1307	*n* = 773

[a] The term 'direct labour' indicates the exclusion of inspectors, production and material control operators and maintenance workers

[b] Calculated on the basis of data supplied by the company relating to the shopfloor workforce in October 1985. All percentages are rounded up or down

A degree of teamwork was also to be found in the Old West body plant. A door hanger working on the Mini described how 'to a certain extent' he worked cooperatively with a mate on the other side of the car using the same tools in the same sequence. By contrast, a Rover 200 worker in the New West doing the equivalent job emphasized that his job was 'independent'. A similar spirit was conveyed by the sheet metal rectifier on the Metro who commented: 'I've got my job; they've got theirs'. He added: 'The supervisors are pretty good. They leave you alone as long as you do the job'.

Table 11.9 Direct labour[a] on Mini, Metro and Rover 200 in body and assembly by date of recruitment (%)

Date of recruitment	Mini	Metro	Rover 200
Up to 1952	6[b]	1	1
1953–67	30	15	4
1968–77	51	47	21
Since 1977	13	37	74
Total	100	100	100
	$n = 356$	$n = 1307$	$n = 773$

[a] The term 'direct labour' indicates the exclusion of inspectors, production and material control operators and maintenance workers

[b] Calculated on the basis of data supplied by the company relating to the shopfloor workforce in October 1985. All percentages are rounded up or down

The relative youth of the Rover 200 workers may be explained by the fact that the track is much less automated than in the case of the Metro. The complaints about intensification amongst the interviewees came not from the Rover 200 workers but from the rather older Metro and Mini workers. A 42-year-old trim worker on the Mini complained: 'We are doing more work with fewer men'. He added that the tools and tasks had not changed. However, a Metro trim worker, five years older sardonically observed: 'The new technology was not [intended] to improve the car but to make you work faster. . . . It has made everything faster but not necessarily better.'

The comments of supervisors in body and assembly, interviewed in 1987, indicated that one of the problems arising from this intensification of pressure was absenteeism. At least one supervisor, working in the CABs, blamed this partly on the relentless monotony imposed by short holidays and the lack of strike activity. The most hard-working and reliable operators were to be found amongst a distinct stratum, it was generally agreed. This consisted of what was described by another CAB supervisor as 'the 23 to 26 year old man with two kids and a mortgage who is trapped'. The best workers were flexible and conscientious, prepared to listen but also make constructive comments. As a paint shop foreman put it, 'I don't want people who are like mice'.

The research indicated that supervisory styles varied from zone to zone. However, almost all supervisors complained of lack of manpower, scarcity of materials and the care that has to be taken in motivating those working under them. The bonus system is plant-wide so that the care and effort of any one work group has a very small impact upon it. The supervisor cannot offer local financial incentives although he may be able to find ways of rewarding cooperative workers with a little extra free time.

The job was made easier by the increased freedom in recent years to move labour around the plant without consulting the shop steward. However, flexibility and team work were very much limited by the willingness of individuals to join in voluntarily. This varied greatly.

POWER TRAIN

One of the senior managers on the power train side expressed the company's current approach to good work practice:

> Quality is the responsibility of the operator. . . . There should be prompt despatch to the next in line who is, in effect, your customer. We should talk to each other [about the work we are doing]. Statistical process control helps to achieve high quality standards. We are introducing it in a number of places. If a job is not done properly the operator should 'flag it up' [i.e. mark it for attention]. He should pick that kind of thing up by gauging frequencies. Each operator has a tag – with a specific colour for each zone – and this can be used to flag incorrect items for the inspector to pick up. Robots won't replace people. Over the past two years we've been training new people for the R8 and the PGI gearboxes. We are gradually improving the training. There's a big change from five years ago [interviewed January 1988].

The transformation described above was in its very early stages when the shopfloor interviews were carried out. There was a noticeably higher level of anxiety among workers in the East works as compared to the South works. A 54-year-old machine shop operator from the East works commented: 'Cooperation is essential but it doesn't always happen. There's a lot of friction on the line. It's frustrating when different people have different outlooks. . . . There's a big age gap. Also different ethnic groups.' A tool setter working on the gear section described himself as 'one of the people they want to get rid of'. Such expressions of insecurity were rarer in the South works.

The apparent difference between the two works may be merely due to the fact that prestigious projects such as FMS and the PGI gearbox had a larger and earlier impact on South works while the new projects in East works were at a much earlier stage of development when the interviews were carried out. Important projects were on stream for the East works including the new 'K' series engine and the new MA gearbox (to be installed in the nearby Cofton Hackett building). Techniques such as low pressure sand casting and precision metal forming are also being introduced. However, these innovations were still in the pre-production stage during the research period.

Just as important may have been the different demographic structures of the two workforces. The East works had a much larger proportion of older workers from the earlier recruitment generations. One of the operators described it as 'the geriatric shop'. The South works was smaller and had a more evenly-balanced population (see Tables 11.10 and 11.11).

In both factories new technology was seen as double-edged. On the one hand, it was cutting jobs and making life more difficult for those

Table 11.10 Direct labour[a] on engine and transmission in East and South works by age (%)

Age	East	South
Up to 26 years	5[b]	12
27−46 years	35	35
Over 47 years	60	53
Total	100	100
	n = 1328	n = 582

[a] The term 'direct labour' indicates the exclusion of inspectors, production and material control operators and maintenance workers

[b] Calculated on the basis of data supplied by the company relating to the shopfloor workforce in October 1985. All percentages are rounded up or down

Table 11.11 Direct labour[a] on engine and transmission in East and South works by date of recruitment (%)

Date of recruitment	East	South
Up to 1952	4[b]	8
1953−67	43	26
1968−77	41	32
Since 1977	12	34
Total	100	100
	n = 1328	n = 582

[a] The term 'direct labour' indicates the exclusion of inspectors, production and material control operators and maintenance workers

[b] Calculated on the basis of data supplied by the company relating to the shopfloor workforce in October 1985. All percentages are rounded up or down

who remained. For example, inspectors were under pressure to extend their role to include not only checking work done but also rectification and direct production. On the other hand, for a small minority automation was the route to greater involvement and commitment. A 34-year-old general machinist recently set on as a power press operator working on the new precision metal-forming technology was pleased to have 'a new experience, a new challenge'. He looked forward to 'learning a lot about tools, design and so on'. He thought his job prospects were good: 'with it being a new job, they've got to make it work'.

Power train supervisors, interviewed a year later than the shop-floor, reported that quite high levels of flexibility had been achieved. In the East works, one man said, 'most people will do most jobs we ask, including cleaning down the machines. We don't abuse it. There is still some demarcation but a setter would help a fitter.' Another commented that some operators would do a bit of labouring. A supervisor working on the PGI gearbox said his people were 'good at working together. I got rid of two who didn't fit in'. Flexibility was, however, limited by a lack of skills in some zones and by the conservatism of older workers. More generally, supervisors in power train had similar complaints to their colleagues in body and assembly. Their ideal worker had familiar characteristics: 'young, married, with kids and a mortgage' (East works supervisor).

CONCLUSION

During 1986 and 1987, as perhaps for some time to come, Longbridge was in an 'in between' state. Management had reaped a number of advantages from the strategies of domination and automation. They were the beneficiaries of a smaller, more subordinate workforce. It was less costly, less wasteful. However, in order to optimize quality, quantity and productivity it was thought necessary to increase employee involvement and commitment. The dilemma was that a workforce experiencing intense downward pressure was not likely to display voluntary initiative on behalf of management on a wide scale.

The example of maintenance suggests that it is not impossible to pull off this trick. However, it apparently only works with fairly small groups who already feel, or can be made to feel, that they are a special elite. This observation is reinforced by the apparent success of training programmes for new technology projects such as the PGI gearbox, FMS, the 'K' series engine, and so on.

The attempt to spawn a dense tissue of quality or zone circles has not come off. The new venture of discussion groups – 'son of zone circle' – is likely to be a slow business. Perhaps some lessons can be learned by looking, finally, at the conditions under which zone circles were most effective at Longbridge. The limited success of the zone circle scheme was heavily weighted towards two parts of the site: the highly automated New West body plant with its relatively young labour force and, quite surprisingly, the 'geriatric' East works. Each had six schemes (out of a total of twenty) in May 1987.

As has been seen, the demographic structure, degree of modernity and type of production found in the two locations are quite different. Why should they both have been in the vanguard of the brief zone circle experiment? This outcome may, perhaps, be a consequence, half intended and half unintended, of management's ability to separate out the two areas from the rest of the Longbridge operation.

Recruits to the New West were a mixture of 'green' labour and carefully vetted volunteers from other shops. Management was more dominant than in, say, the Old West works. At the same time, many of the operators in the East works may have felt especially vulnerable because of their association with the old 'A' series engine at a time when new technology seemed to be overtaking it. The incentive to cooperate with management may have been particularly strong, for a minority at least.

However, just as important as demographic factors, may have been the geographical isolation of the East factory. It is separated from the main site by Groveley Lane. Like the New West, it is out on a limb (see Fig. 11.1). From the air, the Longbridge site describes the shape of a huge question mark. The New West is located at the top left extremity of this interrogative. The East works forms the bottom stem.

It is very much open to question whether either the sense of powerlessness or the sense of being a special elite can be generalized throughout the entire Longbridge site. Longbridge seems destined to remain in its 'in between' state for the foreseeable future. The question mark remains.

NOTES

1 The research upon which this chapter is based was carried out as part of the South West Birmingham Project. The author was principal investigator of this project which examined the consequences of economic restructuring with particular reference to the local factories of Rover at Longbridge and Cadbury-Schweppes at Bournville. The research is financed by the Economic and Social Research Council (D04260006). A number of working papers and other publications arising from this project are listed in the bibliography.

2 Interviews were conducted with sixty-two shopfloor workers during the summer of 1986 as part of a larger project concerned with the impact of economic restructuring upon south-west Birmingham. Employees for interview were selected in such a way as to optimize, as far as possible, the distribution of interviewees by age, date of recruitment, type of work and place of residence. During 1987 interviews were carried out with twenty-six supervisors involved in first-line management. Finally, a small number of interviews were held with production and personnel managers at Longbridge. Interviews were also carried out in a number of households in south-west Birmingham. Eleven of these were with Longbridge workers and their responses have been taken into account within the following analysis. The workers interviewed were all residents of the seven postal districts covering south-west Birmingham, as were over 40 per cent of the shopfloor workforce. The interviews with employees and supervisors were based upon a semi-structured questionnaire. These interviews were carried out by Malcolm Maguire. Other interviews were carried out by Michael Maguire and by the author. The expert help of both Maguires is gratefully acknowledged. Analysis of all interview materials was carried out by the author.

12 Policy implications of trends and changes in the vehicle and components industries: the case of the West Midlands

David Elliott and Patrick Gray

Policies are developed and evolve to reflect the trends and changing structure of industries at local, regional, national and European levels. Institutions at these different levels are engaged in developing specific policies which affect market competition and the production decisions of vehicle and component companies. They also take account of the industry effects of more general economic policies. The policy-making process is further complicated by the fact that the diverse and sometimes conflicting interests of companies, workers, consumers and communities have varying degrees of influence with different political institutions at different levels, at different times. Indeed, the interests of communities are often subordinated to national economic interests or excluded from the policy-making process altogether. This chapter begins by summarizing the international trends and changes in the industry which have most affected European and national policies in the 1980s as a prelude to describing the particular forms of policy and initiatives developed in the West Midlands. It concludes by drawing some lessons from the West Midlands experience and that of national and European networks of local and regional authorities on the adequacy of political structures and institutions to respond to technological and locational transformations within the industry.

INTERNATIONAL COMPETITION AND EUROPEAN POLICY

The major trends and changes in the world vehicle and components industry have been well-documented in preceding chapters of this book and elsewhere. The predominant theme is one of instability attributable to the difference between the scale of Japanese production and the size of the Japanese market. It is this difference and its effects on trade, production and competition elsewhere in the world which has most concerned and continues to influence policy at national and European levels.

By the late 1980s car production in Western Europe was roughly equivalent to the size of the market: US production was just over two-thirds of the size of the US market and Japanese production was nearly two and a half times domestic demand. Two-thirds of Japanese exports were destined for the US compared with less than one-third to Europe. Western European manufacturers export less than 100,000 vehicles to the Japanese market and US exports to Japan are negligible. Western Europe, however, exports 700,000 cars to the US, many in the sports and luxury market segment, compared with imports from the US of only 30,000 vehicles. Although the basic problem of instability in production, markets and trade is widely recognized, there is less agreement on its causes and, more significantly from a policy point of view, on its future industrial and locational implications.

Throughout the 1980s it became increasingly clear that, irrespective of the causes of Japanese competitive success, worsening imbalances in trade in vehicles would not be tolerated by the US and European governments for ever. Consequently, Japanese companies continued to increase market penetration and minimize or avoid punitive action by establishing overseas production facilities. Although Japanese investment in Europe is still in its formative stages, it is considerably further advanced in North America. Honda was the first Japanese company to invest in a North American production facility. It was subsequently followed by Nissan, Toyota, Mazda, Mitsubishi, Isuzu, Suzuki and the South Korean company Hyundai in Canada, all of which have either made direct investments or are committed to joint ventures. By the early 1990s, the combined capacity, including some trucks and four-wheel drive vehicles, of these plants will be approximately 2.4 million vehicles per annum and the possibility exists of Japanese companies producing cars in the US for export to Europe.

A more immediate impact of Japanese investment in the US was the re-invigorated interest of Ford and General Motors in the European market. Ford, for example, continued to make major investments in Europe such as the new engine plant at Bridgend and to increase market share by attempting but failing to buy both Austin Rover in the UK and Alfa in Italy. General Motors, meanwhile, for the first time established a European headquarters in Zurich to coordinate and oversee its European activities, notably Opel in Germany and Vauxhall in the UK. A further implication of Japanese investment in the US is that the pre-eminent position enjoyed by some European manu-facturers in the luxury and sports car segments of the market is no longer unassailable as Japanese manufacturers move steadily up-market.

These then are the major features of international competition which European policy is seeking to address. The response is essentially twofold. First, greater reciprocity in external trade with Japan. Second, encouraging competition within the European industry by removing internal barriers to trade. The main problem in agreeing a European trade policy with Japan is the wide variation in Japanese market penetration of different European countries. In the UK, for example, the share of the home market taken by Japanese imports is roughly 11 per cent, the same as the average for Europe as a whole. In Italy, Japanese import penetration is below 1 per cent; in France it is about 3 per cent; in Germany 15 per cent; in Belgium 20 per cent; and in Denmark, Japanese cars account for one-third of the market. These different degrees of Japanese import penetration make it difficult for Europe to present a united front, as each country seeks to protect a different starting point. The aim at present is a situation where the share of the Japanese market held by the EC motor industry is at least half of the Japanese share of the community market.

Resolving trade imbalances with Japan will ultimately depend less on trade agreements than on equalizing relative competitiveness and it is this which underpins the second main strand of European policy. The move towards a genuine internal market, a Europe of production as well as of trade, is intended to stimulate competitiveness and increase productivity, thereby reducing the advantages currently enjoyed by Japanese manufacturers. The most direct way in which costs of European manufacturers are reduced by the internal market is the removal of fiscal, physical and technical barriers to trade within Europe. Manufacturers have supported moves in this direction except where the removal of barriers threatens the market share or future existence of nationally supported companies. Reluctance to harmonize emission regulations is the most obvious example of this problem with the UK dragging its feet whilst West Germany has met and argued for more stringent standards.

Difficulties in reaching agreements between the different national governments on a wide range of fiscal and technical issues combined with a growing awareness of the significance of the industry in economic and employment terms has led the Commission to consider easing the process of adjustment with compensatory social and complementary technological initiatives, alongside policies for trade relations and the internal market. Karl Heinz Narjes, the European

Commissioner for industry, for example, said in concluding his address to the third conference of regional and local authorities in motor manufacturing areas in Antwerp in 1987 that 'The commission is not insensitive to the social consequences of employment losses in such a vital sector as motor vehicles. This is why in parallel to our internal market programme we will reinforce our social policy in particular concerning retraining and our policy of encouraging regional development' (GOM Antwerp, 1987).

UK TRENDS AND POLICY

The success of the vehicle manufacturers located in the UK is of immense importance to employment in other manufacturing industries. They provide a market for the output of thousands of companies in the metals, plastics, rubber, glass, mechanical engineering and electrical industries (Bessant *et al*. 1984). In 1982 it was estimated that in addition to the 177,000 people employed in vehicle assembly, 270,000 jobs were dependent on the purchases of vehicle companies and another 297,000 people were employed producing components for export. In total the industry accounted for 654,000 production jobs or 2.6 per cent of the UK employed workforce (Mackay *et al*. 1984). Whilst employment in the industry has undoubtedly fallen since 1982, its relative importance to and within manufacturing has arguably increased.

The scale of the industry is such that the traumatic changes which British motor manufacturers underwent in the 1970s and 1980s had an economic significance extending far outside the industry. These changes were made more traumatic by an explicit policy of exposing and subjecting the domestic industry to international competition. The process of adapting to the oil price hikes of the 1970s, to new product and process technologies and the challenge from Japan took place against a backdrop of a long-term decline in investment and output. Prior to the 1970s the British motor industry grew in line with the industries of the other major European countries. But over the following decade, car and commercial vehicle output fell steadily from 2.3 million units in 1972 to 1.3 million units in 1982. Including associated component and materials suppliers, some 270,000 jobs were lost between 1974 and 1984. Plants were closed and BL and Chrysler UK had to be rescued from bankruptcy. The net trade balance of the motor industry swung from a surplus of £1,518 million in 1975 to a deficit of £3,887 million in 1986.

In Britain, in contrast to other countries, the recovery of demand after 1979 was met by imports rather than by increased production. Indeed, with sterling buoyed up by revenues from North Sea oil, Ford and General Motors took advantage of their increasingly integrated European operations to switch production to plants on the Continent and launched into an intensive battle for market share in the profitable UK market. Austin Rover, meanwhile, was unable to maintain its position and closed five of its plants as well as drastically cutting employment at Longbridge and Cowley. Following the decline in UK vehicle production the components industry also went through a dramatic cutback. The only sign of expansion was the news that Nissan was to build a plant in the North-East.

In 1986, the rise in the Deutschmark altered the relative production costs more in favour of the UK. A favourable exchange rate reinforced public pressure on the multinational producers to review their sourcing strategies. After years of making money on imported cars and losing money on cars built in the UK, the situation was reversed, with imported cars and components becoming very expensive. With improved productivity and increased investment in new equipment, the UK once again appeared to be a competitive place to build cars. Ford, General Motors and Peugeot all announced plans to increase UK output and even to recommence exporting from the UK. Car production climbed back towards 1.2 million, compared with a low of 890,000 in 1982, but still remained a long way below the peak figure achieved in 1972. Component producers also experienced increasing demand from foreign and domestic customers.

Prospects for the 1990s appear to be somewhat better than the 1980s with most vehicle companies manufacturing in the UK anticipating increased production. However, whilst output may increase, companies are also certain to want further improvements in productivity to match standards set by Nissan, Toyota and Honda on greenfield sites with new workforces and practices. The ability of other car manufacturers to match these standards will largely determine whether new Japanese capacity adds to or displaces existing plants. A similar argument applies in the components industry where opportunities exist for UK suppliers to compete with their Japanese counterparts who will almost certainly be encouraged to set up operations near the new assembly sites.

Productivity does not improve of its own accord. It depends on long-term investment in people and technologies. Under-investment over a long period was one of the principal reasons for the decline of the industry and a reversal of this trend will take several years to begin to take effect. Amongst the vehicle builders only Ford, Rover, Jaguar and Leyland Daf undertake significant research and development in the UK and the aggregate level of R&D spending in the industry has not risen in real terms in the last fifteen years. A similar situation exists in training where investment in human resources lags behind that of other countries. The implication of this legacy of under-investment is that a considerable effort will be required at all levels within the industry if the UK is to catch up and surpass best standards at home and abroad.

THE WEST MIDLANDS RESPONSE

The brief description of international restructuring and European and UK policy responses given above provides a backdrop to the emergence of local and regional policies across Europe but particularly within the UK. The geographical concentration of the industry meant that several communities underwent a process of painful adjustment to international restructuring. Whereas in the past localities and regions tended to be passive recipients of industrial change, the scale of restructuring encouraged several authorities to adopt a more active stance in terms of advocacy and supportive initiatives.

The West Midlands was in the forefront of these moves partly because it was one of the regions most seriously affected and partly because the UK government's non-interventionist stance ignored the differential local and regional effects.

Relationships between the local authorities and the industry, however, predated the change of government. At the end of the 1970s a motor industry action group consisting of manufacturers and the West Midlands County Council (WMCC), met regularly to discuss issues of common interest. The degree of common interest diminished as the situation within the local industry deteriorated and there was a growing recognition that the interests of the community as represented by the WMCC and those of the manufacturers were not always synonymous. More radical and independent policies and initiatives were required.

In 1981 the WMCC established an Economic Development Committee (EDC) which sought to develop a set of motor industry-related policies and initiatives which were part of a broader social, economic and industrial strategy aimed at tackling under-investment, retarded technology, the collapse in skill training and other economic and social disadvantages which undermined the regional economy (Elliott and Marshall 1989). The main vehicle for implementing the EDC's policies was the West Midlands Enterprise Board (WMEB), a limited liability company established at arms length from local government in order to be able to react more speedily to problems and opportunities for supporting local industry.

Its main areas of work were investment in locally owned manufacturing companies, technology transfer, training, cooperative development and advocacy (Edge 1986). By mid-1988 the WMEB had a total investment portfolio of £20 million of which £10 million was invested in twenty-seven companies. It had also encouraged other financial institutions to invest funds alongside the Board of up to four times that amount. In this portfolio nine companies employing over 2,000 people had a substantial dependence on vehicle manufacturing either as suppliers of components for original equipment or as suppliers of spares and parts to the aftermarket.

Technology transfer was the responsibility of a subsidiary company charged with assisting companies to upgrade and introduce best-practice technology in both product and process. Vehicle components was identified as a priority sector for the initial activities of this company. The WMEB was also a major shareholder in Warwick Science Park which contains a number of companies at the leading edge of R&D in the vehicle industry.

In the area of training the WMEB was responsible for establishing a high-quality skills centre which, amongst other things, provided courses to assist people in upgrading and learning new skills in hydraulics, pneumatics and computer-aided design, all of which are relevant to the needs of the vehicle and components industries.

Finally, in order to be a more effective advocate of local interests the WMEB developed alliances with employers and trade unions in the industry. It facilitated the establishment of the West Midlands Auto Industry Forum which brought together trade unionists with local authorities to exchange information and develop campaigns on issues which affect the industry (WMAIF 1987).

This advocacy and campaigning role as well as the initiatives described above were supported by continuous monitoring and research on major changes in the industry.

In European terms the WMEB was neither unique in its analysis of the problems nor in its policies and initiatives. Neither was it capable of solving or even adequately addressing the problems on its own. Hence it devoted a considerable proportion of its limited resources to working with other local and regional authorities at national and European levels to more towards more comprehensive policies and strategies for the industry.

NATIONAL AND EUROPEAN GROUPINGS OF REGIONAL AND LOCAL AUTHORITIES

Both the UK and European networks developed from conferences held sequentially in Birmingham in 1985. The UK network later assumed the acronym MILAN, which stands for Motor Industry Local Authority Network and has subsequently developed a range of activities including seminars, plant visits, research, briefings for members and representations.

The experience of MILAN's first three years suggests that the network does address needs recognized by the local authorities representing motor manufacturing areas. Membership has grown steadily to around twenty-five member authorities and meetings have consistently been well-attended both by senior officers and by elected councillors. Moreover, several of the councils which were involved in MILAN's establishment, including Birmingham, Coventry, Luton and the West Midlands Enterprise Board, have committed significant officer time and financial resources to promoting the development of the network.

The secretariat for the network has been bought in on a contract basis, first from the Institute of Local Government Studies at Birmingham University and more recently from the Local Government Centre at Warwick University. While inevitably producing certain conflicts of interest, this arrangement has provided MILAN with efficient administration, excellent provision for meetings and seminars and access to high-quality research resources at a minimum cost in terms of bureaucracy.

With the exception (so far) of the Ford plants at Dagenham and Southampton, virtually all of the areas with established vehicle assembly plants in the United Kingdom joined within the first year. Since 1987, two further groups of authorities have joined. First, a number of councils representing counties and districts with vehicle component, but not vehicle assembly, industries became involved. Examples of these are Llanelli in South Wales, Walsall and Redditch in the West Midlands and Sheffield – the latter primarily because of the importance of the motor industry as a market for special steels. These were followed, in late 1988 and 1989, by authorities representing the areas chosen by Nissan and Toyota for their main European car assembly plants – Sunderland and Derby. Thamesdown, the host authority for the planned Honda car assembly at Swindon, was amongst MILAN's founder members.

This expansion of MILAN's membership has brought the network face to face with two of the central issues currently confronting the UK motor industry. The adhesion of the components manufacturing areas has focused attention on the relationship between suppliers and assemblers and hence on the role local and regional bodies can play in supporting investment, training and technology development in this highly fragmented sector. The arrival of Sunderland and Derby has brought to the fore other sensitive issues: in particular the question of the differing interests of established vehicle manufacturers, the new Japanese assembly operations and of components producers who may or may not win contracts to supply to Nissan, Toyota and Honda.

Decision-taking within MILAN has always been on the basis of consensus. This convention has proved a constraint in some areas. For example, it has prevented the network becoming as fully involved with the issue of the environmental impact of the motor car as some members would have wished. On the other hand, it has enabled authorities of various political shades and representing areas with significantly different prospects and economic interests to cooperate fully where they do recognize common interests.

In practice, MILAN has evolved a basic philosophy which appears to have the broad support of all its members. First, the network accepts that its role must be to work with, rather than against, the grain of the market as far as the evolution of the motor industry is concerned. It accepts that changing technology, management practice and world markets mean that continuing restructuring in the industry is inevitable. Second, however, it also believes that public policy at the European, national and local levels can play a significant role in mitigating the harmful effects of industrial change on the communities most directly concerned. Exploring ways in which complementary economic development can be promoted where closures or redundancy are involved is an important part of MILAN's agenda. Third, the network has developed a strong interest in, and support for, the work of the European Commission both in terms of social and regional policy and in terms of industrial and trade policy as far as they address the interests of the motor and components sectors (MILAN 1987).

This European focus has encouraged MILAN to play an active role in promoting the development of the European network. Hitherto, progress has been piecemeal, with support coming from Antwerp (home of GM's Belgian assembly plant), from the north of Italy and more recently from Spain, but with only patchy interest from France and Germany. The pattern of well-attended biennial European conferences is now well established. Organization between conferences, however, has proved more of a problem – in part largely because many local authorities have tended to be cautious about approving expenses for international travel for what is inevitably a long-term project.

Nevertheless, a working group of interested regional and local authorities has been in existence since 1986 and has met periodically in order to prepare for the Antwerp and Valladolid Conferences and to make *ad hoc* representations to the European institutions. A delegation met members of the European Parliament in Strasbourg during the consideration of the Beazley Report on the European motor industry in 1987 and a number of meetings have been held with senior European Commission officials of the Industry, Social Affairs and Regional Policy Directorates General. There is good reason to believe that these contacts have helped to put the issue of the local and regional impact of restructuring in the motor industry on the agenda. For example, when the Commission resolved in 1989 to fund research on the regional dimension of industrial change, the motor vehicle components industry was one of only three sectors singled out for study.

Recently, the prospects for a more coherent approach have improved with the news that the European Commission is to provide 100,000 Ecus to help to fund a small secretariat for the European motor manufacturing local authorities. This is based in Spain and is associated with the Spanish branch of the Federation of European Regions and Municipalities. The secretariat was established following the Fourth European Conference which was held in Valladolid in February 1990. It is also now likely that regular consultations will be instituted between the European Working Group and officials of the Commission. Moreover, the City of Frankfurt has offered to host the following conference in 1991. It is hoped that this will help to stimulate greater interest among German local and regional authorities.

A key problem facing the motor manufacturing authorities in their relations with the EC is that the motor industry does not fit tidily into the Commission's framework for approaching industrial issues. The industry is obviously not in decline in the sense that mining, textiles and shipbuilding have been perceived to be. But it is also difficult to compare it crudely with the new growth sectors such as information technology and aerospace. In fact, it shares important characteristics with both of these types of industry. In the context of the motor industry, policies are needed to support advanced research and development and training and at the same time to promote industrial regeneration and employment opportunities in communities which are faced by closures and retrenchment.

As a result, European-level parameters will often be inappropriate as a basis for determining the priorities for intervention at the local or regional levels. Exactly because motor industry plants tend to be so large and so dominant in their local economies, industrial restructuring may spell calamity for the local community concerned, even when it is sited in a prosperous area which is ineligible for conventional regional assistance. This is perhaps particularly so in the United Kingdom because of the lack of a regional tier of government with economic powers of the kind which exists in the Federal Republic and in Belgium.

MILAN and the European network evolved in the mid-1980s to address the specific needs of a diverse group of motor and component manufacturing communities and to prepare for and respond positively to the economic and industrial changes which were affecting their local areas. Historically, the voice of communities dependent on the motor industries had been muted when compared with those of the companies, trade unions and government. The basic aim of the networks was therefore to work together on behalf of communities which depend on the motor industry and to support the future development of vehicle and component manufacturing.

In times of growth and prosperity, local and regional authorities are important providers of the services and infrastructure necessary to support the rapid expansion of the motor and component industries. However, restructuring, closure and redundancy create economic, social and environmental problems and local and regional organizations have to create new and imaginative responses. Perhaps the most important functions of the networks in this context are the sharing of experiences to better understand the dynamics of the industry and to respond to the problems and opportunities it creates, to advocate supportive policies at national and European levels and to enter into dialogue with government companies and trade unions in order to represent the community interest.

CONCLUSIONS

This chapter has illustrated how the restructuring of the vehicle industry provoked a response in a region severely affected by that process. The fact that the response was limited and inadequate indicates some important weaknesses in political structures which are unable to accommodate the interests of communities and areas alongside those of companies, trade unions and national governments. Informal and formal links between local and regional authorities within and between countries suggest that the commonalities in problems faced at this level are greater than the differences and that there is a need for more effective representation of local and regional community interests at European level. The dominant influence of national governments defending national interests has proved an inadequate basis for Europe to respond to worldwide trends in the vehicle industry in the 1980s: it is likely to become increasingly inadequate in the 1990s. Mechanisms need to be found to allow local and regional interests to transcend those of national governments and contribute towards European policies.

Bibliography

Adams, W. and Brock, J.W. (1986) 'The automobile industry', in W. Adams (ed.) *The Structure of American Industry*, 7th edition, New York: Macmillan.

Afriat, C., de Banville, E. and Chanaron, J-J. (1987) *Rapports entre constructeurs automobiles et fournisseurs aux Etats-Unis*, Paris: Centre de Prospective et d'Evaluation.

Aglietta, M. (1979) *A Theory of Capitalist Regulation*, London: New Left Books.

Agurén, S., *et al.* (1984) *Volvo Kalmarverken efter tio ar*. Manniskorna, tekniken, ekonomin, Stockholm: Radet for utvecklingsfragor SAF-LO-PTK.

Ahlinder, J. (1988) 'Job creation in the automotive industry: the Volvo experience', in Olsen (ed.) *Industrial Change and Labour Adjustment in Sweden and Canada*, Toronto.

Alexander, J.W. and Gibson, L.P. (1979) *Economic geography*, 2nd edition, Englewood Cliffs, New Jersey: Prentice-Hall.

Altshuler, A. *et al.* (1984) *The Future of the Automobile*, Cambridge, MA: MIT Press.

Amin, A. and Goddard, J. (eds) (1986) *Technological Change, Industrial Restructuring and Regional Development*, London: Allen & Unwin.

Amin, A. and Smith, I.J. (1990a) 'The British car components industry: leaner fitter?', in S. Crowther, P. Garrahan and P. Stewart (eds) *Progress to Decline*, London: Avebury.

Amin, A. and Smith, I.J. (1990b) 'Decline and restructuring in the U.K. motor vehicle components industry', *Scottish Journal of Political Economy*, 37, 209–40.

Atkinson, J. (1984) 'Flexibility, uncertainty and manpower management', *Institute of Manpower Studies, Report No. 89*, University of Sussex.

AUEW (1985) *The Way Forward: Proposals of the AUEW Shop Stewards*, Newcastle: H.K. Porter.

Automobile Quarterly (1971) *The American Car since 1775*, New York: E.P. Dutton.

Automotive News (1988) *Market Data*, Detroit: Automotive News.

Bäckström, A. (1988) 'The role of the automotive industry for the Swedish economy and labour market', in Olsen (ed.) *Industrial Change and Labour Adjustment in Sweden and Canada*, Toronto.

Ballance, R.H. (1987) *International Industry and Business: Structural Change, Industrial Policy and Industrial Strategies*, London: Allen & Unwin.

Beauregard, R.A. (ed.) (1989) *Economic Restructuring and Political Response*, Newbury Park, CA: Sage.

Bennett, D.C. and Sharpe, K.E. (1985) *Transnational Corporations versus the State: The Political Economy of the Mexican Auto Industry*, Princeton: Princeton University Press.

Berger, S. and Piore, M. (1980) *Dualism and Discontinuity in Industrial Societies*, Cambridge: Cambridge University Press.

Bessant, J., Jones, D.T., Lamming, R. and Pollard, A. (1984) *The West Midlands Automobile Components Industry: Recent Changes and Future Prospects*, Economic Development Unit, West Midlands County Council, Birmingham.

Beynon, H. (1984) *Working for Ford*, 2nd edition, Harmondsworth: Penguin.

Bhaskar, K. (1980) *The Future of the World Motor Industry*, London: Kogan Page.

Bloomfield, G.T. (1978) *The World Automotive Industry*, Newton Abbot: David & Charles.

Bloomfield, G.T. (1981) 'The changing spatial organisation of multinational corporations in the world automotive industry', in F.E.I. Hamilton and G.J.R. Linge (eds) *Spatial Analysis, Industry and the Industrial Environment*, Vol. 2, Chichester: John Wiley.

Boas, C.W. (1961) 'Locational patterns of American automobile assembly plants 1895–1958', *Economic Geography* 37 (3): 218–30.

Bradbury, J.H. (1985) 'Regional and industrial restructuring processes in the new international division of labour', *Progress in Human Geography* 9 (1): 38–63.

Brown, W. (1988) 'Japan targets U.S. auto parts market', *Baton Rouge Sunday Advocate*, 12 June.

Buckley, J. (1988) 'How Japan is winning Dixie', *U.S. New & World Report*, 9 May, pp. 43–59.

CAITS (1983) *The Manufacture of Electrical Equipment for Motor Vehicles in the Greater London Area*, North London Polytechnic, London: Centre for Alternative Industrial and Technological Systems.

CAITS (1986) *Flexibility: Who Needs It?* Centre for Alternative Industrial and Technological Systems, North London Polytechnic, London, mimeograph.

CAITS (1988) *Japan Comes to Vauxhall*, Centre for Alternative Industrial and Technological Systems, North London Polytechnic, London, mimeograph.

Chaillou, B. (1977) 'Definition et typologie de la sous traitance', *Revue Economique* 28 (2): 262–85.

Chang, K-T. (1989) 'Japan's direct manufacturing investment in the United States', *Professional Geographer* 41: 314–28.

Chethik, N. (1988) 'NUMMI in no-layoff bind', *The Cincinnati Enquirer*, 22 March, p. E-6.

CIS (1978) *Ford: Anti-Report*, London: Counter Information Services.

Clark, G.L. (1986) 'The crisis of the Midwest automobile industry', in A.J. Scott and M. Storper (eds) *Production, Work Territory; The Geographical Anatomy of Industrial Capitalism*, Boston: Allen & Unwin.

Clarke, S. (1988) 'Overaccumulation, class struggle and the regulation approach', *Capital and Class* 36.

Clayton, M. (1987) 'Small towns think Japanese', *Christian Science Monitor*, 11 May, p. 1.

Cohen, S.S. and Zysman, J. (1987) *Manufacturing Matters: The Myth of the Past-Industrial Economy*, New York: Basic Books.

Cole, R.E. and Yakushiji, T. (eds) (1984) *American and Japanese Industries in Transition*, Ann Arbor: Center for Japanese Studies, University of Michigan.

Cooke, P. (1988) 'Flexible integration, scope economics, and strategic alliances: social and spatial mediations', *Environment and Planning D.* 6 (3): 281–300.

Cooke, P. (ed.) (1989) *Localities: The Changing Face of Urban Britain*, London: Unwin Hyman.

Coventry Economic Monitor. Various years, Coventry City Council.

Covried: The Coventry Region Industrial Establishment Databank. Held at the Department of Geography, Coventry Polytechnic.

Cowling, K. (1986) 'The internationalisation of production and de-industrialisation', in A. Amin and J.B. Goddard (eds) *Technological Change, Industrial Restructuring and Regional Development*, London: Allen & Unwin.

Cox, K.R. and Mair, A. (1988) 'Locality and community in the politics of local economic development', *Annals of the Association of American Geographers* 78: 307–25.

Crandall, R.W. (1986) *Regulating the Automobile*, Washington, DC: Brookings Institution.

Crowther, S. and Garrahan, P. (1988) 'Corporate power and the local economy', *Industrial Relations Journal* 19: 51–9.

CSCA (1987) Repertoire Mondiale, Chambre Syndicale des Constructeurs d'Automobiles, Paris.

Cusumano, M.A. (1985) *The Japanese Automobile Industry: Technology and Management at Nissan and Toyota*, Cambridge, MA: Council on East Asian Studies, Harvard University.

Dicken, P. (1986) *Global Shift: Industrial Change in a Turbulent World*, London: Harper & Row.

Done, K. (1989) 'Japanese spring board', *Financial Times*, 13 September, p. VI.

Dunnett, P.J.S. (1980) *The Decline of the British Motor Industry: The Effect of Government Policy, 1945–1979*, London: Croom Helm.

The Economist (1985) 'Another turn of the wheel; a survey of the world's motor industry', March, p. 2.

The Economist (1987) 'Japan tunes up for the '92 Grand Prix', 23 May, p. 72.

Edge, G. (1986) *Priorities for Economic Regeneration in the West Midlands*, Birmingham: WMEB.

Edwardes, M. (1983) *Back from the Brink*, London: Collins.

Egerton, J. and Thomas D. (1983) *Nissan in Tennessee*, Smyrna, TN: Nissan Motor Manufacturing Co.

EIU (1983) *West European Car Replacement Parts Markets: United Kingdom*, London: Economist Intelligence Unit, Multi Client Research Report.

Ellegård, K. (1983) *Manniska – produktion. Tidsbilder av ett produkionssystem*.

Meddelanden fran Goteborgs universitets goegrafiska institutioner, Serie B Nr 72, Goteborg.

Elliott, D. and Marshall, M. (1989) 'West Midland sector strategy', in P. Hirst and J. Zeitlin (eds) *Reversing Industrial Decline*, Oxford: Berg.

Estall, R.C. (1985) 'Stock control in manufacturing: the Just-in-Time system and its locational implications', *Area* 17 February, 129–33.

Ettlie, J.E. (1988) *Taking Charge of Manufacturing: How Companies are combining technological and organisational innovations to compete successfully*, San Francisco: Jossey-Bass.

Expenditure Committee, House of Commons, Session (1986–7) *The U.K. Motor Component Industry*, Report HC 407, London: HMSO.

Feigenbaum, A. (1983) *Total quality control*, New York: McGraw-Hill.

Ford, M. (1988) 'The Motor Industry in South Korea; reacting to trends at home and abroad', *Financial Times*, October 20, p. 210.

Foreman-Peck, J. (1986) 'The motor industry', in M. Casson (ed.) *Multinationals and World Trade*, London: Allen & Unwin.

Forster, J. and Woolfson, F. (1989) 'Corporate reconstruction and business unionism – the lessons of Caterpillar and Ford', *New Left Review* No. 174.

Friedman, A. (1977) *Industry and Labour: class struggle at work and monopoly capitalism*, London: Macmillan.

Friedman, D. (1983) 'Beyond the age of Ford: the strategic basis of the Japanese success in automobiles', in J. Zysman and L. Tyson (eds) *American Industry in International Competition*, Ithaca, NY: Cornell University Press.

Friedman, D. (1988) *The Misunderstood Miracle: Industrial Development and Political Change in Japan*, Ithaca, NY: Cornell University Press.

GOM Antwerp (1987) *The European Motor Industry at the Crossroads*, international conference report, Antwerp: GOM.

Gardner, D. (1986) 'The motor industry in Mexico; aiming for exports', *Financial Times*, 14 October, p. 8.

Gardner, D. (1987) 'The rich pickings in America's backyard', *Financial Times*, 31 July, p. 14.

George, M. and Levie, H. (1984) *Japanese Competition and the Workplace*, London: Centre for Industrial and Technological Systems, North London Polytechnic.

Gertler, M.S. (1988) 'The limits to flexibility: comments on the post-Fordist vision of production and its geography', *Transactions of the Institute of British Geographers, N.S.* 13 (4): 419–32.

Gertler, M.S. (1989) 'Resurrecting flexibility? A reply to Schoenberger', *Transactions of the Institute of British Geographers* 14: 109–12.

Glasmeier, A.K. and McCluskey, R.E. (1987) 'U.S. automobile parts production: An analysis of the organisation and location of a changing industry', *Economic Geography* 63 (2): 142–59.

Gooding, K. (1979) 'How General Motors aims not to be "one of the pack" overseas', *Financial Times*, 17 August, p. 9.

Gooding, K. (1986) 'Motor industry survey; accelerating on road to change', *Financial Times*, 14 October, p. 1.

Gooding, K. (1987) 'South Korea's Hyundai gears up for the big league', *Financial Times*, 20 February, p. 16.

Gramsci, A. (1971) *Selections from the Prison Notebooks*, in Q. Hoare and G. Nowell (eds) London: Lawrence & Wishart.

Green, R. and Schor, A. (1988) 'Small towns work to draw Japanese firms', *The Cincinnati Enquirer*, 8 August, p. D1.

Gwynne, R.N. (1978) 'The motor vehicle industry in Latin America, *Bank of London and South America Review* 12 (9): 426–71.

Gwynne, R.N. (1979) 'Oligopolistic reaction', *Area* 11 (4): 315–19.

Gwynne, R.N. (1980) 'The Andean Group Automobile Programme: an interim assessment', *Bank of London and South America Review* 14 (11): 160–8.

Gwynne, R.N. (1985) *Industrialization and Urbanization in Latin America*, London: Routledge & Kegan Paul.

Gwynne, R.N. (1988) 'The future of the Latin American motor vehicle industry', *Bulletin of Latin American Research* 7 (1): 149–54.

Gwynne, R.N. (1990) *New Horizons? Third World Industrialisation in an International Framework*, London: Longman.

Gyllenhammar, P.G. (1981) *Bilindustrin – infor ett debacle?* Handelsbankens smaskriftsserie 20.

HMSO (1987) *The Motor Components Industry: Minutes of Evidence*, London: House of Commons, Trade and Industry Committee HC 143.

Håkanson, L. and Danielsson, L. (1985) 'Structural adjustment in a stagnating economy: Regional manufacturing employment in Sweden, 1975–1980', *Regional Studies* 19 (4): 329–42.

Hamilton, F.E.I. (1984) 'Industrial restructuring: an international problem', *Geoforum* 15 (3): 349–64.

Harbour and Associates (1982) *Analysis of the Japanese Landed Cost Advantage for the Manufacture of Subcompact Cards*, Berkeley, MI: Harbour and Associates.

Harvey, D. (1987) 'Flexible accumulation through urbanisation: reflections of "Post Modern" in the American city', *Antipode* 19: 260–86.

Harvey, D. (1988) 'The geographical and geopolitical consequences of the transition from Fordist to flexible accumulation', in G. Sternlieb and J.W. Hughes (eds) *America's New Market Geography*, New Jersey: Rutgers University.

Healey, M. and Clark, D. (1984) 'Industrial decline and government response in the West Midlands: the case of Coventry', *Regional Studies* 18 (4): 303–18.

Hedlund, G. and Steen, R. (1985) 'Staten och bilindustrin – en sammanfattning av industri-och handelspolitiken, in *Bilen och bilindustrin i svenskt perspektiv*, Gothenburg: Institute for Management of Innovation and Technology.

Henderson, J. and Castells, M. (eds) (1987) *Global Restructuring and Territorial Development*, London: Saga.

Henrickson, G.R. (1951) *Trends in the Geographical Distribution of Suppliers of Some Basically Important Materials Used at the Buick Motor Division, Flint, Michigan*, Ann Arbor, MI: University of Michigan, Institute of Human Adjustment.

Hermele, K. (1982) *Den drivande kraften. Bilindustrin som exemple*, Stockholm.

Hill, R.C. (1986) 'Crisis in Motor City: The politics of economic development in Detroit', in S.S. Fainstein *et al. Restructuring the City*, New York: Longman.

Hill, R.C. (1987) 'Global factory and company town: The changing division of labour in the international automobile industry', in J. Henderson and M.

Castells (eds) *Global Restructuring and Territorial Development*, London: Saga.

Hill, R.C. (1989) 'Comparing transnational production systems: the automobile industry in the U.S.A. and Japan', *International Journal of Urban and Regional Research* 13: 462–79.

Hill, R.C. *et al.* (1989) 'Flat Rock, Home of Mazda; The Social Impact of a Japanese Company on an American Community', in P.J. Arnesen (ed.) *The Auto Industry Ahead: Who's Driving*, Michigan Papers in Japanese Studies No. 18, Ann Arbor, MI: University of Michigan.

Hill, S.B.P. (1989) *Flexibility and Patterns of Work*, Cardiff: Cardiff Business School.

Holmes, J. (1986) 'The organisation and locational structure of production subcontracting', in A.J. Scott and M. Storper (eds) *The Geographical Anatomy of Industrial Capitalism: Production, Work and Territory*, Hemel Hempstead: Allen & Unwin.

Holmes, J. (1987a) 'The crisis of Fordism and the restructuring of the Canadian auto industry', in J. Holmes and C. Leys (eds) *Frontyard–Backyard, The Americas in the Global Crisis*, Toronto: Between the Lines.

Holmes, J. (1987b) 'Technical change and the restructuring of the North American automobile industry', in K. Chapman and G. Humphrys (eds) *Technical Change and Industrial Policy*, Oxford: Basil Blackwell.

Holmes, J. (1988) 'Industrial restructuring in a period of crisis, an analysis of the Canadian automobile industry, 1973–1983', *Antipode* 20: 19–51.

Holmes, J. (1989) 'The impact of new production technologies on the organisation of labour in the North American automobile industry', in G. Linge and G.A. Vander Kamp (eds) *Labour, Environment and Industrial Change*, London: Croom Helm.

Holusha, J. (1987) 'Chrysler, Mitsubishi pick Illinois site', *New York Times*, 8 October, p. D1.

Holusha, J. (1988a) 'Mixing cultures on the assembly line', *New York Times*, 5 June, p. (3) 1.

Holusha, J. (1988b) 'Ford and Nissan take new route', *New York Times*, 22 September, p. D2.

Huckle, J. (1984) 'Explaining unemployment: an example of political education through geography', *Teaching Geography* 9 (3): 99–103.

Hudson, R. (1988) 'Changing spatial divisions of labour in manufacturing and their impacts on localities', *Nordisk Samhallsgeografisk Tidsskrift* 7: 3–14.

Hunker, J.A. (1983) *Structural Change in the U.S. Automobile Industry*.

Hurley, N.P. (1959) 'The automotive industry: a study in industrial location', *Land Economics* 35 (1): 1–14.

Iacocca, L., with Novak, W. (1984) *Iacocca: An Autobiography*, New York: Bantam Books.

Imrie, R. (1986) 'Work decentralisation from large to small firms: a preliminary analysis of subcontracting', *Environment and Planning A* 18: 949–65.

Jenkins, R. (1977) *Dependent Industrialisation in Latin America*, New York: Praeger.

Jenkins, R. (1987) *Transnational Corporations and the Latin American Automobile Industry*, London: Macmillan.

Jensen, C. (1986) 'Mitsubishi–Chrysler venture eyes S. Ohio', *Cleveland Plain Dealer*, 16 April, p. E1.

Jessop, B. *et al.* (1988) *Thatcherism: A Tale of Two Nations*, Cambridge: Polity.

Johns, R. (1987) 'The Mexican motor industry: compensating for home slump', *Financial Times*, 10 December.

Jones, D.T. (1981) *Maturity and Crisis in the European Car Industry: Structural Change and Public Policy*, Sussex European Papers No. 8, Brighton: Sussex European Research Centre, University of Sussex.

Jones, D.T. (1985) *The Import Threat to the U.K. Car Industry*, Brighton: Science Policy Research Unit, University of Sussex.

Jones, D.T. (1988) 'Structural adjustment in the automobile industry', *STI Review* 3 (April): 8–64, Paris: OECD.

Jones, D.T. and Graves, A. (1986) 'The race for pole position – revolution in the car industry', *Marxism Today* 30: 28–32.

Jones, D.T. and Womack, J.P. (1985) 'Developing countries and the future of the automobile industry', *World Development* 13 (3): 393–407.

Kamath, R. and Wilson, R.C. (1983) *Characteristics of the United States Automotive Supplier Industry*, Ann Arbor, MI: The University of Michigan Centre for Japanese Studies.

Karlsson, C. (1985) 'Bilindustrins framtid – industriell strategi och struktur', in *Bilen och bilindustrin i svenskt perspektiv*, Gothenburg: Institute for Management of Innovation and Technology.

Keeble, D. (1976) *Industrial Location and Planning in the U.K.*, Andover: Methuen.

Kinch, N. (1988) 'Volvo – drommen som blev verklighet', *Tvarsbutt*, No. 2.

King, R. (1986) 'The motor industry in South Korea; exporting to major world markets', *Financial Times*, 14 October, p. 8.

Kraar, L. (1984) 'Detroit's new Asian car strategy', *Fortune*, 10 December, 172–8.

Kronish, R. and Mericlole, K.S. (eds) (1984) *The Political Economy of the Latin American Motor Vehicle Industry*, Cambridge, MA: MIT Press.

Krumme, G. (1981) 'Making it abroad: The evolution of Volkswagen's North American production plans', in F.E.E. Hamilton and G.J.R. Linge (eds) *Spatial Analysis, Industry and the Industrial Environment*, Vol. 2, Chichester: Wiley.

Kuhn, A.J. (1986) *GM Passes Ford 1918–1938: Designing the General Motors Performance Control System*, University Park, PA: Pennsylvania State University Press.

Lall, S. (1980) 'The international automotive industry and the developing world', *World Development* 8: 789–812.

Lall, S. (1983) 'Prospects for automotive transnationals in the Third World', *National Westminster Bank Quarterly Review*, pp. 13–20.

Law, C.M. (1985) 'The geography of industrial rationalisation: the British motor car assembly-industry 1972–1982', *Geography* 70 (1): 1–12.

Lipietz, A. (1980) 'The structuration of space; the problem of land and spatial policy', in J. Carney, R. Hudson and J. Lewis (eds) *Regions in Crisis*, London: Croom Helm.

Lipietz, A. (1986) 'New tendencies in the international division of labour and modes of regulation', in A.J. Scott and M. Storper (eds) *Production, Work, Territory: The Geographical Anatomy of Industrial Capitalism*, Hemel Hempstead: Allen & Unwin.

Lloyd, P.E. (1989) 'Fragmenting markets and the dynamic restructuring of production: issues for spatial policy', *Environment and Planning A*, 21: 429–44.

Lundmark, M. and Malmberg, A. (1988) *Industrilokalisering i Sverige – regional och strukturell forandring*, Geografiska Regionastudier 19, Uppsala: Kulturgeografiska institutionen, Uppsala Universitet.

Mackay, D.I., Sladen, J.P. and Holligan, H.J. (1984) *The U.K. Vehicle Industry and its Economic Significance*, Edinburgh: PEIDA.

Mair, A., Florida, R. and Kenney, M. (1989) 'The new geography of automobile production: Japanese transplants in North America', *Economic Geography* 64: 352–73.

Malmberg, A. (1987) *Industrisysselsattningens regionala utveckling 1870–1980*, Forskningsrapport 93, Uppsala: Kulturgeografiska institutionen, Uppsala University.

Marsh, P. and Collett, P. (1986) *Driving Passion: The Psychology of the Car*, London: Jonathan Cape.

Marshall, N. (1987) 'Industrial change, linkages and regional development', in W. Lever (ed.) *Industrial Change in the United Kingdom*, Harlow: Longman.

Maskell, P. (1982) *Industriens regionale omlokalisering 1970–1980 – omfang, arsager konsekvenser*, Kopenhamn: TRR, Handelshojskolen.

Maskell, P. (1988) 'Att forklara industrins regionala omfordelning', in Anderson and A. Malmberg (eds) *Regional struktur och industriella strategier i Norden*, Uppsala.

Massey, D. (1979) 'In what sense a regional problem?', *Regional Studies* 13: 223–44.

Massey, D. (1984) *Spatial Divisions of Labour: Social Structures and the Geography of Production*, London: Macmillan.

Maxcy, G. (1981) *The Multinational Motor Industry*, London: Croom Helm.

May, G.S. (1975) *A Most Unique Machine*, Grand Rapids, MI: Eerdmans Publishing.

Mericle, K. (1984) 'The political economy of the Brazilian motor vehicle industry', in R. Kronish and K. Mericle (eds) *The Political Economy of the Latin American Motor Vehicle Industry*, Cambridge, MA: MIT Press.

Meyer, P.B. (1984) 'General Motors', Saturn plant, a quantum leap in technology, and its implications for labour and community organising', *Capital and Class* 30: 73–96.

Monopolies and Mergers Commission (1984) *Guest, Keen and Nettlefolds plc and A E plc: a report on the proposed merger*, Cmnd 9199, London: HMSO.

Monopolies and Mergers Commission (1985) *Ford Motor Company Ltd: A Report on the Policy of not Granting Licences to Manufacture or Sell Certain Replacement Parts in the U.K.*, Cmnd 9437, London: HMSO.

Morris, J. (1988) 'New technologies, flexible work practices, and regional sociospatial differentiation: some observations from the United Kingdom', *Environment and Planning D* 6 (3): 301–21.

Motor Industry Local Authority Network (1987) *Local Government and the Challenge of the Motor Industry*, Birmingham: MILAN.

Murray, R. (1985) 'Benetton Britain: the new economic order', *Marxism Today*, November 1985.

Murray, R. (1988) 'Life after Henry (Ford)', *Marxism Today*, October 1988.

Murray, R. (1989) 'Interview in Interlinks', *Interlink*, February/March 1989.

MVMA (published annually) *Motor Vehicle Facts and Figures*, Detroit: Motor Vehicle Manufacturers of America.

MVMA (1988) *World Motor Vehicle Data*, Detroit: Motor Vehicle Manufacturers Association.

Nader, R. and Taylor, W. (1986) 'Roger Smith: Detroit-iron in orbit', in *The Big Boys: Power and Position in American Business*, New York: Pantheon.

New York Times (1988) 'Mazda complains about U.S. parts', 22 March.

Nissan (1988) *Nissan Information Pack*, Sunderland: Nissan.

Oberhauser, A. (1987) 'Labour production and the State. Decentralisation of the French automobile industry', *Regional Studies* 21: 445–58.

Odaka, K. (ed) (1983) *The Motor Vehicle Industry in Asia*, Singapore: Singapore University Press.

OECD (1987) *The Costs of Restricting Imports: The Automobile Industry*, Paris: OECD.

Oliver, N. and Wilkinson, B. (1988) *The Japanisation of British Industry*, Oxford: Basil Blackwell.

Olsson, R. and Broomé, P. (1988) *Alderschocken*, Stockholm.

Pastor, S. (1988) '2 Japanese auto makers to build a $500 million plant in Indiana', *New York Times*, 3 December, p. A1.

Peet, R. (ed.) (1987) *International Capitalism and Industrial Restructuring*, Boston: Allen & Unwin.

Perroux, F. (1955) 'Note on the concept of "Growth Poles",' reprinted in I. Livingstone (ed.) (1981) *Development Economics and Policies*, London: Allen & Unwin.

Piore, M.J. and Sabel, C. (1984) *The Second Industrial Divide*, New York: Basic Books.

Pollert, A. (1988a) 'Dismantling flexibility', *Capital and Class* 34: 42–75.

Pollert, A. (1988b) 'The "flexible firm": fixation or fact?', *Work Employment and Society*, 2 September 1988.

Rae, J.B. (1982) *Nissan/Datsun: A History of the Nissan Motor Corporation in USA 1960–1980*, New York: McGraw-Hill.

Rainne, A. (1985) 'Small firms: big problems: the political economy of small businesses', *Capital and Class*, 25.

Rehder, R.R. (1988) 'Japanese transplants: a new model for Detroit', *Business Horizons* 31 (1): 52–61.

Rehder, R.R., Hendry, R.W. and Smith, M.M. (1985) 'NUMMI the best of both worlds?' *Management Review* 79 (12): 36–41.

Reich, R.B. and Donahue, J.D. (1985) *The Deals: The Chrysler Revival and the American System*, New York: Times Books.

Rhys, D.G. (1972) *The Motor Industry: An Economic Survey*, London: Butterworth.

Rhys, D.G. (1979) 'The components sector', in K. Bhaskar (ed.) *The Future of the U.K. Motor Industry*, London: Kogan Page.

Rich, D.C. (1987) *The Industrial Geography of Australia*, London: Croom Helm.

Roberts, A. (1987) 'GM divisions go it alone in the world', *Dayton Daily News and Journal Herald*, 12 July, p. 1-F.

Rubenstein, J.M. (1986) 'Changing distribution of the American automobile industry', *Geographical Review* 76 (3): 288–300.

Rubenstein, J.M. (1987) 'Further changes in the American automobile industry', *Geographical Review* 77 (3): 359–62.

Rubenstein, J.M. (1988a) 'Changing distribution of American motor-vehicle-parts suppliers', *Geographical Review* 78 (3): 288–98.

Rubenstein, J.M. (1988b) 'The changing distribution of U.S. automobile assembly plants', *Focus* 38 (3): 12–17.

Rubenstein, J.M. and Reid, N. (1986) *Ohio's Motor Vehicle Industry*, Miami Geographical Research Paper, No. 1, Oxford, OH: Miami University, Department of Geography.

Sabel, C. (1982) *Work and Politics: The Division of Labour in Industry*, New York: Cambridge University Press.

Salt, J. (1967) 'The impact of Ford and Vauxhall plants on the employment situation on Merseyside, 1962–1965', *Tidschrift voor Economische et Sociale Geographie* 58: 225–64.

Sayer, A. (1986) 'New developments in manufacturing: the just-in-time system', *Capital and Class* 30: 43–72.

Sayer, A. (1989) 'Postfordism in question', *International Journal of Urban and Regional Research* 13: 666–93.

Schlesinger, J.M. (1988) 'Shift of auto plants to rural areas cuts hiring of minorities', *Wall Street Journal*, 12 April, p. 1.

Schoenberger, E. (1987) 'Technological and organisational change in automobile production: spatial implications', *Regional Studies* 21 (3): 199–214.

Schoenberger, E. (1988) 'From Fordism to flexible accumulation: technology competitive strategies and international location', *Environment and Planning D* 245–62.

Schoenberger, E. (1989) 'Thinking about flexibility: a response to Gertler', *Transactions of the Institute of British Geographers* 14: 98–108.

Scott, A.J. (1983) 'Industrial organisation and the logic of intra-metropolitan location: 1 theoretical considerations', *Economic Geography* 59 (3).

Scott, A.J. (1986) 'Industrial organisation and location; division of labour, the firm and spatial processes', in A. Scott and M. Storper (eds) *Production, Work, Territory: The Geographical Anatomy of Industrial Capitalism*, London: Allen & Unwin.

Scott, A.J. (1988a) 'Flexible production systems and regional development: the rise of new industrial spaces in North America and Western Europe', *International Journal of Urban and Regional Research* 12: 171–86.

Scott, A.J. (1988b) *New Industrial Spaces*, London: Pion.

Scott, A.J. and Storper, M. (eds) (1986) *Production, Work, Territory: The Geographical Anatomy of Industrial Capitalism*, London: Allen & Unwin.

Sheard, P. (1983) 'Auto production systems in Japan: organisational and locational features', *Australian Geographical Studies* 21: 49–68.

Shepherd, D., Silberston, A. and Strange, R. (1985) *British Manufacturing Investment Overseas*, London: Methuen.

Sinclair, R. and Walker, D.F. (1982) 'Industrial development via the multinational corporation: General Motors in Vienna', *Regional Studies* 16 (6): 433–42.

Sinclair, S. (1983) *The World Car: The Future of the Automobile Industry*, New York: Facts on File.

SIND (1980) Svensk bilindustri och dess leverantorer (SIND PM 1980: 20), Stockholm.

Slaughter, J. (1987) 'The team concept in the US Auto industry; implications for unions', *Labour Notes*, Michigan.

Slaughter, J. and Parker, M. (1989) 'Sparks fly on the factory floor', *New Internationalist*, May 1989.

Smith, D. (1988) 'The Japanese example in South West Birmingham', *Industrial Relations Journal* 19: 41–50.

Smith, D. (1989) 'Not getting on, just getting by', in P. Cooke (ed.) *Localities: The Changing Face of Urban Britain*, London: Unwin Hyman.

Smith, D. (1990a) 'Burawoy and Birmingham', in S. Clegg (ed.) *Organisation Theory and Class Analysis*, Berlin: De Gruyter. (In press.)

Smith, D. (1990b) 'Coping with restructuring: the case of South West Birmingham', in M. Harloe, C. Pickvance and J. Urry (eds) *Locality, Policy and Politics*, London: Unwin Hyman.

Smith, D. (1990c) 'Dimensions of flexible specialisation: two case studies', in N. Thrift and P. Cooke (eds) *Capture Britain*, Cambridge: Cambridge University Press. (In press.)

Smith, D. (1990d) 'Restructuring the shopfloor – Austin Rover and Cadbury Schweppes in South West Birmingham', in J. Lovering and R. Meggan (eds) *Restructuring Britain*, London: Unwin Hyman. (In press.)

Sobel, R. (1984) *Car Wars*, New York: E.P. Dutton.

Storper, M. and Scott, A.J. (1989) 'The geographical foundations and social regulation of flexible production complexes', in J. Wolch and M. Dear (eds) *The Geography of Power*, London: Unwin Hyman.

Storper, M. and Walker, R. (1989) *The Capitalist Imperative Territory, Technology and Industrial Growth*, Oxford: Basil Blackwell.

Svensk industri och industripolitik (1988) Stockholm: Ministry of Industry.

Tenorio, R.M. (1988) 'Industria Automotriz: Podria convertirse en maguiladora', *El Financiero*, 26 May, p. 36.

Thoms, D. and Donnelly, T. (1985) *The Motor Car Industry in Coventry Since the 1890's*, London: Croom Helm.

Tolliday, S. and Zeitlin, J. (eds) (1986) *The Automobile Industry and its Workers: Between Fordism and Flexibility*, Cambridge: Polity Press.

Tomkins, R. (1989) 'In wrong gear for goodtimes', *Financial Times*, 22 June, p. 26.

Turnbull, P.J. (1988) 'The limits to "Japanisation" – Just-in-Time, labour relations and the U.K. automotive industry', *New Technology, Work and Employment*, 7–20.

Turnbull, P.J. (1990) 'Industrial restructuring and labour relations in the U.K. automotive components industry: "Just in time" or "Just-too-late?"', in S. Tailby and C. Whitson (eds) *Manufacturing Change*, Oxford: Basil Blackwell.

Uchitelle, L. (1987) 'Japan winning in auto parts', *New York Times*, 1 May, p. D1.

UNCTC (1983) *Transnational Corporations in the International Auto Industry*, New York: Centre for Transnational Corporations, United Nations.

United States Department of Commerce, Bureau of the Census (published annually), *County Business Patterns*, Washington, DC: US Department of Commerce.

United States Department of Transportation (1981) *The U.S. Automobile Industry, 1980*, Washington, DC: US Department of Transportation.

United States Department of Transportation (1982) *The U.S. Automobile Industry, 1981*, Washington, DC: US Department of Transportation.

Vartan, V.G. (1986) 'Car part shift aids suppliers', *New York Times*, 28 July, p. D2.

Vernon, R. (1979) 'The product life cycle hypothesis in a new international environment', *Oxford Bulletin of Economics and Statistics* 41: 255–68.

Walker, R. and Storper, M. (1981) 'Capital and industrial location', *Progress in Human Geography* 5: 473–509.

Wall Street Journal (1988) Advertisement, 21 March, p. 7.

Ward's Automotive Yearbook (published annually) Detroit: Ward's Communications.

Watanabe, S. (1972) 'International subcontracting, employment and skill promotion', *International Labour Review* 105: 51–76.

Watanabe, S. (1986) 'Labour-saving versus work amplifying effects of micro-electronics', *International Labour Review* 125 (3): 243–59.

Watanabe, S. (ed.) (1987) *Microelectronics, Automation and Employment in the Automobile Industry*, Chichester: John Wiley.

Way, A. (1989) 'Manufacturers treading the path to partnership', *Financial Times*, 13 September, p. XVI.

West Midlands Auto Industry Forum (1987) *The Road Ahead*, Birmingham: WMEB.

West Midlands Industrial Development Association (1989) *Vehicle Components Sector Report*, Coleshill: WMIDA.

White, L.J. (1971) *The Automobile Industry Since 1945*, Cambridge, MA: Harvard University Press.

Wickens, P. (1987) *The Road to Nissan*, London: Macmillan.

Wilkerson, I. (1987) 'Influx of Japanese changing styles of Midwest', *New York Times*, 15 February, p. A1.

Wilkinson, B. and Oliver, N. (1988) *Power Control and the Kanban*, Cardiff: UWIST.

Williams, K., Williams, J. and Haslam, C. (1987) *The Breakdown of Austin Rover: A Case Study in the Failure Business Strategy and Industrial Policy*, Oxford: Berg.

Willman, P. and Winch, C. (1985) *Innovation and Management Control: Labour Relations at BL Cars*, Cambridge: Cambridge University Press.

Index